GLACIER: A NATURAL HISTORY GUIDE

Help Us Keep This Guide Up to Date

Every effort has been made by the author and editors to make this guide as accurate and useful as possible. However, many things can change after a guide is published—phone numbers change, hiking trails are rerouted, regulations change, facilities come under new management, and so forth.

We would love to hear from you concerning your experiences with this guide and how you feel it could be improved and kept up to date. While we may not be able to respond to all comments and suggestions, we'll take them to heart and we'll also make certain to share them with the author. Please send your comments and suggestions to the following address:

The Globe Pequot Press
Reader Response/Editorial Department
P.O. Box 480
Guilford, CT 06437

Or you may e-mail us at:

editorial@GlobePequot.com

Thanks for your input, and happy travels!

GLACIER
A Natural History Guide

Second Edition

David Rockwell

GUILFORD, CONNECTICUT
HELENA, MONTANA

A FALCON GUIDE®

Maps: p. vi, courtesy of Glacier National Park; pp. 1, 73, 97, 147, courtesy of Jeremy Schmidt.

Library of Congress Cataloging-in-Publication Data is available.

ISBN: 978-0-7627-3569-3

Manufactured in the United States of America

Distributed by NATIONAL BOOK NETWORK

For Nancy and Isaac

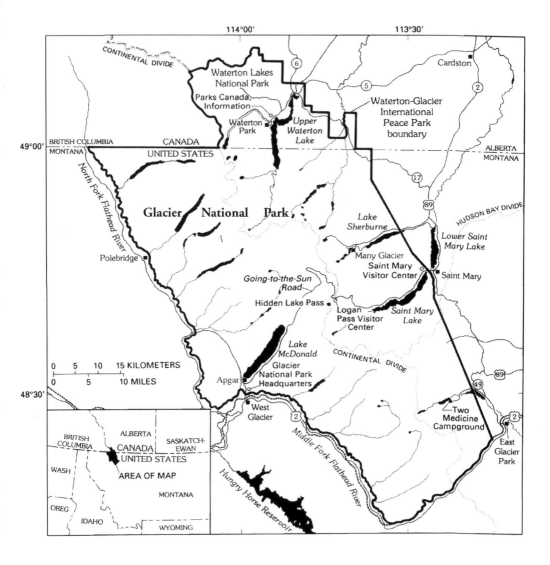

Contents

Acknowledgments

Many people helped with this or the previous edition of this book. I am especially indebted to Joe Weydt for most of the photographs in the book. Thanks to Jerry DeSanto for his willingness to share his knowledge of Glacier's natural history and for his review of the original manuscript. Thanks to the many park managers and scientists who reviewed this edition of the book and offered suggestions, including Jack Potter, chief of science and resource management; Dennis Divoky, fire ecologist; Tara Carolin, ecologist; Daniel Fagre, research ecologist; Richard Menicke, geographer; Steve Gniadek, wildlife biologist; Bill Michels, aquatic ecologist; John Waller, wildlife biologist; and Sallie Hejl, resource education specialist. Thanks to biologist Dave Shea, who reviewed the previous edition of the book and offered a number of suggestions for revisions. Thanks to Don Winston for his help with the geology chapters. To Jerry McGahan and Doug and Antje Baty for their careful readings of the original manuscript, and to Beth Dunagan, the park librarian, for her support, which proved invaluable. To Carl Key, park geographer, for his help and review of the original manuscript. To Jock Pribnow for the many photos he generously contributed. To Susan Kunhardt for her editing of the original Houghton-Mifflin edition in 1995. To George McFarland, Deirdre Shaw, Ann Fagre,

Somer Treat, and Doug O'Looney for help with Park Service photos. To Mark Gahagan, Kate Kendall, Leo Marnell, Jack Stanford, Peter Lesica, Arnold Finklin, Diane Boyd, Steve Arno, Lou Bruno, Robert Horodyski, An Yin, Dan Carney, Diana Tomback, Diane Debinsky, Frank Tyro, Evelyn Bull, Kyran Kunkle, Wendy Clark, Pat Tucker, Bruce Weide, Tom Meier, Phillip Crissman, Rachel Potter, Ira New Breast, Harvey Locke, John Frederick, Steve Thompson, Bonnie Pierce, Fred Vanhorn, Dan Bennett, Tara Williams, and Dave Hadden for sharing their time and knowledge or for supplying photographs. I am grateful to Bill Schneider, Jeff Serena, and Julie Marsh of Globe Pequot for their help and support for the book. And thanks to Rick Balkin for suggesting the project in the beginning. I accept full responsibility for any mistakes.

Introduction

Call it the Crown of the Continent. Or the Land of Shining Mountains. Or *Ahkwaiswílko*, the Kootenai word for a glacier-carved mountain wall. Or call it by its Blackfeet name, *Mistúkisz-Ikanáz(iaw)*, which translates as Mountains of Crystals. The Blackfeet also refer to the Glacier Park terrain as the "Backbone of the World." All these names fit this place, this jumble of peaks that rise up so suddenly from the western edge of the Great Plains and that surprise even the most mountain-wise visitor.

But those names only describe the park as it appears from a distance, as you approach it, say, from the east on U.S. Highway 2, or as you look east toward the Continental Divide from the North Fork Road. Once inside Glacier, things look different. You get swallowed up by mountains. There is grandness, yes, but also detail and a diversity of life beyond what any single word or phrase can impart. You see that the flanks of the mountains are covered with trees, mostly evergreens, but birch and aspen and cottonwood, too, and a deciduous conifer called western larch that turns large patches of the forest bright yellow in the fall. You notice that fjord-shaped lakes extend fingerlike into the very heart of the park, and that the peaks rising above them form almost sheer, mile-tall cliffs. You begin to understand why this place was named *Glacier* Park—not primarily for the small glaciers that linger here today; the name really refers to how all the peaks have been chiseled and scooped out by the mountain-range–size glaciers of the last ice age. Looking up, you see torrents of white water shooting off ledges, falling thousands of feet. You see, on either side of those, parallel rows of avalanche chutes, ridges as jagged and thin as a serrated knife, peaks that remind you of the Matterhorn, and snow; even in August you see snow. And everywhere, there are flowers. Checking your map, you notice the park's one million acres are dotted with hundreds of lakes and that those lakes are connected by hundreds of streams, and you see that there are also networks of trails for getting out and really seeing this place. So you take a hike.

The first hike I took in Glacier National Park was to Iceberg Lake in July of 1973. I arrived at the lake in the evening, after the sun had disappeared behind the Ptarmigan Wall. Still half frozen, the lake's liquid half had slabs of ice the size of school buses drifting in it. On the way back, as the daylight faded, a grizzly bear dashed across the trail a hundred yards in front of me, and I sang "Me and Bobby McGee" at the top of my lungs the rest of the way out. I began to realize that this was a truly wild place.

The North Fork Valley and the Belly River Valley, which lie on opposite sides of the park, are one of the only places in the continental United States with all their predators, that is, all the ones that were here when European-Americans first arrived: wolves, mountain lions, grizzly bears, black bears, coyotes, and wolverines. All are interacting and hunting deer, elk, and moose as they did hundreds, even a thousand years ago. Humans impinge little on their daily lives.

One fall, a friend and I were hiking out of the park along a tributary of the North Fork when it started snowing. A short time later we saw lion tracks on the trail, fresh in the snow. We followed them, and they quickly led us off the trail and into thick timber. Suddenly, we were standing in a place where dirt had been kicked up and leaves scattered. Drops of blood lay on the snow. A few yards farther, we saw swatches of hair, then a dead deer on the ground, its neck evidently broken. The animal had died moments earlier. The lion's tracks circled it, then disappeared into the trees. We hustled back to the trail, adrenaline pumping.

Few of my hikes in Glacier have been so eventful, though most have been equally memorable: a warm evening spent watching a moose and her calf dining on mannagrass and willows along the south edge of Elizabeth Lake; a June hike across an east-side alpine ridge when the draba and candytuft were in full bloom; an afternoon spent beside a creek, overwhelmed by the sweet smell of cottonwood, the flutelike calls of thrushes, and the enormous mountains all around.

So, although Glacier Park, our third-largest national park in the lower 48, is best known for its heart-stopping scenery, it is also a terrific place—one of the best in the Rockies—to contemplate natural history. And not just the lives of wolves and bears and lions. Rock buffs will find the geology riveting. You can run your fingers across mud cracks and ripple marks made one and a half billion years ago, or touch a fault line where the top layer of rock is 1,300 million years older than the bottom layer. You can walk on a glacier, sit on a pillow of lava, or, if you are really into it, search for some of the earliest multicellular fossils in the world. The park's rocks are among the oldest and best-preserved sedimentary rocks found anywhere. How they got here is a story in itself (the formations that make up the park's mountains slid over 50 miles across Idaho and northwest Montana). And then there is the story of the glaciers and the sculpting they did during the last ice age to make this place into one of the most scenic mountain terrains in the world.

Plant lovers, too, will find Glacier a compelling place to explore. More than 1,100 plant species live here. Most are common in the Rockies, but some have migrated from the Arctic and occur there and here and only a few places in between. Others have come from the Great Plains, or the rain forests of the West Coast, or the Great Basin, or the prairies of eastern Washington and Oregon. Few places on the continent have such a mix.

On a hike through an alpine meadow, you might come upon an unusual orange-blooming poppy known as the alpine glacier or pygmy poppy, a species found only here and a few other spots in Canada. In the North Fork you might find a sphagnum fen complete with bladderworts and sundews—carnivorous plants that flourish on a diet of insects and tiny crustaceans. There, too, in the North Fork, you might see orchids: white or spotted lady-slippers, striped or yellow coral-roots, bog-orchids, rein-orchids, or lady's-tresses. Along McDonald Creek, you can hike through an ancient forest with its unique collection of shade-loving plants, some that make their living without chlorophyll. Or lie on your belly above treeline in a bright field of flowers with a flower guide, and take your time identifying a particular species of draba or saxifrage.

There are joys for animal watchers as well—wolverine tracks cutting across a snowfield, a band of mountain goat kids cavorting about in an alpine meadow, spectacularly colored red and blue and white harlequin ducks sailing like rafts over waterfalls and riffles on McDonald Creek. From the forest you might hear the haunting cry of a pileated woodpecker, or, following a trail along a noisy creek, round a bend and encounter a small herd of elk grazing the hillside. Perhaps, like many hikers, you will be startled by a ptarmigan you unintentionally flushed from the tundra or surprised by a snowshoe hare, tawny and alert, regarding you from the undergrowth.

Here, northern bog lemmings scurry along sphagnum-lined runways, pausing now and again to nibble on sedges or willow leaves, while pikas clip alpine grasses and stack them in neat piles to cure, as farmers do with their hay. Here, grizzly bears climb to the summits of the highest peaks to turn rocks for army cutworm moths that have migrated all the way from the Dakotas, and bighorn sheep bang heads in collisions that can be heard a mile away. Wild *is* a good word for this place.

But Glacier Park has also been affected by people. An introduced disease has shaken entire communities. Weeds have crept into meadows. Nonnative fish have been introduced into lakes and streams and are overwhelming the natives. In an effort to protect the forest, the Park Service fought fires here for years. But the practice altered age-old cycles and changed plant and animal communities. Today some fires are managed to benefit plants and animals. Now, new challenges face the park's caretakers. Development of surrounding lands threatens populations of elk, moose, grizzly bears, wolves, and other animals whose seasonal ranges extend beyond the boundary.

This book describes Glacier's natural history, the geology of the park as well as the lives of selected plants and animals from different communities. More important, it explores connections, the threads that tie these organisms to their environment—why a species of columbine grows only on a certain kind of rock, how communities of subterranean insects and crustaceans fertilize river floodplains, how a nut-eating bird has influenced the evolution of a high-elevation pine.

It is a small book about a large and complex and beautiful place, a place where you can still examine and wonder at the natural world, and observe it going about its business as it has done since the beginning. May your visit be rewarding, and may this wild park, the Crown of the Continent, abide.

1

The Rock of the Park

Going-to-the-Sun Road was empty. It was November, and the Park Service had closed it to cars the month before. I walked from The Loop toward Logan Pass under an early sky that was clear and washed of color. A brief snowstorm had swept through the night before and whitened the mountains. A few wisps of clouds still hung on the summits, and as I walked the road toward the pass, the light that had been so soft earlier that morning grew in brilliance and warmth until I squinted to protect my eyes and shed my coat, mittens, and hat.

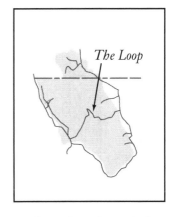

The Loop

I had come to photograph billion-year-old fossils of cyanobacteria imbedded in the rocks cut by this section of road. Along the way, I watched mountain goats move unconcerned across a narrow rock shelf not 20 yards away and gray-crowned rosy finches flit tamely against the rock face as they gleaned seeds from scattered clumps of grass. The quality of the light, the cool freshness of the air, the unsoiled snow, and the innocence of the animals made that part of the world seem new. The rock around me, however, was ancient.

Not far from The Loop, the road cut the cliff to a sheer face. This face is a succession of fine layers, wafers of green and smoky gray rock stacked perpendicular to the cut. The only intrusions on this plywoodlike repetition, aside from the lightning bolts of white calcite that zigzagged randomly through the layers, were fossils—big white-and-pink–tinted columns of hard limestone left behind more than a billion years ago by colonies of cyanobacteria, also referred to as blue-green algae. One intersected the roadcut head-on, and its circular cross section suggested a swirl of petals, a rose encased in a field of green rock. Farther up the road, in a different, buff-colored formation, I found more fossils, dozens of them, some of which resembled sliced cabbage heads.

Back at The Loop, below the first group of fossils, I studied the rock. It was fractured and broken, especially on the margins of the face. Small slabs and chunks of it littered the road. The smallest pieces, those up to an inch thick, snapped in my hands, and I could crumble the thinnest slices almost as easily as one crumbles crisp bread. Most of the fractures ran between layers, and often, where a plank of rock had fallen away, I saw mud cracks and ripple marks on the exposed surface. These appeared fresh, every detail preserved, as if the mud of a rising and falling lake had suddenly frozen and then stood firm against the abuse of time.

These marks, along with the textures, colors, compositions, and structure of the bedrock, reveal like the artifacts of an ancient civilization the history of Glacier Park's mountains—how they were built and how they are being dismantled. They also help explain why living things in the park occur where they do. Soils reflect the compositions of their parent materials. Dolomite, a calcium-rich rock that underlies much of the park, breaks down into a more calcareous soil than that produced from argillite, another rock common in the park. Soil, in turn, helps to shape plant communities. And plant communities determine animal communities. In other words, the focus of my attention—the rocks—had a lot to do with just about everything else I encountered on that beautiful November day.

I picked up a 1-inch-square wafer of rock from the road. It was dull, a light sage green, and fine-grained. This was sedimentary rock of the Snowslip Formation, argillite, about 1.3 billion years old. It was thin, a leaf of a rock, yet it, too, was layered. Without the aid of a magnifying glass I could see at least five tissue-thin layers within the space of a sixteenth of an inch. The story of this modest piece of rock is, at least in a general sense, the story of most of the rocks in Glacier. That story, in its broadest outlines, is as follows:

Just under 1.5 billion years ago, the rock was sediment, a mix of clay, silt, and sand eroded off some barren landscape (a landscape absent of plants) and transported by a river to an enormous shallow body of water something like the Caspian Sea. When the sediment finally settled, it rested on top of 10,000 feet of similarly deposited sediments, at a spot some 50 miles west of what is now Glacier National Park. There, at the bottom of this immense sea, it formed a mud rich in calcium carbonate and quartz. Water levels rose and fell. The mud beneath shallow water rippled under the action of waves. Some was exposed to the air and dried and cracked. Soon more sediment rode in and covered what was there. Deposition continued for hundreds of millions of years, and our few ounces of sediment became buried beneath thousands more feet of sediment. All the while, gravity bore down on the mass, and the entire basin slowly sank deeper into the earth's mantle. Pressure and heat transformed mud into rock—argillite, quartzite, limestone, and dolomite—most of it preserving the marks of waves and desiccation.

Gradually, the basin filled. Deposition stopped. The sea dried, and the millions of layers of baked and compressed sediment sat undisturbed for a billion years. But those sediments were part of a continental plate that was slowly drifting west across the Pacific Ocean, an ocean that, at the time, was crowded with island arcs and small continents. Collisions, dozens of them, were inevitable. Islands the size of New Zealand and Japan smashed into North America one after another, shoving, crumpling, and heaving the crust of the continent into long, corrugated chains of mountains. Rocks folded and faulted and rode over each other. The compression fractured portions of the basin's rocks and thrust a slab 300 miles long and 20,000 feet thick 50 miles across northwestern Montana. A portion of that prodigious chunk would become Glacier National Park. Our inch of thin rock sat somewhere in its middle.

Waves rippled some of the mud that would become the rock of Glacier Park. Top, modern ripple marks in mud deposited in the park in a 1964 flood; above, ripple marks in rock that was mud laid down approximately 1.4 billion years ago. Glacier's rocks are some of the oldest and best-preserved sedimentary rocks in the world. (GLACIER NATIONAL PARK)

This great thrust happened from 60 million to 70 million years ago. Since then, erosion has been at work. Most occurred during the Pleistocene, when glaciers sculpted the park's mountains into what they are today. One of those glaciers filled the McDonald Creek Valley and gouged from its sides colossal pieces of rock. It cut within a few feet of that portion of the layer holding our piece, close enough that a bulldozer building Going-to-the-Sun Road easily finished the job and uncovered it entirely. Once exposed, rain and frost and gravity took over. For the first time in its billion-plus-year history, the layer cracked and flaked and then crumbled. Pieces of it fell away almost daily, until finally, ours dropped at the side of the road.

Looking Back a Billion Years or So

Glacier's rocks are known to geologists as Belt rocks, because the first place they were described was east of the park, near Montana's Belt Mountains. They are among the oldest well-preserved sedimentary rocks in the world. In the park the most senior rocks, those of the Prichard and Waterton Formations, formed about 1.4 billion years ago, when the earth was around 3 billion years old. For perspective, the earliest fossils of land plants appear

Geologic Eon or Era		Geologic Period	Millions of Years Ago	
Cenozoic		Quaternary Tertiary	2	Glacial erosion carves Glacier's peaks.
			63	
Mesozoic		Cretaceous Jurassic Triassic	138 205	North America collides with numerous island arcs. The collisions cause the Rockies to rise up and they thrust Glacier's rocks into place.
Paleozoic		Permian Pennsylvanian Mississippian Devonian Silurian Ordovician Cambrian	240 290 330 360 410 435 500	Erosion removes the rocks deposited during this time from the tops of the rock formations found in Glacier.
			570	
Proterozoic	Late Middle Early		800 1600	The sediments that will become Glacier's rocks are laid down in a great sea or lake.
			2500	
Archean	Late Middle Early		3000 3400	
Pre-Archean			3800 4500	The earth forms.

in rocks that are about 450 million years old (although some scientists now think land plants may have made their first appearance 300 million years earlier). So the first land plants are perhaps a billion years younger than the Belt rocks. Dinosaurs show up in the fossil record about 250 million years ago, and humans come on the scene some 245 million years after that.

Because we tend to think in terms of a few generations, geologic time frames are difficult to comprehend. To try to grasp such enormous spans, imagine that the punctuation mark at the end of this sentence represents one year. One and a half billion of those periods lined up side by side would reach all the way across Montana and halfway into North Dakota, a distance of 750 miles. Stand on the first of those periods, the one touching the Idaho border, and look down that line of dots toward Bismarck. That is roughly the vantage we have when we try to consider events that happened so long ago.

Walk that line, and each step takes you back roughly 650 years. Forty steps and you are 25,000 years before the present, roughly the time, according to most archaeologists, when humans arrived in North America. Walk another mile or so and you are near the beginning of the Pleistocene, the glacial epoch or Ice Age, when Glacier's peaks were fashioned. You would have to walk 27 miles to be present during the time when the Belt rocks were being thrust into their current position. Those 27 miles on a Montana map would put you just east of Libby. If you wanted to travel all the way back to the time when the Belt rocks formed, you might want to take a bus.

From the perspective of one person's lifetime, the mountains of Glacier seem constant, which they nearly are over the course of seventy-five years. Even a rushing stream like McDonald Creek, which is much more dynamic than a mountain, changes its course very little in that amount of time. The earth plods. It requires millions, even tens of millions of years to make mountains and just as long to take them apart. Thrusting a 4-mile-thick slab of Belt rock 50 miles probably took five million to ten million years. Since then those rocks have eroded less than an inch a century. Rock is resolute, but with enough time, even continents move.

Imagining the Belt Basin

One and a half billion years ago, faulting broke the crust of North America in the region of Idaho and Montana. Large blocks of the earth bounded by these faults subsided and formed a basin roughly the size of Arizona. The basin became a catchment for the sediments that would eventually become Belt rock, the rock that makes up Glacier's mountains. Beyond this broad outline, we are still learning about the basin—the earth forces that created it, whether it was open to the ocean, where the sediment that filled it came from, and how long it lasted. The answers to these questions help us understand the history of the continent. For Belt rocks preserve in their layers, better than any other rock in North America, a record of the Middle Proterozoic, the geologic eon in which they formed. Consequently geologists rely on them to develop hypotheses about everything from paleogeography (how the continents were arranged during the Middle Proterozoic) to the history of the western half of North America.

Although there have been half a dozen explanations for the origins of the Belt sediments, two prevail. The first has the sediments accumulating in a marine environment—over tidal flats, in deltas, and in the open ocean. According to it, the basin was part of a continental shelf that extended into a proto-Pacific Ocean. In the second explanation, the basin is an inland sea, a giant lake that lay within the North American continent at a time when it was joined to another landmass. This sea, sometimes fresh, sometimes salty, may have been open to the ocean, but only during the earliest part of its history. Today's Caspian Sea or Black Sea are roughly analogous, except that during the Middle Proterozoic, land plants had not yet evolved so there was nothing to slow erosion. When it rained, the water gushed across the land in gigantic sheets, carrying huge quantities of mud and sand with it. Over eons, the sediments built up enormous fans or aprons thousands of feet thick. Eventually, they filled the basin.

At the foundation of the second interpretation is the theory of plate tectonics, which says that North America and other continents sit on plates that slowly glide across the earth's mantle. The plates are pushed by convection currents circulating in the mantle, much the way dumplings are

Water tumbles over dolomite ledges along Going-to-the-Sun Road. Some geologists believe that the rock of the park formed from sediment eroded off another continent, most likely Australia. (JOE WEYDT)

pushed around by boiling soup. Plate movement is slow—an inch or so a year (about the same speed that your fingernails grow)—but it is ceaseless and, given geologic time spans, enough to ensure momentous change in the geography of the planet.

The movement of plates periodically brings continents together, and the resulting slow-motion collisions are violent. Continental crust crumples, and mountain chains are born. The Appalachians, the Alps, and the Himalayas are examples. Plate movement also pulls continents apart, most often along the relatively weak weld where two plates had previously joined. That side of the process is called continental rifting, and it is occurring right now in Africa's Great Rift Valley. If rifting continues there, East Africa will eventually separate from the rest of the continent and become a continent unto itself.

According to the second interpretation, the Belt Basin was a rift, a place where the continent had stretched and broke and subsided and would ultimately tear apart. Geologic features suggest that what was once the western margin of North America has been married at least once to another continent. And there is good geologic evidence for a cataclysmic separation occurring about 700 million years ago. The inland sea interpretation is also supported by research that shows the Belt sediments generally become finer as you move east across the group, a trend that implies the muds washed in from the west side of the basin (because coarser, heavier materials settle first). Had they been accumulating on a continental shelf, that would have been impossible; there would have been nothing but ocean to the west.

So what was the land mass to the west from which all those sediments eroded? Researchers using radioactive isotopes to date sand grains imbedded in the Belt rocks have found they originated in granite that cooled between 1.64 and 1.86 billion years ago. No granite in North America is of that age. This prompted geologists to look elsewhere for the source—specifically the underlying rocks of Siberia, Antarctica, and Australia because paleogeographers believe those continents may have been connected to North America during the Middle Proterozoic. They found granite in both Australia and Siberia that matches that of the sand grains imbedded in Glacier's rocks. The most recent research, which incorporates additional evidence, now firmly points to ancient rock formations in Siberia. To say that the mountains of Glacier National Park might be made of ground-up Siberia speaks volumes about how the geography of this planet is utterly impermanent.

A Layer-Cake Geology

Whichever continent it was, it gave up a substantial chunk of its terrain to the Belt Basin. The accumulation in the park, cooked and compressed as it is, measures 3 to 4 miles deep. Those 15,000 to 20,000 vertical feet of strata can be divided into twelve formations (and three major groups): the Prichard, Altyn, Waterton, and Appekunny (of the Lower Belt); the Grinnell and Empire (of the Ravalli Group); the Helena or Siyeh; and the Snowslip, Shepard, Mount Shields, Bonner, and McNamara (of the Missoula Group).

These formations are stacked like differently flavored layers of a fat wedding cake and are almost as easy to identify. Blocky Mount Gould, for example, is four-layered: At the base is the Grinnell, a purplish red or plum. Next is the Empire, a dull gray-green layer of pistachio. On it lies the Helena, a buff or cream that might pass as a tier of vanilla; and on the very top rests the Snowslip, a mélange of flavors—mostly pale reds and greens, but also yellows, oranges, and light purples.

Each formation, with its characteristic sediment types, represents different kinds of deposition and a different stage in the history of the Belt Basin. The formations can be read as a mystery novel is read, by piecing together clues to reconstruct a scene, in this case the character of the Belt Basin at a given moment. Cobbles and pebbles of quartz, granite, and feldspar cemented together in a matrix of sand could be interpreted as remnants of channels and longitudinal bars of an ancient braided stream (realizing modern braided streams create the same pattern). Flat, laminated coarse sand may be evidence of flooding across the middle and lower sections of an alluvial apron. Mud cracks record an episode of desiccation, of retreating shorelines. By studying and interpreting the layers and formations, we can piece together the 200-million-plus-year story of the basin.

What follows are descriptions of the Belt formations coupled with explanations of how the rocks may have formed, why they have the colors they do, or why they possess certain peculiar structures. To avoid tarrying too long on this stage of the park's geologic story, I have presented just one interpretation of the Belt Basin: that of a restricted basin with periodic inpourings of ocean water.

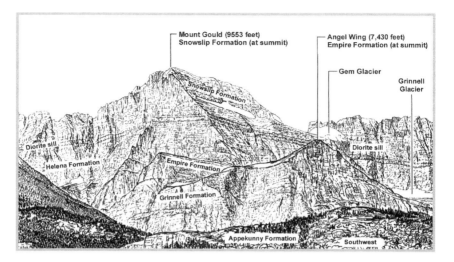

The view looking southward from the Many Glacier area. The various Belt rock formations are labeled. (The formation names under the names of the peaks are for the summit rocks only.) (U.S. GEOLOGICAL SURVEY)

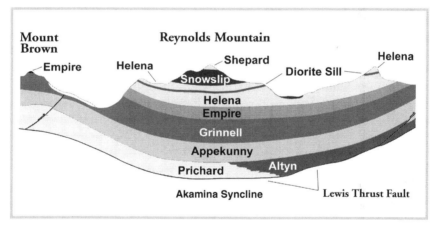

A simplified cross section of the park from Mount Brown to near Siyeh Pass, showing the park's major formations. (U.S. GEOLOGICAL SURVEY)

Putting Down the Foundation:
The Prichard, Waterton, and Altyn

On the west side of Glacier, the lowest and oldest rocks belong to the Prichard formation; on the east side, to the Waterton and Altyn formations. These three formations constitute the basement or underbelly of the

Belt Supergroup. In cross section they hang like a horse's belly. The Prichard shows itself all along the base of the mountains on the east side of the North Fork Valley. The Waterton is exposed only in the far northeast corner of the park, especially on the east flank of Yellow Mountain and farther east of there on Sherburne Peak, where I examined it. The rest of it, an estimated 4,000 vertical feet, is hidden beneath younger rock. Similarly, most of the Altyn is buried. On a geologic map it appears serpentine, a sinuous ribbon that snakes along much of the park's eastern margin. You can see it directly and perhaps best on the south face of Yellow Mountain or at the base of the cliffs cut by Apikuni Falls. Its name comes from a prospector's settlement that was inundated when the dam creating Lake Sherburne was built on Swiftcurrent Creek.

The Prichard is dark green and gray argillite. Argillite is a clay-rich rock, a hardened siltstone or shale (shale is simply hardened mud). Prichard argillite is finely layered. It splits easily. Such ultrathin, smooth laminations of clay and silt tell us the Prichard formed in still waters, well below the reach of waves. At that time, the Belt Sea was young and deep, as deep perhaps as it would ever be.

The Waterton and the Altyn are mostly dolomite, although both contain small amounts of blue-gray limestone. Dolomite is a carbonate rock, like limestone except that it is magnesium-rich. Because of the iron in it, its surface weathers to shades of tan, yellow, and orange. Waterton dolomite, when first exposed, is green or gray; seasoned, it is yellow, orange, brown, and in a few places a rusty reddish brown, even cranberry. Imbedded in the Waterton, near the bottom of what we can see of it, are small blebs of black chert that, like dolomite, weather to rich browns and rusty oranges. Altyn dolomite starts out creamy white to steel gray and weathers tawny, terra-cotta, or salmon, colors conspicuous from a distance. Layers of coarse quartz sand and ripple marks indicate some parts of the Altyn formed in relatively shallow water, when the Belt Sea was receding.

Although dolomite is not uncommon in the world, there are few places where you can see it being created—the Florida Keys, the Bahaman Islands, the Lesser Antilles—and there it is forming in near trivial amounts.

Geologists still puzzle over "the dolomite problem." If more than half the world's carbonate rocks greater than a billion years old are dolomite, why don't we see masses of it forming today? Why is there nowhere in the world a sea with a muddy, dolomitic bottom? Some look at the small amounts of dolomite forming currently from solutions of magnesium percolating through pre-existing limestone and say Precambrian dolomite formed the same way. Others argue that it might also form the way limestone sometimes does, when carbonate minerals, in this case calcium magnesium carbonate, precipitate out of hypersaline waters. Glacier has a lot of dolomite in the Waterton, the Altyn, and in other formations; exactly how it formed, however, remains a mystery.

What was the Belt Sea like when the Altyn was being deposited? Its waters were most likely shallow and warm, and although its shores were barren, its depths were crowded with life—not animals or plants but cyanobacteria, what some people call blue-green algae (even though there is no relationship between cyanobacteria and other organisms called algae). Communities of cyanobacteria coated the muddy bottom of the sea, forming reefs in some places. The structures they left behind, called stromatolites, are abundant in the Altyn.

Modern, dome-shaped stromatolites growing in Hamelin Pool, southwest Australia. The photo was taken at low tide. (PHILLIP PLAYFORD, GEOLOGICAL SURVEY OF WESTERN AUSTRALIA)

Stromatolite means "stone or fossil mat." The name refers to the mat-like accumulations of cyanobacteria that created them. The fossils them-selves, however, are anything but matlike in their appearance and can take the shape of domes, cones, or branched and unbranched columns. The particular form depends on the specific kinds of organisms that created them, on how deep the water was when they formed, and on a host of other factors such as water currents, seasonal patterns, rates of sedimenta-tion, and water chemistry. In various cross sections, stromatolites can look like swirls or eddies of water, intricately branched coral, the pleated leather of a collapsed bellows, irregular tree rings, an open Japanese fan, or the domed cap of a mushroom.

We know a little about how stromatolites form because we can watch modern ones grow. Stromatolite-forming blue-green algal mats thrive today in all sorts of places—in freshwater lakes and streams, on marine tidal flats, near deep ocean vents, in shallow seas, in hot and cold springs, beneath the ice at both poles, and on dry ground. The mats growing in some of these loca-tions are building stromatolites similar to those in Glacier. That suggests that those sites might be analogous, at least in certain respects, to the Belt Sea. There are fossils in the Altyn, for example, equivalent in many ways to struc-tures being produced today by mats of cyanobacteria in the Bahamas. Thus, it is tempting to look to the Bahaman examples as we try to envision the Belt Sea. But there are also budding stromatolites growing in hot springs in Yel-lowstone Park that look just like miniature versions of stromatolites imbedded in the rocks along Going-to-the-Sun Road. Yellowstone's are thriving at tem-peratures of 140°F. The Belt Sea was undoubtedly much cooler.

Stromatolites do not contain mineralized cyanobacteria; most are devoid of any kind of microbial remains. They are, rather, layers of calcium carbonate and sediment built up and trapped by colonies of cyanobacteria. Mats of cyanobacteria convert alternating spurts of growth and sediment into layers of calcite. The cells die and disintegrate almost as quickly as they become coated with lime. In the end all you have are the stacked lamina-tions. The laminations then get buried in mud and eventually turned to stone.

In the Belt Sea, cyanobacteria mats created cone-shaped stromatolites called conophyton. The Helena Formation, which lies several formations above the Altyn, is crowded with them; many are more than 30 feet high. A billion and a half years ago they stood on the sea floor like trees, a cyanobacterial forest of two- and three-story-high, upside-down ice cream cones.

Cone-shaped stromatolites start out as gossamer-thin blankets of filamentous cyanobacteria. The filaments or threads are mucus-coated and glide randomly across the bottom until, here and there, they tangle and form knots, similar to the way tiny wool balls form in the nap of a sweater. The knots protrude above the mat. Other gliding filaments meet them and are deflected upward. Knots grow into tufts as more filaments pile on and become entangled. The tufts become more pointed the taller they grow because the movements of the filaments become less random and more directed toward the light source—the sun—which, because of light scattering, appears to be directly overhead the entire day. In currents, more filaments build on one side, and the cone grows a ridge. Branches occur when filaments knot up on the sides of the cone, and the knots start new growths.

As the mat grows, seasons change. Perhaps more rain falls. The rivers swell and turn brown with mud. The mud washes into the basin, turning clear water murky, and less sunlight penetrates. The mat goes dormant for a while, or at least its growth slows enough that it becomes overwhelmed by sediment, covered with lime and mud. Then the season changes again, the waters clear, and the colony grows a fresh mat. The cycle repeats. Layers build and, if sedimentation continues, the structure, a stromatolite, is preserved.

The cyanobacteria aids this process to its detriment. During photosynthesis, it consumes carbon dioxide and gives off oxygen. The removal of CO_2 causes a chemical reaction that forces lime dissolved in the water to come out of solution and form tiny particles. These encrust the cyanobacteria. They form a chalky glaze over the entire mat, similar to the way plaque coats teeth. The particles adhere to sediment, too, and make the mud limy. In this way the cyanobacteria speeds its own death and helps layers to build. It also makes the sediments limy. Hence, the cyanobacteria that created the stromatolites are responsible as well for a substantial amount of the park's limestone and dolomite.

Most important, the cyanobacteria pumped oxygen into what was, one and a half billion years ago, an oxygen-poor atmosphere. That allowed other life-forms to develop, everything from insects to mammals. So, in a real sense, we owe our existence to the cyanobacteria that built Glacier's stromatolites (and that built other stromatolites in Proterozoic rocks elsewhere in the world).

On a recent hike to Apikuni Falls on the east side of the park, I saw two kinds of stromatolites nested in the Altyn. One had branching columns 8 inches across and 6 feet high. The other was columnar but unbranched, somewhat elongated, and up to 9 feet high. It looked almost like a pleated curtain.

The Appekunny and its Fossils

The Appekunny Formation rests on the Altyn and the Prichard. At Apikuni Mountain, a good place among many to see it, it is almost half a mile thick. On that side of the park it can be seen everywhere immediately above the yellows, browns, and light grays of the Altyn. (The two spellings, Appekunny for the formation and Apikuni for the mountain, arise because the word is Blackfeet, and Indian words were spelled phonetically, hence the multiple spellings. Appekunny was the Indian name of author James Willard Schultz, who lived with and wrote about the Blackfeet, and both the formation and mountain are named for him. In Blackfeet, the word means "scabby or spotted robe"—the root *apik* referring to smallpox.)

The greenest rock in the park, the Appekunny ranges in color from an unusually bright green to jade to olive to a dark grayish green. It has only a few stromatolites, all in the northwestern part of the park. Elsewhere in the formation, impressions that look like strings of beads are thought to be fossils of some early animal. At nearly a billion and a half years old, *Horodyskia moniliformis*, as it has been named, is considered one of the earliest known multicellular fossils in the world.

Most of the Appekunny is finely laminated quartz arenite (a hardened

Fossil stromatolites are abundant in several Glacier Park rock formations. These are in the Helena Formation along Going-to-the-Sun Road. (JOE WEYDT)

quartz sand) and siltite (a similarly pressure-cooked siltstone)—sand and mud deposited in deep water. The rock sparkles when you hold a piece of it up to the light. Toward the top of the formation, though, there is a 190-foot layer of mud-cracked argillite. The cracks and the beautiful mud-chip breccias found there formed on a mudflat. They suggest the Belt Sea had begun to shrink. They mark the first big transition in the history of the basin and, not coincidentally, the end of the Lower Belt.

A Draining and Filling: The Ravalli Group

One afternoon I walked the trail that follows along the north side of McDonald Creek to a place about 3 miles above the lake, to the point at which purple and red rock overwhelms green. This is where the Appekunny Formation gives way to the overlying Grinnell. The red comes

Goat Lick, near Essex, where the red beds of the Grinnell Formation (right) are faulted against a band of dark gray rocks of the Helena, which in turn are cut by a second fault that dropped red and green argillite of the Snowslip. The faults bleed a salty juice that draws goats, elk, and deer. (DAVID ROCKWELL)

from hematite or iron oxide, the same pigment found in red paint. I picked up a piece of the rock that had broken off from a small outcrop above the creek. It was almost as red as a freshly painted barn.

Grinnell rock is mostly thinly bedded argillite and siltite with occasional layers of white quartzite. Loaded with clay, it formed during a period when sea waters were retreating and sediments were exposed to the air and oxidized, which explains their red color, the rouge of rust. After the sea had shrunk considerably, floodwaters laden with sediment poured into the basin across broad alluvial aprons and vast mudflats. They filled depressions and created shallow lakes. Wind whipped up waves that rippled the muddy bottoms. Eventually the lakes evaporated and became mudflats again. They baked in the sun, dried, and cracked. Today, mud cracks and ripples in the rock look no more than weeks, even days, old though they are well over a billion years old.

There is a place where the Grinnell borders two other, younger, formations. At Goat Lick, near Essex, a fault dropped the Snowslip Formation down against Grinnell rock. Caught in the middle is a small, 100-yard-wide block of the Helena Formation. From the Goat Lick Overlook off U.S. Highway 2, you see the three formations lined up: red argillite of the Grinnell against dark gray dolomite of the Helena against green argillites of the Snowslip. The faults that cut these blocks go deep, slicing all the way through the Belt rocks into underlying layers of marine sedimentary rock. Those bottom rocks, laid down in a salty ocean, bleed a mineral-rich juice that migrates up the faults to the surface and dries, leaving a crust of salt. Like a bucket of oats, the lick draws mountain goats, elk, and deer from miles around.

Look for the Grinnell Formation on Mount Grinnell or at Red Rock Point on McDonald Creek, although it can be seen in many places. The pretty blood red, plum, and mauve cobbles so common on Glacier's stream bottoms, for example, are likely from the Grinnell.

The Empire, a thin 500-foot-thick formation, rests on top of the Grinnell. When fresh, as in a roadcut, it is gray to green; it weathers to light green. The rock in the Empire is mostly argillite but contains some dolomite. A bed of coarse quartz sand, probably an old beach deposit, separates it from the Grinnell. The sea was rising again, filling up the basin once more.

The greenness of the Empire (and the Appekunny) comes from a chemical process called reduction, the exact opposite of what occurs when iron rusts. When Empire sediments settled out, they contained as much iron oxide as those of the Grinnell, but because they were underwater and not exposed to oxygen, the iron combined with silica compounds. Then, pressure and heat converted the iron-silicate minerals to chlorite, the green compound coloring the rock. To see the Empire, look at the summit of Angel Wing from Many Glacier Hotel or at the lower part of Scalplock Mountain just east of Essex or at the east side of Mount Peabody.

Midway: The Helena Formation

Piled on top of the Empire is the Helena, one of the most massive formations in the park and probably the most noticeable because it makes up the bulk of so many peaks. It was once known as the Siyeh Limestone, and many still call it that. But the U.S. Geological Survey formally changed the name in the 1970s. The Helena measures about 3,300 feet at its thickest point, which is in the southwestern part of the park. It alternates between dark gray and melting tones of tan and khaki, is heavily jointed (which gives it the appearance of stone blocks), and often breaks into huge slabs and house-size rectangular blocks. It also breaks off in smaller chunks, a characteristic that on more than one climbing expedition has sent chills down my spine. Most of the rock cut by Going-to-the-Sun Road from just above The Loop to Logan Pass and down the other side to Siyeh Bend is in the Helena Formation.

If the sea was rising when the Empire formed, it continued to do so during the deposition of most of the Helena. Then, apparently, the climate changed and began to cycle back and forth between humid and arid. The sea responded with rhythmic risings and fallings. Those cycles show up in the Helena as alternating layers of silica-rich rock and dolomite. During the wet, rainy periods, the sea expanded and became fresher, less saline. Floods washed huge volumes of dark siliciclastic or silica-rich sediment into the basin. Then, slowly, the rains stopped. Decades or centuries of drought prevailed. The sea shrank. Its waters grew hypersaline along the sea margin, saturated with high levels of calcium carbonate. The carbonate precipitated out and attached itself to the clay-rich mud, forming the dolomite or upper part of the cycle. Then, gradually, the climate became humid once more, and the pattern repeated. Much of the rock of the Helena reflects these climate changes in a hypnotizing series of dark and light layers.

Near the upper part of the Helena, a massive, 100-foot-high band of stromatolites is conspicuous enough to see from a couple of miles away. Known as the Conophyton Zone, it does not erode as quickly as the surrounding rock and hence forms sheer cliffs. Looking at these escarpments of fossil cyanobacteria, I imagine a shallow Precambrian sea stretching from horizon to horizon with a bottom of white sand broken by reefs of green stromatolites. Look for the Conophyton Zone on mountains on both sides of Going-to-the-Sun Road east of Logan Pass: On the south side of the road it appears on Little Chief and Citadel Mountains, on the north, on Going-to-the-Sun Mountain and Matahpi Peak. You can study it at close range on the west side of Logan Pass in a roadcut about a half mile below the tunnel. The fossils, both as individuals and as clusters, can be striking and quite beautiful with their sweeping whirls and eddies. Some of the more extraordinary assemblages remind me of Van Gogh's *Starry Night*.

Also present in the Helena is a considerable amount of oolitic limestone. Oolites, or ooids, are tiny, sand-size, egglike balls of calcium carbonate that form in shallow lime-rich water. As waves and currents roll tiny grains of sand near the shore, the sand grains build up layers of precipitated calcium carbonate. The result is small, almost perfectly round pearls of the stuff. Snowballs of precipitate. You can see oolites forming today on the beaches of the Great Salt Lake and in the tidal sand flats of the Bahaman Banks, where they form great underwater dunes. The rock that forms when oolites become cemented together with calcium carbonate is called oolitic limestone, exactly what we have in parts of the Helena.

There are also "molar tooth" structures. They bear this strange appellation because the one who named them thought they looked like the markings in the molar teeth of elephants, and indeed, their squiggly lines and ridges resemble the molar teeth of many animals. But the rocks are not fossil teeth. They are not fossils at all. They probably formed when calcite precipitated in open spaces or in pockets between layers of sediment—in vacant mud cracks, trapped gas bubbles, holes in stromatolites, voids created by rotting plants. The last time I hiked along the Highline Trail, I found some good "molar teeth" about an hour's walk from Logan Pass on the way to Granite Park. Just after I left the forested area I saw, on both sides of the trail, mammoth chunks of Helena limestone bearing these undulating "tooth" marks. I also saw some nice mound-shaped stromatolites.

Just above the Conophyton Zone in the Helena is a sill, a horizontal plate of igneous rock that formed when hot magma from the mantle squirted up through the Belt sediments into the Helena and then oozed sheetlike between layers. Throughout the park, it stands out as a 130-foot black igneous band sandwiched between narrow strips of albino rock. From a distance it is a dark stripe, an even seam that cuts through many of the peaks. When the sill formed, the magma pushed skyward so forcefully that it lifted the overlying sediments 100 feet. It was so hot that it cooked the new limestone both above and below it, bleached it white, and changed it to marble. Cooling rapidly, the magma formed a fine- to medium-grained rock—a mix of feldspar and hornblende called diorite. Look for it a little more than halfway up Mount Gould, the Garden Wall, and Mount Wilbur. Those mountains show it well, but you can see it on dozens of other peaks, too. Along the Highline Trail, the sill becomes richer in light-colored feldspar. It looks like granite, hence the name Granite Park. The name sticks, even though there is no granite in Glacier.

The Top of the Cake: The Missoula Group

The boundary between the Helena and the next formation, the Snowslip, is abrupt. At the point of contact, the Helena is gray to tan, the Snowslip red and green. The Helena, a dolomite, is flush with carbonate. The Snowslip is calcareous and lacks substantial carbonate. The end of the Helena has abundant ooids. Conversely, mud balls and pieces of dried mud cracked into chips and overlapping one another in the manner of shingles or fish scales signal the start of the Snowslip. The change represents another transition in the history of the Belt Basin and marks the beginning of a new rock group, the Missoula. Apparently, the continental crust was beginning to rift again, not to pull apart entirely but to stretch and thin. The basin widened. Most important, sediment now started washing in from the south and southwest, from roughly the direction of what is now the Salmon River country of Idaho. Until now—throughout the deposition of the Prichard, Waterton, Altyn, Appekunny, Grinnell, Empire, and Helena—it had been coming from the west. Rifting, however, changed that by lowering or pulling the northwestern landmass farther away, diminishing its contribution.

The approximately 2,000 feet of the Snowslip can be broken into five major divisions, or members. Members 1, 3, and 5 are maroon to red. Their sediments record periods when the shoreline or beach was building out into the sea from the south. Exposed mud and sand flats stretched far out into the basin. The sediments oxidized to different degrees, creating

Most of Mount Wilbur is limestone and dolomite of the Helena Formation. The summit, however, is argillite—red and green rock of the Snowslip Formation. (JOE WEYDT)

the many hues of red. Members 1, 3, and 5 display mud cracks, mud chips, and ripple marks. The intervening members, numbers 2 and 4, are pale green. They record sea expansions, times when the muds were inundated. The yellows and oranges that occur here and there come from small amounts of weathered dolomite. Mound-shaped stromatolites are common in several of the members, especially in the sandy, green rock of member 2. The Snowslip is named for Snowslip Mountain, a peak at the southern tip of the park famous for its avalanches. There, toward the summit, you can see all five members of the formation. The Snowslip also forms the top half of the Garden Wall and is well exposed around Hidden Lake and from Granite Park to The Loop.

There is no agreement on where the Snowslip ends, but a logical place to draw the line is at a thin bed of coarse white sand that sits like icing on top of member 5. This quartzite beach deposit is covered by a layer of stromatolites. Together, the sand and the stromatolites signal the beginning of the Shepard, a rising sea, and a return to carbonates. The formation is dolomitic and weathers from yellow to dusky orange.

During the early deposition of the Shepard, rifting produced faults that cut through the Belt sediments. Hot mantle magma shouldered its way up through the faults and flowed out across the sea floor. As it hit the water, it cooled quickly and formed lava pillows, similar to basalt domelike structures now found at the bottom of the Atlantic or Pacific, where magma oozes from fissures in mid-oceanic ridges. Except here, the water was shallow—30 to 50 feet deep. We know because the viscous rock billowed high enough to breach the surface. Once exposed to the air, it took longer to cool and moved riverlike, spewing over itself in smooth, ropy flows called pahoehoe, a Hawaiian word. The event is called the Purcell Lava. At Hole-in-the-Wall, its northernmost exposure, the Purcell Lava is 300 feet thick. It thins to 60 feet by the time it reaches Granite Park and pinches out altogether at Huckleberry Mountain. The best places to see it are at Boulder Pass, Fifty Mountain, and Granite Park, where it stands out well from the surrounding rock.

Above the lava, about 100 feet of red strata, oxidized argillite, record a brief drop in the level of the Belt Sea. Above that, the main body of the Shepard, 600 to 1,300 feet of yellow stone, caps many of the park's peaks, including Mount Cleveland, the tallest in the park, and forms the cliffs around Granite Park.

Climb out of the Shepard and you hit red again: the mud-cracked wine reds, brick reds, and rose reds of the Mount Shields Formation. Like the rusted beds of the Snowslip, the lower part of the Mount Shields (members 1 and 2) formed when mudflats and alluvial fans built up and pushed farther out to sea. The top of member 2 is a spectacular creamy pink limestone layer of ooids and small stromatolites left after an interval of sea expansion. Then red again, 1,400 feet of it. More mudflats. Much of the rock here is rippled. The formation is capped by purplish gray and blackish gray-green argillite—another cycle of high water. The darkest mudstone at the top indicates the sea waters had freshened.

Not much Belt rock occurs above the Mount Shields Formation in Glacier Park. Most of it has eroded away. The Bonner Formation, next above the Mount Shields, and the McNamara Formation on top of it are the topmost and most recent of the Belt Supergroup rocks in Glacier. The Bonner is a thin, 840-foot-thick wedge of pink quartzite, a hardened sandstone deposited on an alluvial apron. The McNamara, which is more substantial, is a cracked and rippled gray-green mudstone that records one last drowning and drying of the sea floor. Both formations are exposed in the southern part of the park east of Mount Shields and near the mouth of Coal Creek.

2

Shoving the Park into Place

The laying down of that great assemblage of Belt rock constitutes the first and biggest chapter of the park's geologic history. It ended without major geologic incident about 1.2 billion years ago. For the next 700 million years, not much seems to have happened to the rocks in Glacier Park. To the west, however, in eastern Washington, rifting continued, and the continent that had been stuck to North America (the source of all the Belt sediments) drifted away. Then, about 500 million years ago, during the Cambrian period, sea levels rose and Montana was flooded by ocean waters replete with early marine animals—trilobites, brachiopods, sponges, primitive mollusks, worms, and crustaceans. The Devonian and Mississippian periods followed and left behind more deposits—mostly dolomite and limestone. But throughout those hundreds of millions of years, Glacier's Belt rocks suffered little deformation. They show no signs of torture, record no great episodes of tectonic disturbance—no severe crumpling, no intense folding or faulting, no episodes of mountain building—only some gentle tilting and warping. Of course, erosion worked the rock, washed away entire formations, but only the top ones. Other than that, the Belt rocks rested comfortably.

Until 60 million to 70 million years ago. It is almost as if the rocks had been resting, procrastinating, preparing for the five- to ten-million-year event that would transplant a large chunk of them 50 miles to the east, up and out of the Belt Basin. The chunk to be relocated was titanic—a slab

300 miles long, in excess of 50 miles wide, and up to 4 miles thick. It didn't slip on its own, wasn't pulled by gravity; it was shoved. In the hundred million years preceding the chunk's displacement, North America was crashing into islands the size of Japan. The collisions battered and compressed its crust, lifted mountains, and sent the future Glacier Park sailing, albeit slowly, across northwestern Montana.

Lifting the Rockies

One hundred and eighty million years ago, at the latitude of Glacier National Park, the west coast of America lay somewhere near the Idaho-Washington border. If it had existed then, Sandpoint, Idaho, would have been a Pacific seaport. At that time (the middle of the Jurassic) the west coast of North America ran from the border between the Yukon and the Northwest Territories south, through the middle of British Columbia, Idaho, and Nevada into the Gulf of California. Modern Alaska, the Yukon, much of British Columbia, and all of Washington, Oregon, western Idaho, and western California were absent—yet to be added. Those pieces sat as islands and microcontinents in the Pacific much as Indonesia and the Philippines sit in the South China Sea. At the time, the North American Continental Plate was drifting west. The Pacific plates were sliding under it and being pulled into the mantle. The island arcs, too light to be pulled into the mantle, gathered, one at a time over the course of 100 million years, onto the western edge of North America, fattening it into its current shape.

The sum total of all those islands crashing into the west coast had the same effect as a continent-to-continent collision. It produced forces that raised and rippled North America from Alaska to Mexico. The early Rockies rose up. Even after the islands had stopped colliding (about 80 million years ago), the compression continued. The Rockies kept building—for another thirty-five million years. This later, post-collision phase of mountain building, of folding and faulting, of thrusting and mashing, is called the Laramide Orogeny. It was during the Laramide that the Belt rocks moved into Glacier.

At least two theories account for why deformation continued so long

Aerial view of the Logan Pass area. Logan Pass is center right. The rock that makes up all the park's mountains formed 50 miles to the west and was thrust into its present position by compressive forces that started about 180 million years ago. (NATIONAL AGRICULTURAL IMAGE PROGRAM)

after the last island arc slammed into the continent. The first argues that new terrains added so much igneous rock to the western edge of North America that the crust there grew thicker and hotter and more plastic. Imagine a pile of cool honey poured into a warm wok. As long as it is cool, the honey is glutinous—viscous, like continental crust. It pours into a high mound. But as it sits there and soaks up heat from the wok, the bottom layer becomes more liquid. Honey begins to peel off the top and roll down the sides in thick curtains. They force the lower, more fluid honey to ooze out at the bottom and move vertically, up the sides of the wok. According to this model, the Laramide Orogeny was caused by spreading—the rock oozing out under its own weight. The resulting compression fractured the continental crust, which is more brittle than honey, and thrust great shards of it eastward.

Another theory examines the speed of the colliding plates. Until about seventy-five million years ago, the Pacific plates were smashing into and subducting under the North American plate at a rate of about 2 inches a year. Then, suddenly, the rate tripled. The plates continued colliding at this faster speed, about 6 inches a year, for some thirty million years, then slowed again. Some geologists believe the increase in collision speed compressed the western margin of the continent like an accordion and created the Laramide Orogeny.

The Great Thrust

It could have been a combination of the two, of spreading and plate-induced compression, that broke the Glacier Belt rocks free from their Belt Basin foundation and shoved them to where they now stand at the edge of the Great Plains. The violence began when the compressive strain became so great that the Belt rocks broke, cracked along a nearly horizontal plane, and began to move eastward. In this, a thrust fault, a fracture forms nearly parallel to the surface of the earth. The rock on one side then begins to ride up and over the rock on the other side. The Lewis Thrust Fault, as this one is called, sliced slightly diagonally through the Belt Basin at the level of the Prichard, Waterton, and Altyn formations. Everything above that fault line moved, pushed along by the same compressive forces that caused the fracture.

The movement was spasmodic; the full displacement of Glacier's Belt rocks took millions of years. Lying still for centuries, they would lurch forward 10 or more feet in an instant. In such a moment the entire slab or major portions of it would leap forward and rattle the earth for hundreds of miles around. If you average these explosive quakes over millions of years, the slab sped along at probably less than half an inch a year. Striations on rocks show the direction of the advance was northeast. When the slab finally parked, it sat on top of rock 1,300 million years younger, violating the natural law that says rock gets older as you move down through the earth's strata.

Looking north from Marias Pass, you can see the fault line as it cuts through the middle of both Little Dog and Summit Mountains, a crisp, even, nearly horizontal line with relatively few splays. It is easy for me to imagine it in three dimensions there, as a thrust fault that extends north and south and east and west, as rock riding over rock. Among geologists,

The Lewis Thrust Fault as seen from near Marias Pass. The fault shows up as a thin line of light tan rock about halfway up Little Dog and Summit Mountains. Below the line is Cretaceous-age rock about 70 million years old, above it Altyn limestone that formed some 1.6 billion years ago. (JOE WEYDT)

the Lewis Thrust Fault is perhaps Glacier's single most famous feature, not because it looks spectacular. It doesn't. Rather, this fault's fame derives from its size and from the difference between the ages of the rocks on either side of it. Here 1.6 billion-year-old rock perches above 70 million-year-old rock. One day I hiked up to the fault line, where it cuts across Summit Mountain, and was surprised to see how thin it actually was. In places I could almost cover it with my hand. On top of that line sat Altyn dolomite and the rest of the Belt rock formations; below it was Cretaceous-age Marias River shale. The Altyn is hard rock, as hard as it is old. It resists erosion. It forms cliffs. The Marias River shale is soft and young. It is weak rock that weathers rapidly and crumbles into gentle slopes. Most of it is covered with soil and trees.

Viewed from above, the Lewis Thrust Fault surfaces along a line that runs from Mount Kidd, British Columbia, in the north, to Steamboat Mountain in west-central Montana in the south. In Glacier that line runs just inside the park's eastern boundary. West of it are Belt rocks and the start of the Rocky Mountains. East of it are Cretaceous shales and sandstone hills and the beginnings of the northern Great Plains. The mountains that spring up there, just west of the line, that stand like a parapet against eastern Montana, are rootless in the sense that they are not anchored, not sunk into the earth like most mountains. Rather they perch on top of it, unconnected except by juxtaposition to the rock beneath.

Ever since Bailey Willis, an intrepid geologist and early explorer of the park, discovered the Lewis Thrust Fault in 1901, geologists have considered it one of the world's classic geologic structures. They cite it in freshman geology textbooks. Many come to visit and study it. For a time they thought the Lewis Thrust Fault was the world's largest such fault, although we now know it is not. In lecture halls around the country, geology professors described it: "A perfect example of a thrust fault can be seen in the Rockies in western Montana. There all of the rock in Glacier National Park slid eastward as a great slab along the Lewis Thrust Fault to its current location. The original position of the slab, before thrusting, was 65 to 100 kilometers to the west..." When my instructor gave his version, he placed our textbook on a table in front of the class, then lifted one end of the table until the book started to slide. "This is essentially what happened in Glacier Park," he said, "except that the rock slab—the Lewis Plate—was as long as Colorado is wide."

For a long time, geologists imagined it as this giant, coherent, booklike sheet of rock tobogganing slowly down an east-sloping incline. The motion was due to gravity, not compression. A close analogy, they said, would be a chunk of heavy snow breaking loose and sliding down a roof. They might have admitted that the comparison was a slight oversimplification.

The current theory (accepted since the middle 1980s) describes the Lewis Thrust as a more complicated event. First, compression, not gravity, moved the slab. Second, much of the movement was uphill not downhill (the fault dips 20 degrees to the southwest). Third, the internal structures of the slab are complicated and enigmatic. In recent papers with titles like "Geologic Surprises from a Classic Fault and its Allochthon," geologists report on a series of faults and folds within the slab hitherto unknown. These reveal a confused internal geometry and thus a tortured history, much more tortured, anyway, than previously thought.

Geologists have identified several places where the Belt formations yielded by buckling into multiple small thrust faults. Two are on the east side at Mount Henry and Yellow Mountain; a third is on the west side at Elk Mountain. In all three places the faults are so numerous and so close together they stack like shingles. Another area where the rock is badly deformed is near the east end of Lake McDonald, from Gunsight Mountain to McPartland Mountain. As the Belt rocks were compressed, the Grinnell Formation in this area cracked and split, and a portion of it slid across itself. The rock resisted, and what had been horizontal bedding planes folded like a mangled fender. Grinnell is more flexible, more susceptible to bending than other Belt rock because it is thinly layered and because it abounds in clay. On McPartland Mountain its giant rose-colored curves and swirls look like folds of soft taffy.

Of Synclines and Anticlines

The long episode of crust shortening, the great compression that moved that sheet of rock, did some violence to the slab beyond those many shingled faults at its front end. If you were to cut the park in half along a line that runs from the east to the west and view it in cross section, you would see that its second most prominent structural feature (after the Lewis Thrust Fault) is a giant downward-bowed fold, or syncline. This one is called the Akamina Syncline. It bends the Belt formations, warping them into a trough whose long axis runs north-south through the approximate middle of the park. Earlier, I compared the cross section of the Prichard and Waterton formations to the curve of a horse's belly. They sway that way because they have been folded, as almost all the Belt rocks in Glacier's center have been folded, into a syncline. You can stand in many places in the park and see it simply by following the dipping line drawn by the bedding planes of the formations. Heavens Peak, for example, is on the syncline's west limb, and its strata slopes downward toward the east.

In cross section you will notice the same fold that warps the rock into the trough of the Akamina Syncline curves up to the west into a hump, a structure called an anticline. Anticlines and synclines are a consequence of compression. Push on the edge of a rug and it bends wavelike into a ridge (the anticline) and a trough (the syncline)—an S curve. This particular anticline is called the Flathead Anticline. It runs between and parallel to the Akamina Syncline and the North Fork Valley. The bend of the hump is tighter than that of the trough, so tight that rock within it is intricately bent and broken.

The Creation of the North and Middle Fork Valleys

About 45 million years ago, the forces causing the horizontal compression came to an end, and the continent's crust readjusted by spreading somewhat. That and the force of almost 4 vertical miles of Belt rock bearing down caused several faults to develop. It was the movement along these faults—the Flathead, Roosevelt, and Blacktail—that created the North Fork and Middle Fork Valleys.

The most prominent of the three faults, the Flathead Fault, runs parallel to and about 7 to 12 miles east of the park's western boundary from the Canadian border to Lincoln Creek. At Lincoln Creek it Ys into the Roosevelt and Blacktail Faults, which run all the way past the south end of the park. Thirty-seven million years ago, the Belt formations broke along these lines, and the giant block to the west dropped, slipping in such a manner that it listed like a sinking ship. The crust continued to stretch. Its movement tilted the block and dragged it almost 8 miles to the west. The displacement formed a half-graben, an asymmetrical trough or slanted basin that runs the length of the park's western boundary. Today both the North and Middle Forks of the Flathead River flow through it.

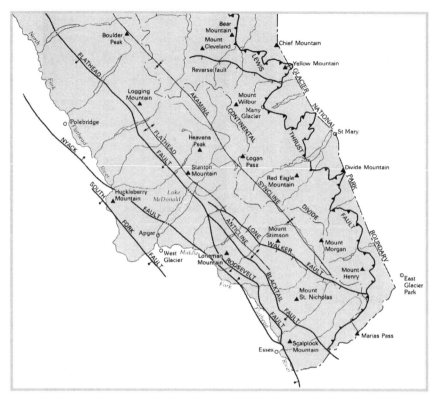

Major faults in Glacier National Park. The Lewis Thrust Fault runs along the eastern edge of the park. The Flathead, Roosevelt, and Blacktail Faults created the North Fork and Middle Fork Valleys. Also shown are the Akamina Syncline and the Flathead Anticline.
(U.S. GEOLOGICAL SURVEY)

Of course the block did not move all at once. It jumped a few yards every century. All the while, erosion worked the Belt formations, which stood as a towering range of mountains immediately to the east. The sediment rolled off them and into the basin, where it settled along streams and at the bottom of lakes and sloughs. The basin filled about as fast as the block was dropping. It filled with sand, silt, and rubble eroded from Belt rock, with volcanic ash exploded from volcanoes, and with organic matter from plants growing in the basin. That mix of material has since consolidated into red-brown and vermilion siltstones and claystones, into variegated maroon and green mudstones, into bluish oil shale and marlstone, into pebble and cobble conglomerates, and into coal—16,000 vertical feet of soft sedimentary stone known as the Kishenehn Formation.

We know from the fossils imbedded in the Kishenehn—fossils of mammals, fish, insects, snails, clams, leaves—a little of what that basin was like then, some thirty-five million years ago. It wasn't Montana, at least not the temperate Montana we know. It was more like Florida or Louisiana—subtropical, swampy, a lowland full of stagnant sloughs, marshes, and dying lakes. Its uplands, hot and humid, supported what must have been magnificent forests. The coal in the North Fork, which occurs sporadically in 6-inch to 3-foot seams throughout the basin, is the product of all that vegetative lushness. North Fork coal burns too cool and puts out too much ash to be of much value, but it was mined during the first decades of this century at a site just across the river from the park, along what's called the Coal Banks.

Oil wells have been drilled in the basin, too. Oil and gas seeps from the ground near Kintla and Bowman Lakes. Speculators sunk two wells at Kintla and along the river a year or two after the turn of the century. Neither produced. Their hope was that the oil was seeping from reservoirs in Kishenehn sandstones and sandy conglomerates, that the source rock was Kishenehn oil shale and coal. Geologists now believe the seeps are linked to the Flathead Fault and that the oil and gas escapes up the fault from marine sedimentary rock thousands of feet below the Kishenehn—from Cretaceous, Jurassic, Mississippian, Devonian, or Cambrian strata. The fault cuts through them all, plunging more than 5 miles into the earth.

These structures—the Lewis Thrust Fault, the Akamina Syncline, the Flathead Anticline, a couple of fold and thrust belts, a series of extensional faults, a basin that holds the North and Middle Forks of the Flathead River—underlie the park, defining it much the way a skeleton defines a bear and distinguishes it from, say, a deer. There are two mountain ranges in the park, the Livingston and Lewis ranges, but they are defined by erosional or surface features rather than by underlying structures. The Akamina Syncline, for instance, cuts diagonally right through both ranges. If you were to draw a line from West Glacier, through McDonald Lake, up McDonald Creek, west around Flattop Mountain, and through the Waterton Valley, everything to the west would be part of the Livingston Range, while everything to the east would be in the Lewis Range. The Continental Divide also cuts across both ranges. It follows the crest of the Lewis Range from Marias Pass north to Flattop Mountain; there it swings west to the crest of the Livingston Range, which it follows into Canada.

3

An Ice-Age Park

People come to Glacier for its surface features: its chains of emerald lakes, its hanging valleys, its knife-edge ridges, towering peaks, and amphitheater-like canyons. The park has been called a geologic opera not for its gentle syncline, thrust belts, or half-graben but for the way its surface has been gouged and chiseled by glaciers. Not the bantam-size glaciers that are here now, but Pleistocene glaciers, Antarctic-size glaciers, ice sheets that began arriving in pulses about two million years ago and retreated as recently as 10,000 years ago. Indeed, the park's name, Glacier, refers to the breathtaking features sculpted by those prehistoric sheets of moving ice.

During the Pleistocene, ice advanced over the continent four times. The Wisconsin Glaciation, the most recent, capped a third of the continent with almost as much ice as now rests on Antarctica, enough ice to lower the current level of the oceans more than 250 feet (because so much water was locked in the continental ice sheets). It is now thought that the Wisconsinan Glacial Interval covered more of North America with ice than most of the previous glacial intervals of the Pleistocene, intervals known as the Kansan and Nebraskan and Illinoian. We know little about those earlier episodes because each one erased most of the evidence of its predecessor. But we know much of the Wisconsinan. Recent work suggests that the Wisconsinan Glacial alone involved multiple glacial advances and retreats separated by as few as 10,000 years. At its height, about 18,000 years ago,

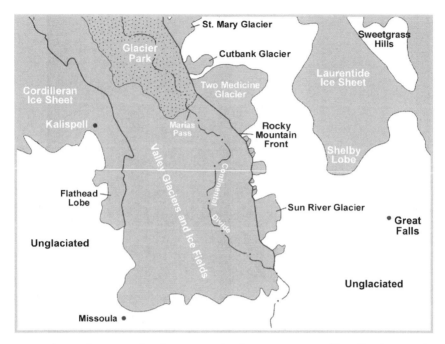

Twenty thousand years ago, the Glacier National Park region was covered by valley glaciers and ice fields. The Cordilleran Ice Sheet advanced from the west, while the Laurentide Ice Sheet approached from the east. (U.S. GEOLOGICAL SURVEY)

ice covered most of northwestern Montana—all but the summits of the highest peaks. Glacier Park's mountains pierced the ice like a rocky, ice-bound archipelago. The Inuit call such islands nunataks. The flanks of those mountains, the parts hidden by ice, were glaciated into the country we know today, sculpted into hanging valleys, finger lakes, Matterhorn-type peaks, and broad U-shaped valleys.

Early in the Wisconsin Glaciation, two ice sheets spread across the continent. The Cordilleran started high in the mountains of British Columbia as a collection of small valley glaciers. As the climate cooled, those ice bodies increased in size. Eventually they merged and coalesced into ice fields. The fields then expanded into an ice sheet that advanced over the Canadian Rockies, sending tonguelike lobes thick enough to bury whole mountain ranges into northern Washington, Idaho, and Montana. An eastern lobe plowed through the Flathead Valley as far as 20 miles south of Flathead Lake. Another sheet, the Laurentide, grew up near Hudson Bay and expanded in all directions—enough to consume nearly all of Canada. It sent a swollen thumb, the Shelby Lobe, southwest across the Montana plains toward Glacier Park.

In Glacier, valley glaciers and ice fields grew until nearly the entire park disappeared beneath thousands of feet of ice. On the west side a huge glacier (called a trunk glacier because it was a main stem that had many smaller glaciers adding to it) poured into the North Fork Valley from the mountains of British Columbia. Ten- and 12-mile-long valley glaciers descended from the Livingston and Whitefish ranges and joined in like tributaries adding to a river. The North Fork Valley vanished beneath ice. Grooves in the bedrock and boulders carried all the way from British Columbia sit atop Huckleberry Mountain and other high parts of the Apgar Range, 3,000-plus feet above the North Fork River. The North Fork Glacier put them there. It rode right over the Apgar Mountains, swallowed them whole along with everything in the valley, then flowed south to join the Flathead Lobe of the Cordilleran Ice Sheet.

Another big trunk glacier plowed down the Middle Fork. It grew up some 60 miles to the southeast in what is now the Great Bear Wilderness, fanned into an ice field at Marias Pass, then flowed down the Middle Fork Valley to the site of West Glacier. Along the way it increased its size and velocity by picking up the valley glaciers dropping out of the Lewis Range to the north and the Flathead Range to the south. At West Glacier it merged with the Lake McDonald Glacier, a titan that had descended from Flattop Mountain. Just beyond there, it joined the North Fork Trunk Glacier. Its other end, near Marias Pass, increased, too, enough to push itself over the Continental Divide and flow east to join the giant Two Medicine Glacier.

The Two Medicine Glacier left the mountains near East Glacier and spread itself like an apron over the plains. There it became the biggest of three big glaciers flowing out of the mountains along the park's eastern boundary. Fed by the ice pouring out of every valley for 37 miles along the Rocky Mountain Front (including the glaciers that bulldozed the Two Medicine Valley), the Two Medicine Glacier sprawled to within 10 miles of the

Shelby Lobe of the Laurentide Ice Sheet. It left, as a measure of its size, a 500,000-acre icing of hummocky rubble—the rocky debris it carried—atop the Marias River Shale. That coating surrounds the town of Browning near East Glacier. Just to the north, a much smaller lobe, the Cutbank Glacier, flowed out of the mountains at Cut Bank and Lake Creeks. A third, fed by valley glaciers from the Divide, Red Eagle, Boulder, Swiftcurrent, Kennedy, and Otatso drainages, filled the Saint Mary Valley and dumped itself onto the plains just south of the Canadian border. Known as the Saint Mary Piedmont Glacier, its ice grew to more than 1,200 feet thick at Lower Saint Mary Lake. Big glaciers lay within the park, too. Blankets of ice more than 1,300 feet thick filled both the Belly and Waterton river valleys. But these mountain glaciers never spilled over onto the plains.

Although ice covered almost the entire park, areas to the north and just 20 to 40 miles to the southwest and east lay unglaciated, ice-free. A large, spiderlike glacial lake many times the size of Flathead Lake sat about 80 miles to the south. Beyond that, the land resembled the interior of present-day Alaska: a treeless mountain country carpeted with tundra—mosses, lichens, alpine flowers, dwarf herbs, and shrubs. Giant bison, two kinds of musk ox, bighorn sheep, caribou, stag moose, horses, camels, peccaries, mammoths, and lemmings grazed there and flourished. Short-faced bears, cheetahs, saber-toothed cats, wolves, and coyote-like canids hunted them. Humans, too. Some of the oldest human bones yet found in North America are from a site in Montana a couple hundred miles south of the park. Carbon 14 dates them to 10,600 (plus or minus 300) years ago; tools and other remains found at other nearby sites are several thousand years older.

In Glacier Park the ice started melting 12,000 to 13,000 years ago and was more than 90 percent gone by 11,000 years ago. The evidence comes mostly from volcanic ash. Mount St. Helens erupted 11,400 years ago, Glacier Peak 11,200 years ago (both are in Washington State). Ash from those eruptions spewed over the park. In areas where glaciers had retreated, it fell on the deposits they left behind. So we know that areas with volcanic ash in post-glacial deposits were ice-free by at least 11,200 years ago. Further evidence comes from radiocarbon ages of organic material dug from bogs. A sample from near the lower end of Bowman Lake suggests the North Fork Valley was completely ice-free by 11,000 years ago. All this tells us that by 10,000 years ago the glaciers in the park had shrunk to the size that the park's glaciers were at the beginning of the nineteenth century. They probably occupied the same cirques and niches.

As the ice rolled back, trees advanced. We know from fragments of plants found beneath Glacier Peak ash that by 11,200 years ago, alder and willow and a few scattered conifers had reclaimed Marias Pass. Flowers and insects, too. Today we find their remains in bog deposits. We know from radiocarbon dating of needles and cones excavated from lake bottoms that by 10,000 years ago, forests—mostly of spruce, larch, and lodgepole pine—had moved back into both the North Fork and Waterton Valleys.

The Remains of the Glaciers

The first plants to come into Glacier after deglaciation seeded themselves in glacial till, the debris picked up, transported, and deposited by the glaciers. As a glacier advances, it carves off and plucks up huge amounts of rock, which it grinds into a heterogeneous mix of boulders, cobbles, gravel, and sand. It carries that debris along until it dumps it at its margins. The unsorted piles are called moraines. A moraine at a glacier's lower edge, where most of the till ends up, is called an end moraine. When a glacier recedes, each lull in its recession is marked with an end moraine. Many of Glacier's lakes formed behind end moraines. The U.S. Geological Survey has identified twenty-five moraines of Pleistocene age in the higher regions of the park (at elevations between 6,200 and 8,000 feet). Most lie in the heart of the Lewis Range, between Sperry Glacier and Triple Divide Pass, and are less than 30 feet high. All support lush alpine tundra communities and stands of dwarf subalpine fir and Engelmann spruce. A good example of a 10,000-year-old end moraine sits 0.5 mile downslope from Sperry Glacier. At its top lies a 4-inch layer of bronze-colored sandy silt—ash that spewed from an eruption of Mount Mazama (the Oregon mountain that cradles Crater Lake) some 6,850 years ago.

An end moraine that forms at the farthest point of a glacier's advance

This young, sharp-crested moraine dates from the last glacial advance, which occurred less than 200 years ago. Many of these younger moraines still have ice cores. (GLACIER NATIONAL PARK)

Glacial striations like these form when rocks imbedded in the bottom of a glacier scrape the underlying bedrock. (GLACIER NATIONAL PARK)

is called a terminal moraine. No good examples of terminal moraines of Pleistocene age exist in Glacier because most of the valley glaciers of that period emptied into the Middle or North Fork trunk glaciers or into one of the large piedmont glaciers along the east side, and those all extended beyond the park. Lateral moraines, formed from till dumped along the margins of a glacier, are common. Both Howe and Snyder ridges on either side of Lake McDonald are large lateral moraines, as are similar ridges along the lower parts of most of the valleys in the park. When glacial till is not dumped into a pile but instead is spread evenly over a valley floor like pickle relish over bread, it is called a ground moraine. Ground moraines form when a glacier retreats without pausing and therefore puts down its load in a continuous, hummocky sheet. When the trunk glaciers melted back in the North and Middle Fork Valleys, they left such a moraine sitting atop the Kishenehn Formation: a rolling blanket of rubble, a chaos of Belt Supergroup rocks in a thin soup of sand, silt, and clay. The thickness of this deposit exceeds 100 feet in places. Glacial till in a ground moraine does not drain well, which explains the abundance of peat and organic mud fens and bogs in the North Fork.

Glacier also has eskers—0.5-mile-long, low, slug-shaped ridges of well-sorted silty sand and gravel deposited by rivers flowing through tunnels at the bottom of the glaciers. A 60-foot-high esker sits just to the west of Lake McDonald's Fish Creek Campground; another lies just to the east. A third esker, in the southeast corner of the park, forms a ridge about a mile west of Green Lake.

Plucking and Abrading: The Work of Glaciers

Collectively, these glacial deposits contain trillions of tons of rock, all whittled from Glacier's mountains and valleys. Glacial ice transfigures the land in two ways: it abrades and it plucks. Abrasion is just what it sounds like. The glacier, its bottom laden with rocks of all sizes, acts as a giant sanding machine. It scratches and polishes everything, smoothes and rounds all protrusions. Glacial scratches are called striations. They are mainly straight and parallel and shallow—only a fraction of a millimeter deep on most surfaces—and they occur in clusters, the kind of marks a comb would make if you pulled it across a slab of butter. Striations record not only the direction of a glacier's movement but also where it flowed. You can find scratched bedrock almost anywhere in the park, and you can find abraded stones in moraines. Striations on stones in glacial till occurred when the rocks imbedded in the bottom of the glacier scraped the bedrock beneath.

Plucking is an entirely different kind of glacial erosion. It is pick and shovel and wheelbarrow erosion—the quarrying work of a glacier. Plucking loosens, picks up, and moves rock, everything from chips to blocks bigger than a house. Through a process called pressure melting, a thin film of water forms on the glacier's underside. Some of it dribbles into and fills fractures and cracks in the bedrock. The water freezes, thaws, and then freezes again—which means it expands, contracts, and expands (ice occupies about 9 percent more space than the same amount of water). The action can shatter the rock. The glacier then picks up the shards and carries them away.

Plucking works in other ways, too. Glacial ice freezes to bedrock, and where that bedrock is heavily jointed or fractured, a common condition in the park, it is often picked up and carted off. Fragments looted in this manner can be substantial—in the magnitude of thousands of tons. In other places, big slabs are broken off and moved simply by the push of the ice. Fluctuations in the pressure that a glacier exerts can also crush, shatter, and crack underlying rock, and those pieces, like everything else not tied down, are hauled away.

A Whittled Terrain

During the Pleistocene, glacial erosion occurred on a colossal scale. It reamed out valleys, scooped out cirques, sculpted hanging valleys and rock walls, and cut cliffs where today water free-falls as far as 2,000 feet. In short, it was mostly ice-age erosion that made Glacier what it is today.

Every valley in the park was shaped first by a stream, then by a glacier. Preglacial streams and rivers cut steep-sided, winding Vs through the Belt formations. Then the glaciers of the Nebraskan, Kansan, Illinoian, and Wisconsin ice ages came along and gouged them deeper and wider, into U

Lake Ellen Wilson is nestled in a hanging valley. Pouring out of it is Beaver Chief Falls.
(GLACIER NATIONAL PARK)

shapes, broad, rounded troughs as straight as boat hulls. Valleys like those that hold Lake McDonald, the Saint Mary lakes, the Belly River, Cutbank Creek, and the Waterton River are among the bigger examples. They have the general profile of a fat canoe because the glaciers had that profile.

But not all bedrock is equal. Mudstone sculpts more easily than limestone, limestone more easily than dolomite, fractured rock more easily than unfractured. The pattern manifests itself in the floors of glaciated valleys as stair steps—treads and risers. Hard rock, soft rock. Where glaciers scooped depressions into the treads, chains of lakes have formed: Lake Evangeline, Camas Lake, Arrow Lake, Trout Lake, and Rogers Lake of the Camas Creek Valley; Ipasha Lake, Margaret Lake, Mokowanis Lake, Glenns Lake, and Cosley Lake of the Mokowanis River Valley. Strings of glacial lakes like these are called paternoster lakes because they rather resemble the beads of a rosary.

Not all glaciers are equal either. Trunk glaciers cut deeper troughs than valley glaciers, and big valley glaciers cut deeper troughs than small valley glaciers. When a small, high glacier is tributary to a large one, it creates a hanging valley—a feeder suspended, sometimes thousands of feet, above the main valley. Bird Woman Falls, Feather Plume Falls, Florence Falls, Virginia Falls—they all tumble, sometimes like water poured from a pitcher, from glacially carved hanging valleys.

Move up any of Glacier's U-shaped valleys to its blunt head and you will be standing in a half bowl, a natural amphitheater, a large hollow called a cirque that looks as if it were made by an ice cream scoop. Cirques begin to form near the tops of mountains even before there are glaciers present. They can start wherever there is a perennial snowbank (a patch of snow that lasts all year). Spring, summer, and fall, the snowbank keeps the ground around it soaked with meltwater. The water flows into cracks and fractures in the rock. It freezes and thaws. The rock breaks and begins to move downslope. With time the snowbank makes its own little hollow. The hollow, when deep enough, begins to shade the snowbank, and the snowbank grows, all the time widening its receptacle. Eventually, what was not much more than a perennial drift becomes deep enough to form a layer of ice at its base, deep enough to begin to move, to flow like a glacier. It is a glacier, small perhaps, but it plucks and moves rock just the same. It eats backward at the slopes that rise above it. They become steep and vulnerable to other kinds of erosion. The wreckage falls on the glacier and is carried away. Over time a cirque is fashioned.

Glacier has hundreds of cirques. Many cradle meadows or ponds, most hold small lakes called tarns. Sometimes cirque glaciers form on several sides of a mountain and whittle it into a spire called a horn or matterhorn (after the famous peak in the Alps). Many of Glacier's peaks are horns— one of them is even called the Little Matterhorn. Of them all, I think Kinnerly is the most spectacular. Sometimes cirque glaciers form on opposite sides of a divide and gnaw toward each other until all that is left is a ridge as thin and ragged as a saw blade, called an arête. The Garden Wall is an arête; so are the Ptarmigan and Pinnacle walls. Because Belt rock is heavily jointed, arêtes in Glacier are ruggedly jagged.

The Glaciers of Our Time

Because all this erosion happened during the Pleistocene, Glacier could be called an ice-age park. Today's glaciers are minuscule in comparison with those of the Pleistocene, and so is the erosion they inflict. They are so small that they are sometimes hard to tell from perennial snowfields, which lack crevasses, debris bands, and bluish white glacial ice. Today's glaciers hide in cirques and well-shaded niches above the tree line, where they may build small moraines and do a little plucking and abrading, but nothing close to the scale of what happened during the Pleistocene.

Since the Pleistocene, slight climatic shifts have caused the glaciers to cycle through several periods of modest growth and recession. The last episode of growth or advancement came in the late eighteenth and early nineteenth century during a period of mild regional cooling. But that cold spell ended sometime before 1850, and the park's glaciers and snowfields have been in dramatic decline ever since. In 1850 the park contained about 150 glaciers. By 1966 only 37 were large enough to merit being named on maps. In 1993 a survey of aerial photographs showed the largest occupied only 28 percent of their original area, and many of the smaller ones were no longer big enough to be called glaciers or had simply disappeared. By then, the area within the park covered by ice and permanent snow had shrunk from about 38 to 10 square miles. Not only had the area shrunk, but the glaciers have also grown thinner by hundreds of meters. A glacier like Grinnell now may have less than 10 percent of the volume it had some 550 years ago (at the end of the Little Ice Age). Today, just twenty-seven glaciers remain in the park. U.S. Geological Survey scientist Dan Fagre, who has been observing this decline since 1991, says the glaciers of Glacier National Park may be gone within our lifetimes.

We know from tree ring studies that the moraines fronting all of the glaciers left in the park date to that last advance, which ended around 1850. Unlike the older, Pleistocene moraines, which in some instances sit just downslope from them, these younger moraines have sharp crests. They are steep-sided and unstable. They are also taller than the older moraines—up to 130 feet taller—and unvegetated. Many still have ice cores. None has a layer of volcanic ash.

From those moraines, we know that in 1850 the Mount Jackson area had twenty-seven glaciers—Sperry, Harrison, Blackfoot, Pumpelly, Logan,

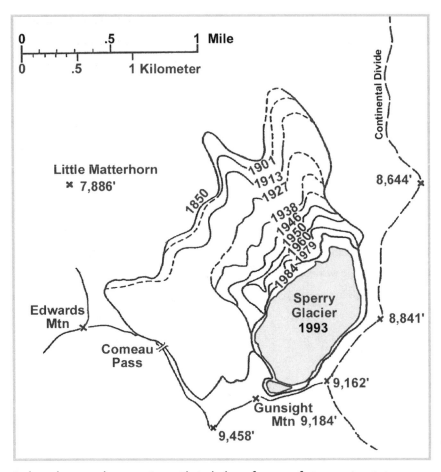

In the mid-nineteenth century, Sperry Glacier had a surface area of 960 acres. In 1984 it occupied only 250 acres, the shrinkage due to a mild warming trend that started around 1850. (U.S. GEOLOGICAL SURVEY)

and Red Eagle among the largest—and that they occupied roughly 5,300 acres. By 1979 only eighteen glaciers remained in that area, and they covered just 1,830 acres. Logan, Red Eagle, and fifteen without names had altogether vanished or ceased to retain the characteristics of active glaciers, and so became classified as stagnant ice masses. Harrison and Pumpelly had each melted into two pieces, Sperry into three, and Blackfoot into seven. All but two of the pieces were big enough to be called glaciers, but only one, the western half of Blackfoot, was large enough to name. It now goes by Jackson. Since 1979, Harrison Glacier has lost 12 percent of its area, and it is now less than 35 percent of what it was in 1850.

The retreat had started as early as 1860. By 1914 scientists had documented shrinkage, although most of the glaciers still touched their terminal moraines. Then, in 1918, the weather in northwestern Montana changed. The summers grew hotter, and precipitation fell off. The pattern continued for twenty-five years. Sperry Glacier went from 840 to 318 acres, Grinnell from 480 to 280 acres. The Blackfoot melted into pieces. Although the weather began to cool in the mid-1940s, the melting has continued, albeit more slowly, to the present. When measured in 1983, Sperry and Grinnell were 250 and 225 acres, respectively. In 1993, just 217 and 215 acres.

Of all the glaciers in the park, we know the most about Grinnell because it is one of the easiest to visit. It sits just 6 miles southwest of Many Glacier Hotel in a cirque on the east side of the Garden Wall, between Mount Gould and Mount Grinnell. The earliest photographs of it date to 1887, twenty-three years before Glacier became a park. In these photos the glacier had two sections, an upper and a lower, connected by an ice fall. The next photo, taken in 1900, shows only a small change. In thirteen years the glacier had lost some thirty-five acres of ice, or about 6 percent of its total size. That year the lower section measured about 515 acres, the upper about 50. By 1927 the lower had melted to about 415 acres, and the ice fall had disappeared; what had been one glacier became two. The lower piece, the larger of the two, retained the name Grinnell. Because of its shape, the upper portion was called the Salamander.

One does not often get to see a natural, high mountain lake come into being. But in 1927 a park naturalist reported "[a] lake of small size has formed on the north side of the [lower] glacier, between the ice front and the moraine. The face of the ice is a steep hill down which streams rush continuously." The "lake" was then more pond than lake and probably only a couple of acres in size. But it was growing and filling the space vacated by the glacier. By 1950 it was twenty acres, large enough to name. First it was called Grinnell Lake, later Upper Grinnell Lake. The last survey, taken in 1968, measured it at thirty-one acres.

These two photos, taken from the same vantage, show how dramatically the glaciers of the park have shrunk during the last century. Top, Boulder Glacier in the summer of 1932 (GEORGE GRANT); above, the same scene in 1988 (JERRY DESANTO).

While the park's glaciers have continued to shrink, most have not yet stagnated. The ice, even in Sperry and Grinnell, moves. At Sperry it creeps downhill at a rate of about 12 to 20 feet a year. Grinnell ice moves 30 to 50 feet a year. That's more than an inch and a half a day. How is it that the ice of both glaciers is moving forward, yet the glaciers themselves are retreating? The answer has to do with the balance the glaciers strike between ice added and ice lost. Snow that falls at the upper end of a glacier accumulates. That is, more snow is added in winter than melts in summer, and so snow and ice build from year to year. Farther downslope, temperatures are slightly higher, and less snow falls. Here, summer melt exceeds winter gain, and there is a net loss of glacial ice. Ice flows from the upper part to the lower. If more ice is flowing down a glacier than is melting, the glacier advances. If the opposite is true, it retreats or shrinks, in spite of the fact that ice is constantly moving forward.

The movement is not uniform. Generally, the ice in the center of a glacier moves faster than the ice on its sides, something you can test by lining up boulders across the surface of the glacier. If, when you start, your boulders form a straight line perpendicular to the direction of flow, within two or three years the moving ice will reshape the line into a shallow U-shape. I say generally because just the opposite is true of Sperry Glacier. It moves faster at its western and eastern margins than it does at its middle, a circumstance due most likely to the unevenness of the underlying bedrock. Usually ice moves faster at the top and middle of a glacier than it does at the bottom, where friction from the bedrock slows it down. If you drill a hole vertically through the ice so that it penetrates the entire glacier, and insert a plastic pipe into it, within several years the moving ice will bend the pipe almost into a J (the hook will not be completely defined).

At a depth of greater than 130 feet, the weight of the ice causes the atoms within individual ice crystals to rearrange themselves in layers generally parallel to the surface of the glacier. The realignment allows the ice to deform and to move without fracturing, in other words, to behave like a liquid. When the glacier flows over uneven terrain, the deep ice bends like soft iron. The shallower ice remains brittle, however, like ice on a lake. It cracks, forming crevasses up to 120 feet deep. Transverse crevasses are

Crevasses such as these in Sperry Glacier are sometimes hidden beneath snow, making travel on the glacier dangerous. (GLACIER NATIONAL PARK)

caused by changes in the slope of the underlying bedrock. Longitudinal crevasses are caused by different rates of flow within the glacier—ice on the margins moving slower than ice in the center, for example. Both kinds of crevasses can be treacherous, even on relatively small glaciers, such as those in the park. Crevasses are often concealed, for example, by snow bridges that can easily fail under the weight of a hiker.

The glaciers here may be small, and the impact of their erosion all but imperceptible; nonetheless, they color our view of the park. Literally. The rock flour produced by rock grinding against rock dyes many of the lakes and streams to shades of green and blue—from the color of a robin's egg to perfect aqua to apple green to a strange kind of milky green. The particular hue depends on the amount of rock flour in the water, how deep the lake is, and the angle of the sun at a given moment. (The color is not due to the color of the rock but rather to the refraction of sunlight by the rock particles. Similarly, particles in the atmosphere give the sky its blue color). From the top of Mount Siyeh, Cracker Lake, fed by meltwater from Siyeh Glacier, looks like a milky turquoise stone; the view is one of my all-time favorites.

Where to See Geology

Going-to-the-Sun Road

From just about any vantage in Glacier Park, you can see spectacular geology—glaciers, arêtes, matterhorns, thrust faults, billion-year-old fossils, U-shaped valleys, paternoster lakes. Glacier is primarily a wilderness park, which means most of it can be reached only by trail, also the best way to see geology. But Going-to-the-Sun Road provides a good introduction to the rock of the park and the processes that shaped it. In the 50 miles between Saint Mary and West Glacier, you pass through eight different Belt formations. You see dozens of classic glacial features, catch a glimpse of a modern glacier, have the opportunity to inspect molar tooth structures and stromatolites, and get a close-up look at the diorite sill, the dark belt of igneous rock seen on many of the park's mountains. Plan on making at least half a dozen stops along the way. You may also want to take a short hike along the Highline Trail.

In the first 6 miles from the East Entrance to Rising Sun, the Going-to-the-Sun Road passes through a hodgepodge of different rocks, a rubble deposited by landslides, glaciers, and streams. Underlying this mix is **Marias River Shale,** a dark-gray marine mudstone about seventy million years old. Half a mile past Rising Sun, you cross over the **Lewis Thrust Fault** (hidden here by a stream deposit), and suddenly you are in Belt rock, strata more than a billion years older than the Marias River Shale. Now the formations become progressively younger as you drive toward Logan Pass. The first formation is the **Altyn,** visible in roadcuts for the next mile. A gray formation of dolomite and limestone, the Altyn weathers to shades of tan or terra-cotta when exposed. Some stromatolites can be found here, but these fossil structures are better seen closer to Logan Pass. After the Altyn comes the **Appekunny Formation,** and the roadcut at Dead Horse Point is a good place to examine it. A dull green to gray rock, the Appekunny, a siltite, was deposited when the Belt Sea was deep. In the absence of oxygen, iron in the sediments combined with silica minerals. Heat and pressure converted those compounds to chlorite, the green compound that now colors the rock.

Just beyond Going-to-the-Sun Point, the road enters the **Grinnell Formation,** the park's famous red rock, which is mostly argillite and siltite and is full of mud cracks and ripple marks. The sediments forming the Grinnell collected in shallow water. When exposed to the atmosphere, iron in the mud oxidized to form the mineral hematite (Fe_2O_3), the same pigment that colors red paint. The road stays in the Grinnell for about 2 miles. The pull-offs are good places to look at this red rock.

After leaving the Grinnell, you pass through about a half mile of the Empire Formation, a green rock poorly exposed on this part of the Going-to-the-Sun Road. A better place to see it is on the other side of the pass. There is one worthwhile stop here, though. The **Jackson Glacier** Overlook affords the best view of a glacier that you will get from Going-to-the-Sun Road. Although Jackson Glacier is 5.5 miles distant, with binoculars you can see **moraines** and **crevasses.** You also get a good view of a **cirque**, the large amphitheater-shaped bowl holding the glacier. In the 1850s this piece of ice was actually the western half of the Blackfoot Glacier (which is not visible from the overlook), but melting has divided the two. Because the climate has grown warmer and drier over the last hundred years or so, the Jackson Glacier has retreated and lost more than 80 percent of its surface area.

Just a quarter mile beyond the overlook, Going-to-the-Sun Road passes into the **Helena Formation,** and there it stays for the next 11 miles, until just before The Loop west of the pass. The Helena is mostly dolomite and limestone, a smoky gray rock when newly exposed but tan or buff when weathered. This extensive formation makes up much of the park.

As you approach Logan Pass, look for Reynolds and Clements Mountains, two good examples of glacier-whittled **horns** or **matterhorns.** Both have summits carved into steep-sided blocky spires.

At Logan Pass, the visitor center has a good exhibit on **glacial geology.** The Highline Trail to Granite Park also begins here. This easy, scenic hike is about 7.5 miles long and offers a chance to see molar tooth structures, stromatolites, the Purcell Lava flow, and various glacier-carved features.

Close-up of the Lewis Thrust Fault. The hammer's base rests below the fault in Cretaceous rubble; the head leans on Belt Rock. (GLACIER NATIONAL PARK)

If you take the hike, look for **molar tooth structures** after you have walked for about an hour. You'll find them in the big blocks of Helena limestone along the trail. As you continue north, watch the rocks for **stromatolites** as well. This is the upper Helena, which has abundant stromatolites. About 0.75 mile before you reach the chalet, outcrops of the **Snowslip Formation** become visible in their various shades of pink and green. At Granite Park, you can see the **Purcell Lava** flow, pillows of once-molten rock that cooled in the Belt Sea. From the chalet you can either return the way you came or, if you've arranged a ride, hike down to The Loop.

A hike in the other direction, from the visitor center to the Hidden Lake Overlook, is also worthwhile. The trail through the lower meadow is underlain by **Helena Formation,** while the upper meadow passes over **Snowslip** rock. There are several sharp-crested, steep-sided glacial **moraines** at the base of Clements Mountain. These were deposited sometime between 1700 and the mid-1800s. So recent are they that they lack soil and vegetation and may even contain ice cores. Clements Mountain itself is topped by rock of the **Shepard Formation** and is mostly oxidized argillite and yellowish gray dolomite. To protect sensitive plants, please stay on the boardwalk or designated trails.

Virginia Creek cuts through the Grinnell, Empire, and Helena formations on its way to Saint Mary Lake. (JOE WEYDT)

Continuing on from Logan Pass, the Going-to-the-Sun Road cuts diagonally across the Garden Wall, an **arête.** Arêtes form when two glaciers gnaw away on opposite sides of a ridge, forming a jagged knife-edge wall of rock. Looking out to the west from the road, you see the McDonald Valley, which has a U shape from the ice-age glaciers that plowed through it. Stop at The Loop if you want to examine rocks of the **Snowslip Formation.** Mostly argillite and siltite, the Snowslip ranges from pale red to purple to dull green and yellow. You'll notice some nice pink and green stromatolites here, too. The Loop is within the trough of the **Akamina Syncline,** which explains why the Snowslip Formation occurs here, seemingly below the Helena. (The strata slope down toward The Loop so that the Helena, which you have been seeing since you left Logan Pass, disappears beneath the Snowslip here. Below The Loop, you regain the Helena for another 2 miles.)

A half mile below The Loop, the road passes through a tunnel. One hundred yards below the tunnel is a roadcut where the **diorite sill** is exposed. This dark band of igneous rock is prominent on many of Glacier's mountains. It formed when molten rock oozed up from the earth's mantle and spread between layers of the Helena Formation, in places cooking and recrystallizing the limestone into marble.

One of the easiest places to see **stromatolites,** the fossil structures produced by communities of cyanobacteria that grew in the Belt Sea, is just over 0.5 mile below the tunnel. There are two parking areas on the right side of the road, one opposite the roadcut, the other 100 yards below it. The roadcut is part of what's called the **Conophyton Zone,** a massive 100-foot-thick, cliff-forming band of stromatolites 1.3 billion years old. This zone occurs throughout Glacier in the upper part of the Helena. Once you learn to recognize it, you can pick it out on mountains miles away. Here, look for stromatolites in the shape of branched and unbranched columns. Others resemble halved cabbage heads or the domed caps of mushrooms.

Green and gray argillite and siltite of the **Empire Formation** are exposed in a roadcut 1.3 miles below the stromatolites. Red Rock Point, another 4.5 miles farther, is, thanks to the clear waters of McDonald Creek, a wonderfully scenic place to again examine rock of the **Grinnell Formation.** There are no signs identifying this stop, so you will need to watch your odometer.

U.S. Highway 2

If you are traveling U.S. Highway 2 on the south end of the park, two stops are worth your while. Heading east, the first is Goat Lick, 2.9 miles beyond the turnoff to Essex. Hike down the short asphalt trail to the Goat Lick Overlook. Two **faults** are visible in the cliff on the opposite side of the river. Farthest to the right is the red Grinnell Formation. Next to it is gray rock, the limestone of the Helena Formation, a block of which has moved down along a deep-running fault. The Helena is then cut by a second fault that dropped pink and green argillite of the Snowslip Formation. The faults bleed salty solutions that attract mountain goats, deer, and elk, which is the reason most people stop here.

The second stop is 14 miles farther, at the summit of Marias Pass. Here at the Continental Divide and for the next 0.5 mile along the highway, look north to Little Dog and Summit Mountains. A little more than halfway up the mountains, you can see the **Lewis Thrust Fault,** one of North America's most famous geological features. Above it is Altyn limestone, a Precambrian sedimentary Belt rock deposited more than a billion years ago. Beneath it is Cretaceous-age shale about seventy million years old. All the rocks above the fault actually formed 50 miles west of where they now sit. They were shoved into their current position after a series of island arcs smashed into the western edge of North America about 100 million years ago. While the fault appears as an almost straight line, the sole of the Lewis Plate (the slab of rock above the fault) has been cut by a complex system of faults and folds that have only recently been described.

Grinnell and Sperry Glaciers

Sperry and Grinnell Glaciers are two of the park's most accessible and studied glaciers. Both glaciers have retreated steadily since the mid-nineteenth century and are now only a fraction of the size they were when people started measuring them. Still, they offer visitors a chance to see a living glacier and various glacial features—**moraines, cirques,** and **crevasses.** A word of caution: Stay off the glaciers themselves. Snow can hide deep crevasses.

Sperry Glacier sits on Gunsight Mountain just below the Continental Divide and can be reached by a trail that starts from near Lake McDonald Lodge. The trail is 10 miles long, the hike strenuous (you gain about 4,500 feet). Most people will want to make an overnighter out of it, camping at the designated camp area near Sperry Chalet before making the final 4-mile ascent to the glacier. When last measured ten years ago, Sperry Glacier was 250 acres, a little more than a quarter of what it was a century ago.

Grinnell Glacier is easier to reach, 5 miles from the trailheads on both the north and south sides of Swiftcurrent Lake. Beyond Josephine Lake, the trails join and climb 1,500 feet to the glacier. Along the way, you can look down on Grinnell Lake, the water of which is made extraordinarily green by **glacial flour**—rock ground up by the glacier and carried into the lake by meltwater. At the glacier, you will see Upper Grinnell Lake, partially impounded by a large **moraine** and crowded with icebergs calved from the glacier. This lake was born in 1927. Before 1927, Grinnell Glacier was connected by an ice tongue to **Salamander Glacier,** the long finger of ice halfway up the Garden Wall. In surface area, Grinnell Glacier is only 35 percent of what it was in 1850.

4

A Place to Live

If you are a tree that likes dry feet, as the drought-hardy limber pine does, you might settle in comfortably on the east side of the park, which has some of the harshest sites in Montana capable of supporting trees. Or, if you are a bird, say a chestnut-backed chickadee that prefers wet old growth, you could make a home among the big redcedars and hemlocks of McDonald Creek, where the weather is as cloudy and damp as a Washington rain forest. Or, should you be an arctic plant, like carpet pink, arctic willow, or mountain sorrel, life could be good on one of Glacier's high, stony, cold ridges. The park supports plants and animals native to the Rocky Mountains, the Great Plains, the Great Basin, the Pacific Coast, and the Arctic. From chorus frog to mountain goat, hummingbird to ptarmigan, sagebrush to liverwort, an immense array of organisms have a place to live in Glacier Park.

Habitats abound here. The glaciers have seen to that. During the Pleistocene, they created a mountain terrain so sliced up that even short linear distances—a mile or two—encompass changes in elevation of more than a mile. Glaciers cut a landscape so rugged and with so many nooks and crannies that any given elevation offers every choice of exposure, soil condition, moisture level, snow depth—in short, a multitude of micro-habitats. In this park, if there is anything, there is a variety of living spaces.

Elevation, Topography, and Soils: Defining a Niche

Elevation determines, more than any other local factor, how living things are distributed in the park. As you move up a slope, temperatures decrease about 3.3°F for every 1,000-foot gain in altitude. Precipitation, on the other hand, increases with elevation because when air is cooled, it retains less water. But the interference of geography and winds make precipitation less predictable than temperature. The amount of increase, for example, varies from 10 to 16 inches for every 1,000-foot gain in elevation. In general, plant communities tend to change with elevation, although topography, soils, fires, floods, insects, diseases, and an array of lesser influences complicate the picture—considerably.

Let's look at topography. Basins and slopes exist at all aspects and elevations. Each offers a slightly different set of growing conditions for plants. South-facing slopes are warmer and drier than north-facing slopes because they receive more sun; hence, treeline is often several hundred feet higher on a southern exposure than it is on a northern exposure. At certain times of the

The mix of prairie and forest in the valleys and on the east side provides homes for a diverse array of insects, birds, and mammals. (GLACIER NATIONAL PARK)

year, ridgetops tend to be warmer than cirques—up to 20°F warmer—because cold air sinks and pools in basins. Windswept terrain is drier than wind-sheltered terrain because wind blows away snow cover and desiccates both soils and vegetation. Concave slopes are generally nearer the water table than convex slopes. Most leeward slopes have a deeper mantle of soil than windward slopes. All these factors affect where plants grow.

Speaking of soils, they are part of the equation, too, although their influence is usually not as profound as that of topography. Soil is the link between the living and nonliving parts of the environment, the bridge between plants and rock. The depth and extent of roots, the amount of water and nutrients roots can extract, depend on soil. On the east side of the park, for example, topography has evolved two types of soils, each supporting its own grassland community. Stony and well-drained hilltop soils grow junegrass, rough fescue, wheatgrass, and phlox. On the sides of those same hills and below, the soils are better developed, deeper, more loamy, and better able to retain water. Here the community changes to blunt sedge, needle and thread grass, chickweed, some fescue, and yarrow. Soil chemistry can also limit plants. Jones columbine, a small, purple alpine flower that flourishes on the east side of the park, is sometimes called limestone columbine because it grows only on limestone and dolomite, presumably because it requires soils high in lime. Alpine dryad is another lime lover; you won't find it growing on soils formed from Purcell Lava because they lack calcium carbonate. Alpine larch, on the other hand, is a high-elevation, deciduous conifer best adapted to acidic soils derived from granite. It doesn't do well in Glacier Park, where soils are born of sedimentary rock, much of it dolomite and limestone, which is basic (that is, the opposite of acidic). In most of the park, pure stands of alpine larch are small and few. The nearby Bitterroot Range, in contrast, is granite-based, and there alpine larch thrives in expansive, pure, open stands on north-facing talus slopes.

The Influence of Fire

Fire also shapes the distribution of plants and animals. Before the advent of organized fire suppression, fires swept through some areas of the park as frequently as once every twenty-five years. H. B. Ayres, the first forester to

Fireweed, aspen, and lodgepole seedlings sprouted soon after the 1988 Red Bench Fire. Frequent fires play an essential part in Glacier's natural history. (MARK GAHAGAN)

describe the Flathead region and the area that would become Glacier, noted how much of the land showed signs of large burns. In 1900 he wrote of the North Fork: "Evidence of severe and repeated fires is abundant. Actual prairie making has been accomplished. Throughout the valley, burns are found varying in destructiveness according to the intensity of the fires, which have ranged from slight, creeping surface fires to those that have swept through the tree tops, and even fires that have rendered the land barren." Of the Middle Fork he wrote, "The upper portion of the valley is very nearly all burned over, and the fires have been severe and repeated." And he described major fires east of the divide that had helped sustain the grasslands there: "The fire of 1885, starting from an Indian camp on Rose Creek, with a strong wind from the southwest, swept the whole wooded side of the ridge to the foot of Lower Saint Mary Lake, covering an area of about 10 square miles in a few hours. Most of the trees were killed, only a few clumps being left here and there. Restocking has been very imperfect; small areas here and there have now an abundant growth of lodgepole pine and [Douglas fir], but grass, willows, and aspen occupy most of the old burn."

Plants and animals in this part of the Rockies evolved with fire and have adapted to it in various ways. Some plants and fungi are only seen in large numbers after a fire: rock harlequin or pink corydalis, Bicknells geranium, dragonhead, and of course, morels. Some depend on periodic fire to maintain or regenerate themselves. Lodgepole pine, ponderosa pine, western larch, western white pine, and whitebark pine would decline and eventually disappear from Glacier Park if all fires were suppressed. A number of animals would suffer, too. Grizzly bear habitat would deteriorate. Bears gorge themselves on huckleberries each summer and autumn to help sustain them through the winter. Low to moderate severity fires induce the plants to resprout and increase productivity. Bushes in forests that haven't burned for fifty years or more are notoriously poor producers. Many of the other foods the bears eat also do best after a fire. The same could be said of fruiting or forage plants favored by moose and elk and many birds.

Until several decades ago, the Park Service aggressively fought fires in Glacier to protect wildlife and forests, and the Forest Service put out fires on adjacent lands, preventing those blazes from ever entering the park. But these efforts brought about some unintended consequences. With fewer fires, vegetation patterns in the park underwent changes. For example, in Big Prairie and Round Prairie, lodgepole pine spread at the expense of bunchgrasses, sedges, and herbs (broad-leaved plants) that are of more value to wildlife. On both sides of the divide, conifers are invading grasslands and are crowding out aspen groves. Fire suppression also helped reduce the forest mosaic, making it less diverse. But a century of suppression only postponed the inevitable, and the fire seasons of 1994, 1998, 1999, 2001, and 2003 have helped return wildland fire and its many beneficial effects to the park.

The Major Zones of Vegetation

Given all these complicating factors, we can still divide the park into several distinct zones, with their own particular climate, plant and animal communities, most within a given elevational range. Discussed in detail in the chapters that follow, these are the valley bottom and aspen parkland zone, a

The vegetation in the foreground of this view of Thunderbird Mountain is characteristic of much of Glacier's upper subalpine zone. (GLACIER NATIONAL PARK)

mosaic of bottomland forests, grasslands, and aspen groves; the montane zone, a narrow belt of low-elevation ponderosa pine, Douglas fir mixed with lodgepole pine and western larch, and redcedar-hemlock forests; the sub-alpine zone, which includes middle- and upper-elevation spruce-fir forests and treeline communities; and above that, the alpine-arctic or tundra zone. Climb a mountain in the park and chances are you will pass through all four. Vegetation zones on such a climb are similar to what one encounters on an 1,800-mile trip from the park north to the Arctic Circle. This is because average temperatures decrease as you travel farther north, just as they drop as you go up in elevation. Hence the progression of communities one passes through is similar over both journeys.

A Surprising Diversity

Glacier National Park has one of the most diverse combinations of plants and animals found anywhere in North America. Here, the flora of the northern Rockies meets that of the Great Plains, the central Rockies, the Pacific Coast, and the Arctic. Some of the trees in Glacier are at the eastern edge of their range, some of the grasses are at their western limit, and some arctic-alpine plants occur no farther south. Northern bog lemmings live alongside pygmy shrews; Pacific tree frogs share creek bottoms with grizzly bears; and until European-Americans arrived, herds of caribou and mountain bison grazed the park. Alaskan beetles, west coast beetles, and beetles from east of the Great Plains have been found living side by side with beetles native to the Rocky Mountains.

What is it about this place that invites such diversity? Triple Divide Peak suggests one answer. Nowhere else in the nation does water tumble off a mountain into three continental drainage systems—the Pacific via the Columbia, the Gulf of Mexico via the Missouri, and Hudson Bay via the Saskatchewan River. Because drainages often serve as corridors along which both plants and animals migrate, the stream courses leaving the park provide an avenue for many of these eastern, western, and northern elements to reach the park. They settle in alongside species native to the northern Rockies.

Pleistocene glaciation has also affected the distribution of living things.

Plants found mainly in rain forests on the Pacific Coast thrive in the McDonald Creek Valley, thanks to inflows of moist, relatively warm Pacific air. (JOE WEYDT)

Outside of a few isolated mountaintops north or south of the park, Arctic rock-jasmine, stalked-pod crazyweed, Arctic bellflower, and four-angled moss heather occur only in the Arctic and in Glacier National Park. How did these little islands end up in Glacier and almost nowhere in between? Perhaps Arctic and alpine communities were similar in the northern Rockies before the last glaciation; perhaps the ice-age glaciers wiped out everything between the Arctic and Glacier Park except for what lived on a few unglaciated mountaintops, and these survivors constitute much of what we consider today to be Glacier's "arctic element."

A scarcity of suitable habitats may also help to explain the distribution. In the Rockies many of these arctic species are found only on calcareous soils—soils high in calcium and magnesium. Glacier's high country is mostly calcareous dolomite and limestone. Perhaps the plants live where they do in part because of their lime-loving nature.

West coast plants and animals also flourish here, in the redcedar-hemlock community along McDonald Creek. The wet Pacific maritime winds blowing in from the coasts of Washington and British Columbia retain a big chunk of their moisture all the way to the Continental Divide. This happens only in the Glacier area of the Rockies where there are no high mountain ranges to the west to capture the moisture before it arrives. When air masses move up and over mountains, they cool. Moisture condenses and falls as rain or snow. The result is that the southwestern part of the park, particularly around McDonald Creek, is wet and relatively warm enough to sustain many of the same plants and animals that live on the rain-soaked sides of the Cascade and Coast ranges of Washington and British Columbia. Which brings us to the subject of weather, a big factor in determining where plants and animals live in the park.

Weather in Glacier

Experienced hikers in the park know to come prepared for all types of weather. It may be 95°F one day and in the 30s the next. In the high country it is common for summer nighttime temperatures to drop into the 20s. In August of 1992 a winterlike storm dumped a foot of snow in the Belly

Parts of the park receive huge amounts of snow. In some places, 800 to 1,000 inches fall each winter. (GLACIER NATIONAL PARK)

River Valley. And Glacier is famous for its winter storms. In winter, Pacific and continental air masses often collide along the Continental Divide, creating fierce blizzards with 100-mile-an-hour gusts. In general, the east side of the park has wider temperature swings than the west side and is windier, and the northern part of the park is drier than the southern. But just as the terrain is varied in any given region of the park, so is the weather.

Most of the park's precipitation falls in winter, brought in by maritime storms. From November to March, those North Pacific air masses bring low clouds, high humidity, and lots of snow to both sides of the divide. West Glacier, at 3,200 feet, gets 29 inches of precipitation a year. Cirques along the Continental Divide just a few miles east of West Glacier receive more than 100 inches of water annually. Both amounts are high for the Rockies.

Along the Continental Divide in the park, the average annual snowfall is 800 to 1,000 inches. One thousand inches is more than 80 feet of snowflakes. You can begin to see why glaciers still repose in cirques and sheltered areas on some of the higher peaks. The actual depth of the snowpack is much less—roughly 20 percent of the total snowfall—because of settling effects, melting, and the wind. Most years, the park accumulates these high amounts from relatively light snowfalls that last many days, as opposed to single storms that dump huge amounts, although the latter happens from time to time, too; in January of 1972, 44 inches of snow fell on Summit in one day.

On the west side, rainfall decreases as you travel north due to a rain shadow cast by the Whitefish Range to the west. Polebridge, 20 miles northwest of West Glacier and 400 feet higher, only gets 22 inches of precipitation (compared to West Glacier's 29). That's why a dry Douglas fir forest community grows around Polebridge, while a wet western redcedar–western hemlock community grows at the same elevations on McDonald Creek near West Glacier.

If you look just at average annual precipitation, the east side of Glacier Park appears to be as wet as the west side because maritime air carries and spills moisture across the Continental Divide. Thirty inches of precipitation falls on Saint Mary and East Glacier, for example. Grinnell Glacier, which accumulates snow blown off the surrounding mountains, gets 150, the highest in the park. Still, the east side, especially at its margins, seems drier than the west. Two-thirds of the park's forests occur on the west side, and dense stands of redcedar and hemlock grow near West Glacier, while locales at the same elevation near Saint Mary support mostly Douglas fir, lodgepole, limber pine, or no trees at all. One reason for this is wind. The east side is known for its exceptionally warm chinook winds during the winter and its dry summer winds. Both parch the soil and desiccate plants. The effect of the maritime air masses declines quickly east of the park boundary; Browning gets but half the moisture East Glacier does at nearly the same elevation, yet the two communities are only 12 miles apart.

During the summer the maritimes are more stable because an enormous high-pressure cell known as the Pacific High generally lies just off the West Coast. It is a fair-weather system that moves northward in early summer and then south again in the fall. When it is in its northern position, it blocks storms moving south from the Gulf of Alaska, storms that from late fall to early spring bring heavy precipitation to the northwest coast and

Glacier Park. Also, as summertime Pacific air moves inland from the coast across the state of Washington, it heats, causing clouds to dissipate. Most do not reach Glacier, which is why July and August skies in the park are mostly clear and dry.

On the east side, dry continental air dominates. In summer it is warm and dry, in winter bitter cold and even drier. With no barriers to their southward movement, continental air masses pour down from the Arctic along the east front of the Rockies like water rushing from a collapsed dam. They can lower January and February temperatures to as much as 40°F or 50°F below zero (minus 55°F is the record low). Occasionally, some of this frigid, bone-dry air crests mountain passes and spills over into valleys on the west side. Because it is so cold and therefore dense, it rides under the maritimes and pushes them higher; the mix brews fierce blizzards with heavy snows and winds that can easily reach 100 miles per hour.

Also on the east side, low pressure systems can pull Pacific air down the mountains and cause what are known as chinooks, an Athabascan Indian term that means "snow eater." As it descends, the air heats and dries—the opposite of what happens when the maritimes rise over the windward, or west side. Those winds, also gusting to speeds of up to 100 mph, can force temperatures to jump 30° to 40° in a few minutes. They melt whatever snow is on the ground and desiccate soils. Plants, too, can be dehydrated. Temperatures drop quickly when one of these chinooks is replaced by a sweep of Arctic air. In Browning in 1916, the temperature dropped 100° (from 44°F to -56°F) in twenty-four hours, a national record for temperature change.

In the summer, air from the interior of Canada and Alaska (as opposed to the Arctic) brings fair, sunny, and dry weather to the east side for most of July and August. Still, summer is the season for thunderstorms. From June to August the park gets about fifteen days of lightning, and thunderstorms start nine or ten fires a year. Ninety percent of those fires occur west of the Continental Divide, where most of the trees are.

So precipitation, temperature, wind, topography, soils, glaciers, fire, rock, other organisms—all these elements and a host of others work in concert to influence where a plant grows or an animal lives in the park. It is because all these factors vary so much that such an unusual and diverse array of organisms lives in Glacier. Together they make for an extraordinary natural history.

5

The Aspen Parklands

Straddling two worlds, I stood on the shoulder of Highway 49 near Two Medicine Lake late one April morning. On the east side of the road stretched the aspen parklands, a hilly patchwork of whites and browns. Cream-colored aspen. Russet prairie grass. Patches of snow. Leafless limbs of buffalo berry, serviceberry, wild rose. And a stiff west wind. On the west side of the road, looking into the park, was green—the dark blue-greens of conifers, of lodgepole pine, limber pine, Douglas fir, subalpine fir, and spruce. The forest stretched 2 miles, from the road to the flanks of the mountains. Above it was brown stone and sparse, low-growing vegetation, snow, and then clouds. The two worlds, aspen parkland and coniferous forest, met there at the road. Bridging them from above, a bald eagle rose from a swale in the foothills to the east, passed slowly overhead, and then dropped into the timber to perch on the broken top of an old spruce snag.

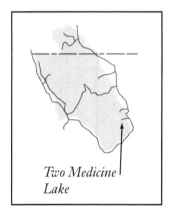

Two Medicine Lake

What Makes a Parkland

Aspen parklands are a wonderful mix of quaking aspen groves, brushy thickets, and open prairie. They border most of Glacier's eastern edge.

Aspen parklands, a mix of aspen groves, prairie, brushy thickets, and scattered stands of conifers, border almost all of Glacier's east side. (JOE WEYDT)

Although most lie east of the boundary, on the Blackfeet Indian Reservation, they extend into the park as narrow fingers or islands scattered amidst stands of lodgepole and limber pine, Engelmann spruce, and Douglas fir. Moose, elk, white-tailed deer, grizzly bears, black bears, coyotes, wolves, and mountain lions move in and out of these pockets of grass and aspen and drift back and forth across the park boundary as if it didn't exist. Most of these animals spend several months outside of the park, foraging or hunting or seeking shelter within the aspen-grassland community; they could not survive without those areas. So I include them, although they mostly lie outside of the park.

Most prairie in Glacier occurs in the Saint Mary, Many Glacier, and Belly River Valleys. Three percent, or about 3,100 acres, of those three drainages support grassland. Whereas aspen and conifers take the more moist and sheltered places, open prairie claims most of the south and southwest slopes, where there is greater exposure to sun and wind, more evaporation, and higher soil and air temperatures. These patches of prairie are a hybrid between the foothill prairie of southwestern Alberta and the foothill grasslands found in the North Fork of the Flathead. Grasslands a little farther east, on the Great Plains, are drier and lower than those of the parklands and support a slightly different grass community.

Here on the east side of Glacier, the most common grasses are rough fescue and Idaho fescue. But junegrass, needle and thread grass, and timber oatgrass also thrive. So do herbaceous plants like yarrow, phlox, and smooth aster, mountain-dandelion and anemone, rosy pussytoes, northern gentian, and stoneseed. Others, like thin-leaved owl-clover and crazyweed, grow here, too, along with penny rattle, Oregon grape, goldenrod, bedstraw, strawberry, sticky purple geranium, meadow rue, and camas.

Thickets of brush—buffalo berry, shrubby cinquefoil, and wolf willow on stony, well-drained soils and snowberry, wild rose, and serviceberry in shallow depressions—fringe the edges of these prairie meadows. This latter community often gets its start in ground disturbed by small mammals. The burrows of badgers, pocket gophers, voles, ground squirrels, and mice break up the sod, loosen the soil beneath, and offer opportunities for the seeds of shrubs to germinate and the young plants to gain a roothold. Badgers and pocket gophers are especially adept at throwing up mounds of fresh earth, which snowberry is quick to colonize.

These islands and tongues of prairie and brush are surrounded by groves of quaking aspen and small stands of black cottonwood that hug protected coves and crannies and many of the bottoms. Wind, especially warm, dry winter and spring chinook winds, sculpts these stands. They desiccate and kill branches and buds and generally stunt trees. The result is that the aspen growing in sheltered places stand taller than those exposed to winter gales. Where a grove raises itself from the hollow above the level of the plain, its top is often made flat by the winds. For the same reason, trees near the upper edge of a slope are often shorter than those in the middle or at the bottom. Wind, more than soil or precipitation, limits the growth of aspen trees on the east side. Aspen on the west side, spared these parching winds, grows faster, taller, and straighter.

Wind also accounts for the absence of ponderosa pine on the east side, although the land seems well suited for it. Ponderosa pine is especially susceptible to winter drought. In winter, 70- to 100-mile-per-hour chinook winds are common. They blow off the mountains and raise temperatures 40°F or more in a matter of minutes. Any snow or ice protecting the needles of pines quickly melts. And because the chinooks are dry, they dehydrate the exposed needles. The trees can't replace the moisture they lose; their trunks and roots are too cold—at or near freezing. The trees die, and their needles turn red, giving rise to another name for the effects of winter drought, red belt. Limber pine, which grows on the east side, has evidently evolved ways of getting around red belt. Its roots are better at absorbing water during cold temperatures, and it can close the stomata (the small breathing pores) on its needles and thereby retain its moisture. Many of the conifers you see growing on exposed sites or scattered among the aspen groves on the east side are limber pine, although white pine blister rust has taken a heavy toll on the species in recent decades. About a third of all limber pine trees in the park are dead from the rust, and more than 75 percent of the remaining live trees are infected.

Glacier's Deciduous Forest: The Aspen Groves

In some of the aspen groves bordering the coniferous forest, you won't see many new aspen trees coming up. What you will see are young shade-tolerant conifers—Douglas fir, Engelmann spruce, and some limber pine—invading older aspen stands. On these sites, as the conifers increase in number and grow in size, they shade more and more of the aspen trees, which require plenty of sunlight. Soon the aspen will die out. It's a relatively short-lived tree anyway, and in competition with conifers it can't regenerate.

Aspen produces seeds, but they lack stored food and have no protective coating and therefore are viable only for a week or two after they hit the ground. If the moisture and temperature conditions are not exactly right, the seeds die. Consequently, aspen trees in Glacier Park do not rely much on seeds to regenerate. Instead they depend on root suckers—sprouts from the roots of existing trees. Because of this, aspen trees within a grove are usu-

One of the most drought-resistant trees in the northern Rockies, limber pine thrives on many of the windiest ridges on the east side, places where no other trees grow. (GLACIER NATIONAL PARK)

ally clones; that is, they are genetically identical. Their crowns and trunks have similar shapes, their bark has similar patterns, and because they enter winter dormancy together, their leaves all change color at the same time in the fall. Because the trees are united by a single root system, each aspen grove can be considered to be one plant. And though individual aspen stems are short-lived, the clones are not. Many aspen clones in the West are thought to be at least 10,000 years old. According to scientists, the oldest is more than one million years. Keep in mind that clonal ages refer to the age of the individual genomes, not actual physical tissue.

While fire easily kills aspen trees, the roots usually survive. Fire, in fact, stimulates aspen roots to sprout. And because it opens up the canopy by killing overstory trees, including invading conifers, it creates ideal growing conditions for root suckers. A new grove, genetically identical to the one preceding it, quickly becomes established. Without periodic fires, however, aspen adjacent to the coniferous forest has a tougher time reproducing and, in some situations, will surrender territory to longer-lived and more shade-tolerant Douglas fir and spruce trees.

Aspen trees within a grove are generally clones and hence have similar bark, trunks, crowns, and leaves. The trees in neighboring groves often look quite different. (GLACIER NATIONAL PARK)

Outside of the park, on the edge of the plains, aspen groves border patches of grassland. Here, too, fire suppression has had an effect. A recent Park Service study of historic photos dating back to 1890 reveals that shrubs and aspen trees are encroaching on grasslands in several areas. A few miles farther north, in the vast Canadian aspen parklands—a broad belt of aspen and prairie sprawling from Alberta to Manitoba—the climate is slightly drier, and there fire is even more of a factor in the maintenance of aspen-grove boundaries. Canada's efforts at fire suppression have caused aspen trees to spread like weeds—the species now occupies in excess of 60 percent more ground in south-central Alberta than it did sixty years ago. In Glacier, however, the expansion of aspen has not been as extensive. Apparently, fire, strong, desiccating winds, and damage by rabbits, elk, and other animals have been more effective at holding aspen in check.

Fire suppression has also allowed conifers to encroach onto east-side prairies. The same study that found shrub and aspen encroachment found conifers gaining ground at Two Dog Flats, Red Eagle Meadows, the south side of Spot Mountain, Swiftcurrent Ridge, and some of the Belly River prairies. The study's authors conclude that prescribed fires could help maintain the park's fire-dependent (grassland) communities.

Some Birds of the Parklands

Thanks in part to the aspen, I have consistently seen more species of birds on the east side than on the west side (the same is true when it comes to plants and butterflies). The mix of aspen, prairie, and coniferous forest makes for a lot of habitats, and each supports a distinct community of birds. On a summer day's walk through prairie and broad-leaved and coniferous forest, you can hope to see some 230 different species of birds. Classic birds of the shortgrass prairie—savannah, clay-colored, and vesper sparrows; meadowlarks; and brown-headed cowbirds—occupy grasslands within the park. Where there is a pond or lake or marsh, solitary sandpipers, long-billed curlews, marbled godwits, and willets nest. They prefer to feed in and near the shallow waters of ponds, lakes, and marshes, where they probe the mud for aquatic insects, snails, and worms. Veerys, white-crowned sparrows, lazuli buntings, black-headed grosbeaks, dusky and least flycatchers, orange-crowned and yellow-rumped warblers, and solitary and warbling vireos inhabit the aspen and brushy thickets, gleaning insects, berries, and seeds from the foliage of both shrubs and low trees. A little higher, where the aspen groves dissolve into coniferous forest, varied thrushes, Townsend warblers, pileated and three-toed woodpeckers, and golden and ruby-crowned kinglets forage in trees for spiders, insects, sap, and berries.

Even within the aspen there is variety in the habitat. Some groves have shrubs in the understory, others grasses and herbs. Some are mixed with conifers. Some border ponds and streams. Some are old, rife with insects and disease, and falling down. Each type of grove attracts its own group of birds. Of all of them, the aspen-conifer mix holds the greatest diversity because it encompasses so many kinds of living spaces and foods.

Aspen is susceptible to heart rot, and many healthy-looking trees are rotten on the inside, infected with wood-decaying fungi that turn solid heartwood soft and spongy. The trees suffer, but cavity-nesting birds profit.

They profit from both these living-but-fungus-infected trees and standing dead trees or snags. There are two kinds of cavity nesters. Primary excavators like woodpeckers and sapsuckers pound out new nest sites each year. Chickadees and nuthatches are also capable of hollowing their own cavities if the wood is soft enough. Other birds nest in holes vacated by these primary excavators. Hooded and common mergansers; buffleheads, goldeneyes, and wood ducks; kestrels and merlins; flammulated, western screech, northern pygmy, and northern saw-whet owls; western flycatchers; tree and violet-green swallows; house wrens; and mountain bluebirds all nest in existing holes. Woodpeckers also provide housing for flying squirrels, red squirrels, big brown bats, and martens. Most secondary cavity-users could not survive in an area without woodpecker cavities, and for that reason woodpeckers are keystone species in these habitats, creatures that have a profound influence on the organisms around them.

Northern flickers, red-naped sapsuckers, and hairy and downy woodpeckers seek out aspen, preferring it over other deciduous species or conifers for both nesting and feeding. Because they feed on the ground as well as in trees, flickers are often seen at the edge of the aspen stands, near pockets of prairie. They peck holes in aspen to find wood-boring insects like poplar borers, ghost moths, and bark and ambrosia beetles. Sapsuckers, which show a strong preference for fungus-infected trees, employ a different feeding strategy. They drill an orderly series of small holes in aspen bark and then return to feed on the sticky, sugary sap that oozes out and the insects attracted to it—bees, wasps, flies, ants, beetles, butterflies, moths. Sapsucker tongues are not long and covered with spines like the tongues of most woodpeckers but short and fringed with hairs, a design that works well for a sap-licking bird. Sapsuckers also eat the sweet, inner bark of aspen. Their holes are entry points for fungi, which as far as a red-naped sapsucker is concerned is for the better. Red squirrels, flying squirrels, chipmunks, warblers, hummingbirds, and wasps and hornets visit sapsucker wells to eat and drink, and the sapsuckers try their best to keep them at bay.

One species found in the aspen parklands, the ruffed grouse, is especially dependent on aspen. The North American range of this chicken-size

On the way to Grinnell Glacier, the Belt formations are easy to see in the Garden Wall and surrounding peaks. The diorite sill stands out as a dark ribbon on many of the park's mountains. (JOCK PRIBNOW)

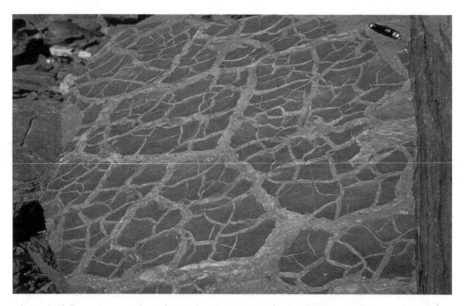

Almost 1.5 billion years ago, the Belt Sea shrank. Portions of its muddy bottom were exposed to air and cracked. Buried under sediment, the cracks were preserved. This is a piece of the Grinnell Formation. (GLACIER NATIONAL PARK)

Fossil stromatolites in the Helena Formation near Grinnell Glacier. These cross sections of dome-shaped stromatolites resemble sliced cabbage heads or raindrops on a quiet pool. (GLACIER NATIONAL PARK)

Mount Wilbur and the ridges behind it have been shaved into arêtes, or jagged knife-edge ridges and mountain crests. Pleistocene glaciers chiseled Glacier's mountains into a variety of shapes. (JOE WEYDT)

Most of Glacier's streams flow clear, but creeks downstream from glaciers often have a milky opalescent hue caused by rock flour suspended in the water. (GLACIER NATIONAL PARK)

Soils are still forming from Belt rock in much of Glacier. The glacier that gouged this valley 20,000 years ago left nothing but rock behind. (JOCK PRIBNOW)

Geology determines where many plants will grow. Jones columbine is often called limestone columbine because it grows only on soils derived from limestone or dolomite. (GLACIER NATIONAL PARK)

Limber pine thrives on some of the harshest sites on the east side, places where no other trees can grow because of the effects of winter drought. (GLACIER NATIONAL PARK)

Grizzly bears, wolves, elk, and moose are among the park animals that migrate onto parklands along Glacier's eastern margin. (JOE WEYDT)

Lower subalpine forests blanket many valley bottoms between 4,000 and 6,000 feet. The most common trees in this zone are lodgepole pine, western larch, Douglas fir, Engelmann spruce, subalpine fir, and whitebark pine. (JOE WEYDT)

Fireweed, sometimes growing 6 feet high, is one of the first plants to move in after a fire. Although the wind carries its seeds throughout the park, it becomes dense only in areas where there is little competition from other plants. (GLACIER NATIONAL PARK)

Two Dog Flats in bloom. Weeds threaten to crowd out the native plants on this elk winter range. Many of the exotics are not eaten by wildlife. (GLACIER NATIONAL PARK)

Glacier lilies grow profusely in many places in the park. Bears love them, and it is not uncommon to find digs in subalpine meadows like this one, where grizzly bears have turned the soil for the plant's small bulbs. (JOE WEYDT)

Above: Along the streambanks, the flower-covered stems of globe mallow sometimes reach 5 feet high. Globe mallow also appears after a fire and on disturbed sites along roadsides. (GLACIER NATIONAL PARK)

Right: Wild blue flax has delicate flowers; wind often causes the petals to drop. In Washington and Oregon, Indians used blue flax to make thread and fishing line. In Glacier Park, the plant likes dry, stony soils and grows from the prairies to the alpine. (GLACIER NATIONAL PARK)

Above: In wet areas, such as along streams, Lewis' monkeyflower grows profusely. Its late summer blossoms attract caddisflies, moths, and hummingbirds. Fattened on nectar from monkeyflower and other plants, the moths become food for grizzly bears. (GLACIER NATIONAL PARK)

Left: The bright green rosette of leaves at the base of this wintergreen plant are full of chloroplasts, the tiny structures that hold chlorophyll. The plant grows in the deep forest where only a small amount of sunlight penetrates. (GLACIER NATIONAL PARK)

Above: Ruffed grouse build nests beneath aspen groves, lining them with preened feathers. After the eggs hatch, female ruffed grouse aggressively defend their chicks against predators. (GLACIER NATIONAL PARK)

Right: Preferring coniferous forests that include plenty of aspen, red-naped sapsuckers are right at home in Glacier's aspen parklands and valley bottoms. Dozens of other birds use sapsucker nest holes after the sap-suckers leave. (GLACIER NATIONAL PARK)

This male yellow warbler has just delivered a meal to his offspring. Cowbirds often parasitize warbler nests by laying eggs for the warblers to raise. Cowbirds now threaten the survival of several warbler species, thanks to human-caused habitat changes that favor cowbirds. But many yellow warblers have learned to bury cowbird eggs in the bottom of their nests. There, the eggs cool off and die. (GLACIER NATIONAL PARK)

Rufous hummingbirds use spider silk as glue to hold their nests together. Besides lichens, building materials include mosses, bud scales, shredded bark, and leaves. Rufous hummingbirds use the same nests for several years, making repairs when necessary. (GLACIER NATIONAL PARK)

A small number of harlequin ducks, rare throughout much of their range, spend summers on fast-flowing, turbulent stretches of McDonald Creek. They winter on the Pacific Coast. (GLACIER NATIONAL PARK)

In spring and fall the ptarmigan's plumage is a mix of brown and white, like the tundra itself. During that time of year, ptarmigan are hard to see because they stay close to patches of snow.
(GLACIER NATIONAL PARK)

A group of cow elk cross a foggy meadow. Elk winter at low elevations but spend their summers in the high country. Hikers may see them in some of the park's high, remote basins. (GLACIER NATIONAL PARK)

Above: Largely because of trapping, lynx are now rare in Glacier even though their principal prey, the snowshoe hare, is abundant. (GLACIER NATIONAL PARK)

Left: Pine martens are kitten-size members of the weasel family, eating everything from rodents and insects to berries and seeds. They patrol the canopies of Glacier's mature forests. (GLACIER NATIONAL PARK)

Wolves started denning in the park again in 1986. Since then several packs have occupied the North Fork Valley, and now visitors hear their howls when they camp there. All of the predators that roamed the Glacier area when European-Americans first arrived are now present in the park. (GLACIER NATIONAL PARK)

bird is almost identical to the range of quaking aspen, and over almost all of its range—95 percent of it—aspen is the ruffed grouse's main food. In spring the birds feast on buds and catkins; in summer and fall they eat the leaves; and in winter they turn to the twigs and buds, especially the male floral buds, which are high in protein. Ruffed grouse consistently select the aspen buds with the highest protein and potassium contents, which usually grow high in the tree. In the park the ruffed-grouse–aspen association is not quite as strong; on the east side the bird is often found in the coniferous forests, though those forests generally have at least a small aspen or cottonwood component.

Ruffed grouse choose dense, pole-size stands for breeding and nesting sites, probably because a closed canopy extends more protection from red-tailed hawks, goshawks, and great horned owls—three of the bird's major predators. Ruffed grouse hatchlings are precocial—that means they are covered with down, open-eyed, and mobile the minute they leave the egg (songbirds, on the other hand, are altricial—hatched naked, blind, and completely helpless). So they leave the nest right away and follow their mothers around. The hens show them food and steer them into areas with more open canopies and dense, shrubby understories. Chicks consume only insects for the first five weeks, and brushy understories harbor more bugs than any other part of the parkland. As the summer progresses, the hens guide their broods farther and farther downslope until, at the end of the summer, they are in the bottoms along the streams and rivers. In late fall both males and females and their offspring journey back upslope into pure stands of aspen or mixed stands of aspen and conifers. They often roost in the conifers.

In spring the cocks display and drum to attract females. In the fall they may drum to set up winter territories. They sit on downed logs to do this, territorial perches they return to year after year. The drumming, which anyone who has spent time in a northern woodland in the spring has probably heard, is a series of low-pitched, hollow-toned thumps that first accelerate then quickly decelerate. The males make the sound by cupping their wings and beating them against the air in a rapid forward and then upward

Horned larks are found in open country and can be seen in the parklands year-round. (GLACIER NATIONAL PARK)

Ruffed grouse, common on the east side, eat mostly aspen leaves, buds, catkins, and twigs. (GLACIER NATIONAL PARK)

motion. If, in the spring, a female responds, the cock immediately begins to display by raising his crest and neck feathers, fanning his tail, and strutting.

The grouse's drumming is a way around a serious problem: how to go about attracting a mate while living on the ground in the middle of a forest. Obviously one solution would be to sing and to sing loud. But high-pitched sounds, such as those crooned by songbirds, don't carry well from a forest floor; they're absorbed and scattered by foliage, tree trunks, and rocks, obscured by other sounds like running water or wind, and blocked by hills and ridges, all of which probably explains why forest songbirds choose treetop perches to serenade from. Sounds that travel well from the forest floor, suffering the least distortion, absorption, or scattering from their surroundings, are low-frequency sounds—booms, croaks, and the like. Wing drumming produces a very low-pitched sound that can be heard a quarter to half a mile away, far enough, anyway, to be effective. Grouse make other sounds to communicate messages over short distances, such as the soft murmurs between a hen and her chicks and the sharp clucks the birds emit when alarmed.

Beavers and Hares: Give and Take in the Aspen

Beavers, like ruffed grouse, are fond of aspen. They eat it in preference to alder, maple, even willow. In winter they rely mostly on it and other members of the willow family. An adult beaver will dine on between two and four pounds of aspen bark a day. That translates into about 200 trees a year. And that's just meals. Beavers also cut aspen for their building projects—cottonwood isn't dense enough and willow has stems and limbs that are too thin. Neither is as ideal for dam and lodge construction as aspen, although they will do if aspen is absent. In the parklands you can consider anything within 500 feet of a stream to be good beaver habitat.

Because beavers harvest so much aspen, their populations in aspen groves are unstable. They move in, build a series of dams and lodges, clear-cut all the available aspen and willow within reach, then leave. But beaver

A beaver dam. Most of the streams on the east side support healthy beaver populations. (JOE WEYDT)

and aspen evolved together, and the aspen is well adapted to the presence of beavers. Unless a grove's roots are flooded, it will resprout. Like fire, though on a smaller scale, beavers renew an aspen stand. They also create places for marsh plants, aquatic insects, migratory birds, and predators.

Snowshoe hares also come and go in the aspen. Although snowshoe hares spend their winters in the coniferous forest, they disperse into the aspen parklands in summer. New aspen growth is choice food for hares—it is less resinous than the branches of young conifers—and the parklands harbor other succulents and shrubs the hares prefer.

While the highs and lows are not as pronounced in Glacier as in the northern boreal forest, snowshoe hares are famous for their population cycles. Their numbers peak about once every ten years, and if the peak is great enough, the hares can overbrowse aspen and other plants. Continuous overbrowsing will eventually kill aspen clones, but the trees have evolved a defense. They suddenly begin sprouting shoots high in terpenes and phenolic resins—compounds that evidently taste bad and lower the ability of snowshoe hares to digest protein. The shoots also contain antibodies capable of upsetting vitamin production in hares. So, just as the hare population reaches its highest levels and its food demands peak, one of the animal's most preferred and abundant foods abruptly becomes inedible. The hares turn to other plants, which they quickly overbrowse. Food grows scarce. Meanwhile, predators gather—hawks, owls, coyotes, lynx, and weasels. The hare population crashes. Browsing pressures decline, and the aspen stops producing its repellent resins, which are rich in carbon and require considerable energy to make. The carbon, and the energy, is channeled back into growth processes, and the aspen renews itself.

The response of aspen trees to the cycles of beavers and hares are examples of how organisms evolve together and how the activities of one can alter the growth and development of another in sometimes surprising and sophisticated ways. In spite of the periodic ravages of beavers and hares, aspen persists. Indeed, as a short-lived tree, it benefits by sprouting new trees.

Glacier's Lost Buffalo

The east-side aspen parklands are also home to muskrats, porcupines (which, mysteriously, have become almost absent in recent decades), red-tailed chipmunks, western jumping mice, deer mice, and three species of ground squirrels—Columbian, Richardson, and thirteen-lined. Prowling after them are predators like coyotes and red foxes, bobcats and cougars, least and short-tailed weasels, and minks. Vagrant shrews, masked shrews, and silver-haired bats chase smaller quarry. Black bears and grizzly bears also hunt the parklands for roots and greens and berries, and for the calves of elk, deer, and moose. They once took bison calves, too, when they could, not from bison native to the Great Plains but from a little-known cousin of the plains bison known as the mountain or wood bison. Only one explorer reported actually seeing bison in what is now Glacier, in 1815, but we know they were there. Their trails were still visible in the early part of this century, showing that they must have existed in great numbers. Bones have turned up in every valley on the east side from Two Medicine to Waterton at elevations up to 5,600 feet. Bison skulls decorated many of the ranger stations in the twenties and thirties. After a flood in 1964 widened and cut new channels on most of the streams in the park, a whole new crop of skulls and other bones turned up, protruding from cut banks and washed up on gravel bars. Most ended up for sale in museum shops in Browning.

The buffalo we are most familiar with, the plains bison (*Bison bison bison*), lived on the prairie. They like open country and had ranges of hundreds of square miles. They may have occasionally grazed the edge of the park but evidently stayed out of the wooded canyons and didn't visit the higher elevations. The buffalo of Glacier, the mountain bison (*Bison bison athabascae*), sometimes called the wood bison, wintered in valleys like Saint Mary and Belly River and summered in the nearby timbered country at higher elevations. They preferred woodlands and aspen parklands to the open prairie and probably never left the park—in fact, an individual may have spent its entire life in a single drainage. Mountain bison still survive in Wood Buffalo Park, Alberta. They are smaller than the plains bison by a couple hundred pounds and darker in color. They have a heavier and curlier coat, a larger skull, heavier horns, and a shorter beard, and are apparently more timid. When they see a human they run for cover, even though they are protected. Mountain bison are also less gregarious, forming bands of only five to thirty animals. They are considered more primitive than the plains bison; their skeleton is closer to that of the ancestral form, *Bison occidentalis*.

Mountain bison became extinct in Glacier Park around 1840. They had the unfortunate habit of congregating in mountain valleys during the winter. At those times the herds must have been easy prey for human hunters, especially after the Blackfeet acquired horses and trappers and mountain men arrived. Waterton Lakes National Park, just across the international border from Glacier, keeps a herd of about twenty plains bison near Lower Waterton Lake in a fenced enclosure of about 1 square mile. The Blackfeet tribe has talked of restoring plains bison to reservation lands adjacent to the park; they have herds now on the prairie.

Bears in the Parklands

On the east side grizzly bears den in the park, but they spend, on average, about half their nonhibernating time outside Glacier, feeding in the aspen

Grizzly bears often emerge from their dens the first week of April, but they stay in the snowy high country until about the first of May. (GLACIER NATIONAL PARK)

parklands on the Blackfeet Indian Reservation. The parklands provide an abundance of both food and cover for silvertips, some of the best grizzly bear habitat in Montana.

Grizzly bears emerge from their high-elevation dens in early April but stay in the snow-covered high country until May. When I first learned this, I wondered why a grizzly bear would linger for a month in the snow and ice after six months of not eating. Weren't they hungry? Why weren't they in the valley bottoms, looking for spring greens along the creeks? But until May, there is little down low for them to eat, and the snow in the high country is too soft for them to travel well. So they stay in the high country, digging through snow for the whitebark pine cone caches of squirrels, foraging for carrion, and relying on body stores until about the first of May, when some of their favorite foods start sprouting in the parklands.

Bear foods in the foothills in May include the buds, leaves, and catkins of aspen and willow and the roots, leaves, and flowers of glacier lilies—bears love glacier lilies. If they are lucky, they might find some carrion—a winter-killed elk or deer perhaps—and sit on it for a week or so. They will eat ground-nesting birds like ruffed grouse if they can. As the groves green up, their diet will expand to include wild rye, bluegrass, and brome grass. They'll concentrate on the wettest parts of the parklands where they'll graze clover and sedges, dandelion and sweetvetch, cream-flowered peavine, cow-parsnip, lovage, angelica, and equisetum. They'll turn soil for ants, mice, ground squirrels, and sweet-root. They'll visit the bone yards of ranches for carrion—the rotting carcasses of cows and sheep. All these foods appear in grizzly bear scats collected from the aspen parklands.

It's tough to generalize about the eating habits of grizzly bears. What grizzly bears eat depends on what they've been taught to eat by their mothers. Some east-side bears leave the aspen parklands around the first of July to climb to the tops of mountains in the park to lap up ants and army cutworm moths, while others stay low in the parklands, first eating succulents, then berries—chokecherries, buffalo berries, serviceberries, and rose hips. In August these bears head back into the subalpine zone in Glacier for the huckleberry crop. By late October, they and many of the bears that left for the mountaintops return to the aspen parklands.

Researchers working just to the south of Glacier see similar patterns among the bears they radio-collar. In fact, they believe two kinds of grizzly bears live along the east side of the Rocky Mountains—lowland bears and backcountry bears. The lowland bears leave their high-elevation, back-country dens and migrate into the lowlands—the aspen groves, limber pine savannas, and prairie—where they stay until autumn, until it's time to den again. Back-country bears leave their dens in the mountains and migrate into the lowlands but only stay through the spring. In June they return to the high country, where they remain until fall. A few return to the lowlands for berries in August and September, depending on the state of the huckleberry crop. (Grizzlies show the same kind of patterns on the west side of the park along the North Fork.) On average, female grizzlies on the east side range over about a 35-square-mile area in search of food. Males cover more than twice that much ground. The size of their home range depends on the resources available. The maximum home range size for a grizzly bear is roughly 600 square miles.

Food habits of individual bears also vary from year to year. Grizzly bears are flexible. They adapt to changes in their environment. If buffalo berries are scarce in a given year, they move a little lower and eat chokecherries. One year when vespid wasps were plentiful, researchers found dozens of scats in the aspen parklands chock-full of big yellow wasps. One radio-collared male ate nothing but vespid wasps. Then, the next year, when wasps were less abundant, researchers didn't find a single scat with wasps in it.

Grizzly bears generally mate on their spring range, which on the east side of the park is the aspen parklands. Their breeding season begins as early as the third week of April, peaks in late May, and ends around the last of June. A courtship lasts anywhere from a week to twenty-five days. The two bears are together most of that time.

I've watched grizzly bears courting in Alaska and Montana. They spend a lot of time lounging around in tall grass, lying on top of each other, playing, sleeping together. During these times the bears seem genuinely affectionate, even joyful. Males sometimes court more than one female. Females at times court more than one male. It is not unusual for a group of males to hang around an eligible she-bear for days on end. Some males will haze a female out of her spring territory into some remote, high-elevation site, apparently to avoid competition or to escape real or perceived threats.

Black bears also make thorough use of the aspen parklands. They, too, feast on grasses, forbs, and berries. They eat more insects than grizzlies, especially ants. Like grizzlies, they take an occasional moose calf if they can. Unlike grizzlies, black bears climb aspen trees—many of the aspens on the east side are scarred with their claw marks—to get at catkins and new leaves and to rob bird nests of their eggs or young. Grizzly bears eat catkins, too, but they tend to bend the more flexible trees over or browse what they can reach by standing. On occasion, a grizzly will prey on black bears; the hair shows up in collected scats. Black bears often den low, near their fall feeding sites; many spend their winters in the aspen parklands, curled in natural hollows or in holes they've dug into banks. Grizzly bears den much higher, well above the upper limit of aspen, in the subalpine or alpine zones.

The Ups and Downs of Wintering Elk

As the bears are searching for den sites, elk—hundreds of them—move into the aspen parklands from the high mountain meadows where they spend their summers. They congregate on winter ranges in the Belly River, Swiftcurrent, Saint Mary, and Two Medicine Valleys. They move back and forth across the park boundary onto the Blackfeet Indian Reservation or, in the case of elk in the Belly River herd, into the Waterton Valley in Canada. Once they are out of the narrow valleys of the park, elk from the various herds are able to associate with one another—elk from the Saint Mary Valley mingle with elk from the Swiftcurrent Valley, which mingle with elk from the Belly River. Some may wander down into Two Medicine. The herds are not distinct in winter. They travel and mix. All winter they graze the fingers and islands of bunchgrass prairie, concentrating on windswept knolls and ridges blown free of snow. When the snow gets deep—deeper than about 20 inches—they move into the aspen stands and browse twigs and shoots. They seem to prefer aspen and serviceberry over other woody plants. They eat aspen root suckers, browse branches up to about 6 feet high, even chew the bark off mature trees (to see evidence that elk gnaw aspen bark, check the trees on the margins of Two Dog Flats). Elk can digest at least half of the bark and extract some nutrition from it. Aspen bark is especially high in vitamin K. They also graze any understory grasses not buried in snow. When spring comes, they disperse into the high country— back into Glacier Park, the females having their calves along the way.

How much time the elk spend out of the park depends on a combination of factors: the weather, their numbers, the condition of the range, and hunting pressure on the Blackfeet Indian Reservation. Hunting is now restricted on the reservation so that the elk can spend more time out of the park, which is beneficial for the elk because there is little winter range within Glacier. Tribal members hunt elk in areas adjacent to the park, but only during three months in the fall, and with a limit of one elk per person per season. Except for the slightly longer season, those regulations are similar to the hunting regulations enforced by Montana Fish, Wildlife & Parks elsewhere in the state. Also, the Boulder Ridge, prime winter habitat for elk descending from the Saint Mary and Swiftcurrent Valleys, has been designated an elk refuge where only a few permits (about ten) are issued to hunters each year. Elk from Saint Mary and Swiftcurrent Valleys are now seen frequently on the Babb Flats and as far east as Duck Lake.

The number of elk wintering in each of the valleys has fluctuated over the years, a response more to the policies of the Park Service and the Black-feet tribe than to the cycles of nature. When the park was established in 1910, for example, only a small number of elk wintered in the Saint Mary Valley, and many believe that in pristine times, that is before 1850, there were very few elk on the east side (and even fewer on the west side where there is less winter habitat). The numbers increased slightly over the first few decades of this century because the establishment of the park afforded some protection from hunters. Also, in the early years, the park instituted a predator control program designed to remove with traps and strychnine and rifles "bad animals" like cougars, bears, coyotes, and wolves so as to protect "good animals" like deer, sheep, moose, and elk. The numbers of

All winter long, elk feed in the pockets of prairie and in brushy thickets and aspen groves along the east side. (GLACIER NATIONAL PARK)

cougars and bears declined. Wolves disappeared almost entirely. When, in 1932, rangers officially started keeping track of the number of elk wintering in the valley, they counted fifty-five. Most of these animals stayed in the bunchgrass meadows along the northeastern periphery of Saint Mary Lake, where high winds kept the snow from accumulating. To encourage elk and deer populations, the Park Service fed them. The elk herd increased and continued to increase for the next eighteen years. In 1950 the Park Service counted 560 elk.

Meanwhile, hunting on the reservation increased, so the elk tended to stay more in the park. The Park Service became concerned because the winter range in the Saint Mary Valley could not support such a large herd without access to the reservation. The elk trampled and overgrazed the meadows, eroded the soils, and chewed browse lines across the aspen stands. So in 1953 the Park Service did an about-face. It adopted a program of "direct removal and harassment"—some animals were shot, and others were scared off the range. After a dozen years, 200 elk wintered in the valley.

Then, in 1965, the policy changed again, this time to one of natural regulation. Elk in the Saint Mary Valley would not be fed. Nor would they be removed or harassed. The elk were on their own. Herds would increase or decrease as nature, not humans, decreed. Of course tribal members still hunted elk outside the park, but the Park Service had no authority there. During the first years of this new policy, the number of elk in the Saint Mary herd declined, partly because of hunting but also because of a mass drowning in 1968.

The winter of 1968 was unusual. Saint Mary Lake had frozen as usual, but on January 19 a warm chinook blew in. Gusts exceeded 100 mph, and the ice on the lake disintegrated. An arctic front followed, and open water refroze into clear, smooth ice. Early February was balmy with nine days of temperatures up to 55°F. The ice began to rot again, and sometime during those nine days the elk broke through. Then it got cold and the lake froze again. The carcasses—cows, calves, and yearling males—were found trapped beneath the ice about 500 feet from the shore. Limbs protruded through the ice, and great shards of ice were frozen into the tangle, indicating the animals had struggled wildly. More elk were scattered around the periphery of this main clump. Forty animals died. That spring and summer, twenty-six bloated carcasses floated to shore. For aesthetic reasons the Park Service hauled many of them away. Bears and bald eagles consumed the remainder.

Hunting pressure on the Blackfeet Reservation caused the number of elk wintering in the Saint Mary Valley to continue to drop until 1970. That winter rangers counted fewer than ninety animals. Then the Blackfeet Tribe closed off Boulder Ridge, a prime elk wintering area, to hunting, and the trend reversed. Fewer than 300 elk wintered in the area in 1980, and by 1994 the estimate exceeded 600. In 2006, according to Dan Carney, biologist for the Blackfeet Nation, around 2,000 elk were using the area. Some of those animals have created a browse line on the aspen trees rimming Two Dog Flats by trimming twigs and foliage, a sign that the size of the winter elk herd may be exceeding the carrying capacity of the meadow.

The Blackfeet tribe deserves praise for the way it has managed elk on the east side of the park. They have monitored populations closely, controlled poaching, invoked seasons, and set up reserves (in addition to Boulder Ridge, the tribe has limited hunting in another large area southeast of the park). Their efforts are helping to ensure a strong elk population on Glacier's east side.

A Homecoming for Wolves

For a while some of the elk wintering in the parklands fell prey to wolf packs. Wolves, which historically helped keep elk and deer populations in check, returned to the parklands after being absent for fifty years, but their stay was short-lived. There had been occasional sightings of individuals or pairs or, more often, tracks—wolves drifting down from central Canada—but not until 1986 did a pair actually den close to the park, near Horse Lake. Those wolves hunted the aspen parklands in and out of Glacier; their tracks went up and down the east side—in the park near Saint Mary and Two Medicine Lakes, on Piegan and Red Eagle Passes, and at East Glacier. They hunted elk, moose, white-tailed deer, jackrabbits, beavers, ground squirrels, mice, and, when they were on the Indian reservation, cattle. Another pair of wolves denned in 1986 in the North Fork Valley on the west side of the park. That North Fork population has been there ever since. But on the east side, wolves have had a harder time because of the ranching that goes on here so close to the park.

What happened to the Horse Lake Pack is a replay of what happened to wolves all over the West in the last century. Briefly, the story goes something like this: In 1984 and 1985 wolf sightings from the east side increased. In the spring of 1986, personnel from the Animal Damage Control (ADC) Division of the U.S. Department of Agriculture, conducting a routine aerial hunt for coyotes, spotted a large black wolf in an aspen grove near Horse Lake, just east of Saint Mary. A few days later they found an unoccupied den—quite possibly the first den south of the Canadian border on the east slope of the Rockies in more than half a century.

The following year the wolves denned again in the same area, and that spring they started killing cattle. Soon thereafter, the ADC, charged with protecting livestock from predators, went into action. The agency set snare traps and began regular aerial patrols. Within a few months, they had eliminated the entire pack—four adults and three pups. Two they shot from the air, another two died or were shot in their traps, and two more were captured and shipped off to a zoo in Minnesota. A rancher reportedly killed the seventh.

Why this pack of wolves chose to den where they did—outside of the park—is a mystery. Perhaps they arrived during the winter, when elk and deer were numerous in the parklands, and stayed to den and raise pups. In spring the elk and most of the deer left for the middle and high elevations of Glacier Park. In their place came livestock; ranchers use the aspen parklands as summer pasture. When wild ungulates became scarce, the wolves simply replaced them with domestic ones—cows.

The Horse Lake Pack's demise had one positive outcome. Public outrage over the killing of seven animals listed as an endangered species spurred the ADC in 1988 to adopt an Interim Wolf Control Plan, a set of guidelines for managing "wolf control actions." That plan and subsequent updates should prevent the kind of slaughter that occurred on the east side of Glacier Park in 1987. They committed more agency funds for equipment, training, and personnel for control operations. The ADC now attempts to relocate livestock-killing wolves to remote areas where they are less likely to get into trouble.

In 1993 and 1994 another pack of wolves denned on the east side, just a few miles north of the Canadian border in the Belly River drainage. The pack included at least six wolves, among the adults a female collared in the North Fork Valley a year earlier. Their winter territory included much of the eastern boundary of Waterton Park, especially the lower parts of the Belly River and Lee Creek Valleys and areas along Glacier's east side. In summer the wolves moved farther up the Belly River, hunting inside Glacier Park. But this pack, too, was soon entirely killed off, this time by Canadians. Since then, wolves have been reported in every major drainage including the Many Glacier, Cut Bank, St. Mary, Belly River, and Two Medicine. But there has been no verified denning activity east of the Continental Divide within the park, although pack activity has been observed in the St. Mary, Many Glacier, and Belly River Valleys. In 2006, for example, two packs were observed on the Blackfeet Reservation. It is obvious wolves are trying to recolonize the area, and at some point it is probably inevitable that another pack will den there; whether they will last is another question.

The situation for wolves on the east side is far from ideal. The animals from the Horse Lake and Belly River packs were outside of the two parks as much as in. Both Waterton and Glacier are bordered by private ranchland, and in spite of the fact that wolves had not denned in or near Waterton since about the 1920s, wolves are not protected in Alberta. Landowners can legally shoot them on sight, as can any hunter with a big-game permit. Hence they are scarce. If one or more of those wolves that are occasionally sighted along the east side of the park started killing cattle tomorrow, they could meet the same fate as the wolves of the Horse Lake and Belly River packs. Seeking a remedy, the wardens at Waterton and private and public agencies (the group includes Canadian Parks and Wilderness Society, the Federation of Alberta Naturalists, Parks Canada, Alberta

Fish and Wildlife, the Waterton National History Association, and the Alberta Cattle Commission) have set up a compensation fund to pay ranchers for livestock lost to wolves (like a similar program funded and managed by the Defenders of Wildlife in the United States). They also encourage landowners to cooperate with the park and provincial wildlife authorities when they do have problems. With a little luck, the agencies can identify and remove offending animals without wiping out a pack or, possibly, the entire east-side population.

6

The North Fork Valley Bottom

I saw my first grizzly bear in the North Fork Valley. I was maybe ten or twelve, and my father and I were fishing the North Fork of the Flathead River in the fall. As often happens when I fish, the river—the dance and music of clean, swift water rushing over red and green stones—and the chance of fish— cutthroat or bull trout—had sucked me in completely, and I thought of nothing else. I moved slowly, carefully, over the slippery bottom, casting into riffles and pools, concentrating all the time on the water, on the bright-cobble-bottomed stream and its promise of fish.

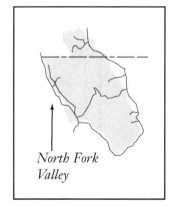

North Fork
Valley

"Bear!" my father shouted. He pointed his rod upstream, past me. The bear, up to her belly in the rushing water, stood on my side of the river, a stone's throw away. Her fur was the color of coffee with cream on her shoulders and back, darkened on her flanks and rump where it lay wet and flat against her body. Water dripped from her chin. Head lowered, she regarded us for a few moments, then turned, and in two bounds fled the water and vanished into the trees.

The river bottom is a prime place for grizzly bears in the spring and fall. I've often found their digs on the islands and dry channels amid cottonwood, willow, and thin-leaved alder, places where they've turned the earth for the tubers and roots of wild onion, milk vetch, kinnikinnick, and crazyweed.

The North Fork Valley, on the park's western edge, is 32 miles long by 4 miles wide. It holds the North Fork of the Flathead River and is home to animals big and small—everything from thousand-pound moose to pygmy shrews that weigh less than a dime. It encompasses an assortment of habitats: spruce and cottonwood along the river; bunchgrass and shrub meadows and lodgepole pine savannas on flats above the river; aspen groves, willow thickets, wet meadows and fens on river silt deposits, and the old deltas of tributary streams; Douglas fir and ponderosa pine forests on dry upland slopes; and on higher ground, a dense coniferous forest of lodgepole pine, western larch, Engelmann spruce, and subalpine fir.

The Living River

The North Fork of the Flathead River forms the western boundary of the park, a movable line that meanders snakelike across a broad floodplain. As it meanders, the river renews itself. It rearranges its bed, puts cobble here, deposits gravel there, cuts earth from the outer edge of bends and dumps it on the inside—undercuts 200- and 300-year-old spruce trees or carries away big chunks of shrub- and grass-covered bank. Periodically it floods and washes over the floodplain and strips the land of vegetation. It dumps silt, forms new gravel bars, cuts new channels, and leaves old ones high and dry. Peachleaf and river willows are among the first to colonize newly exposed cobbles and gravels. Black cottonwood follows. Kootenai and Blackfeet Indians rubbed the sweet, pleasant-smelling resinous buds of black cottonwood into their skin and hair for perfume. Equisetum, sometimes called horsetail or scouring rush, finds a home on sandy soils. So does elegant hawksbeard, rockcress, Jacob's ladder, golden aster, yellow dryad, fireweed, silverleaf-phacelia, and goldenrod. They're all pioneers on North Fork floodplains. The fragrance of wolf-willow, a species of olive, wafts

The floodplain of the North Fork of the Flathead River. The trees along this section burned in the 1988 Red Bench Fire. (JOE WEYDT)

through the valley in early summer, a sweetness some find cloying. As soils develop and shade increases, other plants move in—thinleaf and sitka alder, red-osier dogwood, snowberry, buffalo berry, starry Solomon's-plume, early blue violet, vetch, groundsel, blanketflower. In time, white spruce arrives and, spared further disturbance, ultimately forms a full canopy. Cottonwood surrenders the site to what becomes a bottomland spruce community, the dominant type of vegetation on the North Fork floodplain. But the cottonwood will be back; it will return with the next fire or flood or swing of the river.

The level of the river fluctuates with the seasons. The plants that pioneer on floodplain gravels must survive periods when their roots and lower stems are inundated for days or weeks at a time. The seeds of black cottonwood and willow germinate best when covered with water, and the plants actually grow fastest when flooded, as long as the water is fast-moving and rich in oxygen. Stagnant water, water low in dissolved oxygen and high in silt, slows growth. Many floodplain plants have small pores in their leaves and openings in their bark to breathe in extra oxygen, which they transport to secondary "flood roots." These roots store the air in small pockets to be used by submerged parts of the plant. And during floods, the cells in the leaves and roots of these plants change the way they exchange gases by using otherwise toxic by-products of respiration for growth.

Different species of spruce interbreed easily, and most of the spruce growing on the North Fork Valley bottom are hybrids between white and Engelmann spruce. The park is in the heart of the hybridization zone for the two species—white spruce from the north and Engelmann spruce from the south. White spruce (*Picea glauca*) is a hardy tree of northern and eastern Canada and the northeastern edge of the United States, where it can grow under relatively arid conditions. Engelmann spruce (*P. engelmannii*), on the other hand, is primarily a subalpine, Rocky Mountain species that likes it wet. In Glacier Park white spruce and the hybrid are best suited to the North Fork floodplain and the drier bench communities just above the floodplain. Engelmann spruce, or hybrids with strong Engelmann characteristics, grow higher, at sites above 4,000 feet.

Big Meadows, Wide Savannas, and Sweeping Forests

At the edge of the floodplain, on ground that is slightly higher and drier, the community changes to a mix of hybrid spruce, lodgepole, Douglas fir, ponderosa pine, quaking aspen, and common and creeping juniper. Farther still from the river and out of the bottomlands, the forest thins in places to a savanna—a grassland with scattered trees, mostly lodgepole pine. In places, savanna gives way to large meadows, or what some call prairies. Some Glacier meadows are extensive enough to have their own names: Round Prairie, Big Prairie, Lone Pine Prairie, Dutch Creek Prairie. The largest, Big Prairie, is about 1 mile wide and 4 miles long. Round Prairie, not at all round, is about 0.5 mile wide and 0.75 mile long. The rest are smaller.

The meadows represent pockets of a vegetation type known as foothills grassland. They contain a few plants from the prairies of eastern Washington and some species from the Alberta prairies north and east of the park. Rough fescue, bluebunch wheatgrass, prairie junegrass, Idaho fescue, Richardson's needlegrass, timber oatgrass, and Kentucky bluegrass, an introduced species, intermingle. Big sagebrush, too. But because of fire suppression, lodgepole pine has steadily gained ground in North Fork meadows over the last fifty years.

Grasslands exist in the valley because of fire and aridity. The area gets only about 22 inches of precipitation a year—caused by a rain shadow cast by the Whitefish Range just to the west. Also, the porous soils hold little water. The grasses are drought-hardy. Their root systems are seven to ten times larger than their aboveground portions and quickly suck up all the available moisture. Most years, the grasses leave no water for tree seedlings. Trees that get a start during a wet year have difficulty surviving subsequent dry years; a 1968 drought killed lodgepole that had invaded portions of the meadows forty years earlier.

Still, lodgepole has made inroads onto the prairies, especially at the edges, where shade and wind shelter from bordering trees holds some moisture in the soil. Before 1900, periodic fires killed most of these trees when they were still saplings; prairies in the North Fork burned every nine to twenty-six years. Some of those fires were ignited by lightning; others were set by Indian tribes such as the Kootenai. But after the park was established, fires were suppressed, with mixed success. Now, thanks to prescribed burns, most of the prairies have burned since 1992, reversing the loss of ground to lodgepole and ponderosa pine trees.

Between 1992 and 2005 the Park Service set eleven prescribed fires, which together accounted for approximately 700 acres. The goal was to help maintain the dry meadows against the invasion and encroachment of lodgepole pine and nonnative plants. The fires succeeded in dramatically reducing lodgepole pine densities, but second burns are now needed to reduce the seedlings that reestablished after the first of those burns. At the same time the fires invigorated the grasses. Grasses have most of their biomass underground, and unlike other plants, they grow from their bases rather than their tips. Consequently, the sensitive, growing parts of the plant are protected during a fire. Far from being damaged, grasses often come back stronger after a blaze, free of the layers of dead grass that build in the years when there are no fires. Herbaceous plants also benefit. Typically, if you return to a burned area the summer following the fire, you will see a spectacular mass flowering of yellow penstemon, lupine, geranium, and others, a response to the addition of nutrients.

In Big Prairie, ponderosa pine also survived the flames. Ponderosa pine evolved with frequent fires. It has thick, corky bark that protects its sap wood, thick twigs and large buds that resist burning, high and open foliage, deep roots, and a habit of bleeding pitch after a fire to seal wounds. Other species that occupy habitats where fire is infrequent lack these adaptations; both western redcedar and western hemlock, for example, have thin bark and shallow root systems and are killed by even low-intensity fires. The average fire frequency in a mature redcedar-hemlock stand is from 300 to 400 years.

But while the Park Service started burning Glacier's prairies only in 1992, we should not think of prescribed burns as something new. Today's managers are only recovering a practice tribal people in the region knew and used expertly for millennia to maintain and improve habitats for both wildlife and humans.

Prairies in the North Fork Valley are dry and so are the montane forests that surround them. Stands of ponderosa pine and Douglas fir grow in the area, in a narrow zone on west- and southwest-facing slopes above the river at elevations below 4,000 feet. These two species dominate two of the driest forest communities west of the Continental Divide in the northern Rockies. Ponderosa pine, the more drought resistant of the two, is at the northeast limit of its range in Glacier Park and occurs only in a few isolated pockets in the North Fork, most of them between Polebridge and Anaconda Creek. Trees in those stands are generally 200 years old or older. Lone Pine Prairie is named for the most ancient one in a Glacier prairie. It lived there for perhaps 700 years but died around 1990 as a result of injuries sustained in the 1988 Red Bench Fire. A number of these bigger ponderosa pines and western larch are what the Park Service calls "Indian-scarred trees." Their trunks have scars where Native Americans, probably Kootenais, cut the bark away to get at the cambium layer, a sweet-smelling food high in vitamins.

Like the prairies in the North Fork, stands of ponderosa pine depend on frequent fires—not severe fires that roar through the canopy but low-intensity fires that scorch the forest floor and kill less fire-resistant, competing trees. Without fire, ponderosa pine would disappear from the park—gradually, yes, but vanish nonetheless, its place assumed by Douglas fir and spruce trees. For these reasons, the Park Service has successfully extended its prescribed fire program from the prairies to the forests. Manager-lit fires in ponderosa pine communities have now burned some thirty-eight acres.

Perhaps more importantly, the Park Service can now use *naturally* ignited wildland fires to accomplish specific, predetermined objectives in specific areas—as long as certain conditions are met and the objectives and areas have been previously outlined in the park's Fire Management Plan. The official name for this approach is "wildland fire use." It allows the Park Service to take an intelligent approach to wildland fires, that is, to craft an appropriate management response to one of the park's most fundamental ecological processes.

Since the fires of 2003, a person might well ask whether there has been too much fire in the park, especially in an area like the North Fork. But events like the historic fire season of 2003 have occurred in the past and will again. Steve Barrett, a prominent fire ecologist who has studied the North Fork, reports that most of his study area (60,000 acres) burned in the twenty-eight-year period between 1655 and 1683. The forest ecologist H. B. Ayres, one of the first to study the area, reported in 1900 that much of the North Fork had recently burned (the result of the 1852, 1866, and especially the 1889 fires). Obviously fire has played an enormous role in the vegetation dynamics of the North Fork. Even if we wanted to keep it out, it is unlikely we could.

A Fen Is Not a Bog

Dry as it is, the North Fork Valley bottom also has its wet areas. Beavers create pockets where rushes and sedges, white alder and willow, and other water-loving plants grow; these moist sites make up some of the most productive wildlife habitat in the park, especially for moose and grizzly bears. In other places, where the ground is level and the water table high, wet meadows and *Sphagnum* fens have formed. A fen is a wetland plant community much like a bog—an area where poor drainage, low levels of oxygen in the water, and low temperatures lead to a buildup of dead plant material. The difference between a bog and a fen is that bogs acquire all of their mineral nutrients through the air—from rain and snow—so they are nutrient poor. Fens, on the other hand, get nutrients from both precipitation and groundwater. With waters more fertile and less acidic than that of bogs, they support a greater diversity of species. A bog, for example, might shelter fifteen species of plants, a fen anywhere from twenty to seventy.

About fifty plant species live in the McGee Meadow Fen. Fewer grow in Johns Lake Fen, which is closer to being a bog. Six species—rope-root sedge, pale sedge, buckler fern, green-keeled cotton-grass, Hudson's Bay bulrush, and mountain bladderwort—are considered rare in the northern Rockies. Indeed, eighteen of Glacier's species included on Montana's Sensitive Plant list live in fen habitats. Fens also harbor many species of algae and insects, too. Northern bog lemmings prefer fens over other habitats. Small as they are, these wetlands add tremendously to the variety of life found in the park.

On the short hike to Johns Lake Fen, you can admire *Sphagnum* moss in its delicate shades of pale green, olive, mallow pink, salmon, wine red, and rust. There it generates a thick, water-soaked mat of peat. Like many other mosses, *Sphagnum* receives all its mineral nourishment from rain, or rather from the tiny particles of dust that raindrops pick up as they fall. The plant is expert at soaking up calcium, sodium, and other mineral ions. In return, it releases hydrogen ions into the water. Hydrogen ions are the stuff of acid. By producing acid, *Sphagnum* makes the water too acidic for many other aquatic species, which explains why it dominates. The acid

McGee Meadow, a wet meadow adjacent to the McGee Meadow Fen, harbors rare and sensitive plants. (JOE WEYDT)

does something else as well; along with low levels of dissolved oxygen in the water, it limits bacterial decay. Thus, as the *Sphagnum* grows and dies—it has the peculiar habit of growing from the top while dying at the bottom—dead moss accumulates as peat. Over centuries, tons of it collect. Like a giant sponge, the mat stores rainwater—some species can hold twenty-five times their own weight in water. (Indians used *Sphagnum* as diapers.) This ability to absorb large amounts of water keeps the fen environment wet, even during dry times.

Fen water can be relatively poor in minerals, but many fen plants have adaptations that help them get nutrients elsewhere. Orchids such as bog candle, Alaska and one-leaf rein-orchid, and green and slender bog-orchid draw nourishment from symbiotic fungi living on their roots. The fungi draw minerals directly from the peat and make them available to the orchids.

Other plants have turned to gobbling insects and small crustaceans to obtain nutrients. Bladderworts are small, floating, rootless plants with bright yellow, snapdragon-like flowers. Their buoyant bladders are lethal traps for water fleas, isopods, mosquito larvae, and fish fry. Bladderworts attract prey by releasing sugar from special glands. If an animal then brushes against hairs that protrude from pores on the bladder, a trapdoor releases and water rushes in, sucking the organism along with it. When the bladder is full, the door snaps shut again. The whole process takes less than two thousandths of a second. Once the prey is caged, special glands secrete digestive enzymes. Bacteria living in the bladder aid the process, which takes from fifteen minutes to two hours. Afterwards, cells in the bladder pump the water out and reestablish a partial vacuum—the trap is set again. Large prey, such as mosquito larvae and fish fry or tadpoles, are often caught just by the head or tail. Still, the plant is able to ingest them—in segments, the wriggling animal triggering the bladder door over and over again.

The sundew, another carnivorous plant of the fen, employs different tactics. At its base, beneath a modest ivory-colored flower, a rosette of leaves glisten with gland-tipped, tentacle-like hairs that emit droplets of a sticky mucilage. The droplets sparkle in the sun like dew and attract insects such as damselflies. When an insect lands, the droplets act like flypaper. The hairs or tentacles fold around the insect, then bend slowly inward and deposit the catch in another part of the leaf where digestion takes place. How fast the tentacles move depends on how much the victim struggles. The plant can engulf a small, squirming bug within a minute and a half but might take hours or days to completely entangle a dead fly. If a tiny pebble or twig is dropped on the leaf, the tentacles may not move at all, or they may begin to fold but then open again. As with the bladderworts, sundews secrete enzymes to digest their victims. They also emit an anesthetic to stupefy their prey. Once digestion is complete, the tentacles on the leaves bend back. The plants can survive and reproduce without eating insects, but not as well. If insects are unavailable, sundews bypass seed-making and rely instead on asexual forms of reproduction, which they accomplish through tubers, axillary buds, and leaf buds.

Birding in the North Fork

On a recent birding trip to the North Fork, I found three kinds of wood-peckers in spruce groves along the river: the northern three-toed, the hairy, and the downy. It was spring, and the downy woodpeckers were drumming. By rapidly hammering their bills on a dry or hollow tree or stump for a few seconds, these birds communicate with their mates and advertise or patrol their territories. Other birds accomplish the same through song. I also caught a brief glimpse of a pileated woodpecker. At 15 inches, this is the second-largest woodpecker on the continent after the ivory-billed. Though wary, they are hard to miss even at a distance, looking, as they do, something like a real-life Woody the Woodpecker with their long, black body, heavy bill, and prominent, bright red crest. They drill big, distinctive, rectangular holes high in standing dead trees. Each pair of pileated woodpeckers requires at least 100 acres of dense forest for their nesting territory and more than 500 acres for foraging. Their drumming is loud and slow relative to that of other woodpeckers. One naturalist described it as a mellow-sounding roll "to which the whole wooded heart of the forest makes echoing response—a solemn and ancient sound."

One can also see red-breasted nuthatches, ruby- and golden-crowned kinglets, varied thrushes, solitary vireos, red crossbills, and yellow-rumped warblers in the North Fork bottoms. White-winged crossbills also visit, although I have yet to see one. The strange crossed mandibles of these birds—both red and white-winged—are specifically adapted for extracting pine nuts from cones. At a brushy spot near the McGee Meadow Fen, amidst dogwood, alder, and hawthorn, I saw or heard yellow, orange-crowned, and Wilson's warblers; warbling vireos; a Lincoln's sparrow; an American redstart; and a common yellowthroat. I watched the yellowthroat—a male—as he flew in a territorial or courtship display. Several times he ascended 50 to 100 feet, let out a strong but dissonant and garbled warble, then descended quietly to a perch (female yellowthroats immediately take cover when the males perform this ritual). Perching, he called *witcheby, witcheby*. I was glad to see the redstart; they, like many other warblers, have become rare across much of their range over the past

Pileated woodpeckers live year-round in the park. In winter they depend heavily on dormant ants for food; their favorite is carpenter ants. (GLACIER NATIONAL PARK)

few decades, mostly because of a loss of habitat—in their winter range in the tropics as well as in places like Montana. All of Glacier's warblers, except the yellow-rumped (known to some as the butter-butt), migrate to and from the tropics; it is thought they evolved in southern zones and took to migrating to escape competition from other tropical birds. Most are in Glacier for only a few months, just long enough to breed and raise young.

Near the fen itself, you can see red-winged blackbirds, northern waterthrushes, soras, and snipes. If you are very, very patient, you might spot a LeConte's sparrow, a small, difficult-to-see insect eater. Farther north in the valley you could even come across a hawk-owl, a day hunter more associated with the muskegs of northern Canada than the forests of Montana. Since about 1990, a handful of people have seen nesting pairs within the perimeters of the Red Bench, Moose, Robert, and Trapper Fires; in Glacier the bird is selecting post-fire habitats, nesting in them two to ten years after the fire. Incidentally, 1990 was the first year (that we know of) that hawk-owls bred in Montana.

Bird-watchers have observed more than 200 species of birds in the North Fork Valley. Of those, around 115 nest here. A number are year-round residents. Others visit for short periods during spring or fall migrations. How all these species distribute themselves across the valley bottom depends to a large degree on the vegetation. Generally speaking, the greater the number of plant species that grow on a piece of ground, the greater the number of bird species that use it. For example, only a few species will nest on new sand and gravel bars—areas recently scoured by the river and sparsely populated with plants. Similar sites that are overgrown with cottonwood saplings and willow bushes will host a few more species. But the oldest floodplain communities, areas dominated by mature cottonwood and spruce, have the most nesting birds. As riparian plant communities get older and more complex and diverse, the number of foods and niches increase, and therefore the number of birds feeding, breeding, and nesting in them grows.

The North Fork Valley is a good place to watch birds. Great blue herons stalk the waters of the North Fork and surrounding backwaters for young cutthroat and bull trout. American dippers bob on river boulders

A dipper with a mouthful of stonefly. (GLACIER NATIONAL PARK)

and wade beneath the icy waters of the North Fork in search of aquatic insects. Spotted sandpipers and killdeer search the cobble washes of the shoreline for terrestrial bugs. Sparrows—Lincoln's, song, fox, white-crowned, and chipping—flit about in search of seeds and berries among the shrubs and herbs beneath the cottonwood stands. With them are dark-eyed juncos, red-eyed vireos, Swainson's thrushes, McGillivray's and orange-crowned warblers, western tanagers, veerys, and dusky, least, and willow flycatchers.

The dippers are my favorite, for they seem to be such enthusiastic little birds, always bouncing or flitting from one river rock to another or diving headlong into a current. They captured John Muir's heart, too. Of the dipper, he wrote, "He is the mountain streams' own darling, the hummingbird of blooming waters, loving rocky ripple slopes and sheets of foam as a bee loves flowers, as a lark loves sunshine and meadows. Among all the mountain birds, none has cheered me so much in my lonely wanderings—

none so unfailingly. For both in winter and summer, he sings, sweetly, cheerily, independent alike of sunshine and of love, requiring no other inspiration than the stream on which he dwells."

Dippers, slate gray and small—about the size of a blackbird—dwell and sing on all the streams in the North Fork Valley. The otters of the bird world, they make their living by plunging into rushing waters, where, fully submerged, they walk the bottom and search rocks for insects, mollusks, crustaceans, flatworms, and, occasionally, fingerling fish. They do the same in winter, sometimes strolling beneath the ice. Their legs are unusually strong. But their feet are unwebbed, so they use their wings to propel themselves where currents are swift. They actually fly underwater and can forage easily in currents too swift and deep for people to stand in. They have been known to dive 30 feet for a fat stonefly. Their song, in contrast to their *bzeeeet* alarm call, is as unforgettably clear and bright as the streams they inhabit.

To conserve heat, dippers' bodies are protected by a layer of insulating down, which in turn is covered by more than 6,000 soft feathers. The plumage is so dense that it is difficult to saturate, especially given that they coat it, as they preen with their bills, with a waterproofing oil secreted by a gland near the base of their tails. Other songbirds have oil glands near their tails, but the dipper's is ten times larger. A third eyelid, a thin, milky membrane that closes horizontally across the eye, shields the cornea from splashes and the spray of rapids and waterfalls. Small, moveable flaps of skin close the nostrils when the bird is submerged.

One of the most curious characteristics of dippers is their habit of bobbing or dipping once they climb out of the stream onto a rock. Why they do it remains a question, but they do it continually, up to forty times a minute. One naturalist, who noticed the movement seemed to mirror the dancing movements of the stream, the rises and falls of the rapids and riffles, suggested rapid dipping might improve the bird's ability to see, either into the water or across its surface. An alternative explanation is that it serves to disguise the bird from invertebrates that otherwise might flee. In other words, by bobbing, the bird blends better with its surroundings, making it more effective as a predator.

Dippers nest on rocky ledges and crevices near a stream and return to the same nest site year after year—a favorite nesting place is behind a waterfall. Muir loved the nests: "[It] is one of the most extraordinary pieces of bird architecture I ever saw . . . about a foot in diameter, round and bossy in outline, with a neatly arched opening near the bottom, somewhat like an old-fashioned brick oven, or Hottentot's hut. It is built almost exclusively of green and yellow mosses, chiefly, the beautiful fronded hypnum that covers the rocks and old drift logs in the vicinity of waterfalls. These are deftly interwoven and felted together into a charming little hut and so situated that many of the outer mosses continue to flourish as if they had not been plucked."

I share Muir's appreciation for these exuberant little birds. Full of vigor, they are as lively as the streams they frequent.

As with birds, the distribution of small mammals matches that of plant communities. Young river habitats with sparse vegetation support few species, but the ones that are there, like deer mice and voles, are abundant. Those species seem to be attracted to the debris piles left behind by frequent floods and the greens that sprout from the nutrient-rich river sediments. Older spruce communities, on the other hand, harbor many more species—squirrels, voles, hares, bats, and several kinds of mice—but in smaller numbers.

Where rodents are plentiful, so are predators, and the North Fork river bottom has a diverse array, among them Cooper's, sharp-shinned, and red-tailed hawks; harriers, merlins, kestrels, and goshawks; great-horned, barred, pygmy, and saw-whet owls; and foxes, wolves, coyotes, black bears, bobcats, minks, martens, and weasels.

The Shrews

The smallest predator inhabiting the floodplain is a shrew, a pygmy shrew. It is also one of the rarest creatures in North America. They share the North Fork with three other kinds of shrews: The wandering shrew and the masked are common, the water shrew less so. All, including the pygmy, look a little like runty, pointed-nosed mice, but shrews are altogether dif-

Forests of the North Fork Valley provide homes for a number of small animals from bats to shrews to squirrels. (JOE WEYDT)

ferent from mice; in fact, they are not even rodents but are more closely related to moles and hedgehogs. More primitive than rodents, they have smaller brains and, like reptiles, genital and urinary tracts that merge into a single opening called a cloaca. And shrews eat insects. They climb and burrow some but spend most of their time aboveground ferreting out food amidst a tangle of grasses and herbs.

Shrews have high metabolic rates and therefore voracious appetites. Their respiration rate is twenty-five times greater than that of humans (their excited hearts have been known to beat as fast as 1,320 times per minute). They hunt night and day, winter and summer, and must put down a healthy meal every two or three hours or starve. Pygmy shrews consume more than twenty-five different kinds of creatures, among them beetles, flies, butterflies, ants, springtails, mites, spiders, woodlice, centipedes, snails, slugs, and grasshoppers—beetles seem to be a favorite and have the best overall food value, as they are both high in energy and low in water. Pygmy shrews, however, unlike other species of shrews, avoid earthworms, perhaps because earthworms are so big, relatively speaking. A big earthworm dwarfs a pygmy shrew, which, at an eighth of an ounce, is the smallest mammal on the continent. A pygmy shrew chasing and attacking a grasshopper is as dramatic as a wolf pulling down a moose.

Northern water shrews, because they are semiaquatic, eat everything pygmy shrews eat plus a host of aquatic organisms—mostly stonefly, mayfly, and caddisfly larvae, but occasionally small fish and tadpoles. They inhabit the banks of streams and ponds and often swim in pursuit of food. The water shrew, the second-largest shrew in North America, is almost twice as big as a pygmy shrew. Well adapted to a life in and out of the water, its toes and paws are fringed with stiff, silvery hairs that increase the surface area of the paws just as webbing does on a duck's foot; the ventral sides of its tail sport a row of stiff bristles that serve the same purpose as the keel on a boat; and its fur traps air, a modification that increases insulation and repels water but makes diving more difficult. I once saw a water shrew near an alpine lake in the Mission Mountains, just south of Glacier. I was resting on a mat of heather beside a small but swift stream when something mouselike appeared from the bank and dove, without a hint of hesitation, into the icy water. It swam, fully submerged, along the bottom for about five or ten seconds, then shot back out, groomed itself hurriedly, and disappeared into the sedges growing along the bank.

Like whales and bats, water shrews, wandering shrews, and masked shrews use ultrasonic sounds—high-frequency, low-intensity pulses on the order of 30 to 60 kHz—to orient themselves in unfamiliar territory, to locate prey, to detect predators, and to communicate. The sounds reflect off various surfaces and tell the shrew where it is in relation to those surfaces. Scientists believe shrews, which have poor eyesight and hunt at night as much as during the day, use the sounds to construct an acoustic image—to "see" gaps in vegetation, burrows, insects, approaching predators. The ultrasonic shrieks may also serve to mark territories, like the howls of wolves.

A Mammal of Which We Know Little

One other small mammal of the North Fork deserves mention. The northern bog lemming is a grayish brown, short-tailed, volelike rodent closely related to true arctic lemmings. They are rare in North America; scientists searching for them have collected only about fifty over the past century. As a consequence we don't know much about them; they may in fact be one of the least known mammals on earth. What they eat, how far they travel, how long they live, and their population densities and reproductive rates are unknown. Apparently, their preferred habitat is a thick, wet mat of *Sphagnum* moss, and we presume that, like many other rodents, they develop rapidly, reproduce early and often, and live short lives. The biologists I visited with believe a high percentage probably become food for predators—one Glacier Park study found bog lemmings made up 1 to 2 percent of the diets of pine martens, though they made up only 0.2 of 1 percent of the small mammals captured by the field workers who did the study, which says something about who's the better lemming catcher.

Like arctic plants in Glacier, bog lemmings are considered ice-age relics. Lemmings were probably common during the Pleistocene but then declined after the ice melted and the climate warmed. *Sphagnum*-dominated fens are widely spaced now, and the ability of bog lemmings to migrate is limited. A population at a given fen may have been isolated from other bog lemmings for perhaps 10,000 years.

The Largest Deer

North Fork fens, willow-lined meadows, and shallow lakes bordered by sedges and tender mannagrass are good places to look for moose. All the moose I have seen in Glacier have been belly-deep in wet areas like these, although North Fork moose spend most of their time in drier, upland habitats.

Moose are the largest members of the deer family. Shiras moose, the relatively smaller subspecies found in the northern Rockies of the United States, can weigh up to 1,000 pounds and stand more than 6 feet tall at the

Water provides a refuge for moose fleeing predators like wolves and bears. Moose also frequent wet areas to forage and have been known to dive as deep as 18 feet for aquatic vegetation. (GLACIER NATIONAL PARK)

shoulders. They also have long ears and a bulbous nose, bigger heads and longer legs than other members of the deer family, and a prominent shoulder hump, all of which cause them to appear ungainly. They are not; an alert or suspicious moose can move almost silently through dense brush and, when frightened, gallop as fast as 35 mph.

Male moose carry large antlers, the largest of any member of the deer family, and their antlers are broadly palmate or shovel-like, as opposed to being branched beams like those of deer and elk. The rack of a mature bull, which is grown and shed each year, can stretch 4.5 feet from one end to the other; the size depends on the individual's age, genes, and nutritional health, as well as the amount of lime in the soil. Male ungulates invest considerable energy in antler growth. For moose, it is almost as much as females use during pregnancy.

Antler growth starts early in the spring, initiated by the pituitary gland when days get longer. Growing antlers are covered with and nurtured by a soft, reddish, velvety membrane, a network of small blood vessels. In August or September a surge of testosterone acts to cut off the blood supply, and the velvet dries and begins to shed. To speed its removal, moose scrape their racks against trees and shrubs. When free of their furry coat, the fresh antlers are almost ivory white, except for a few bloodstains. Over the next few weeks they turn progressively darker, so that by September, they are the color of mahogany or cocoa.

The rut begins in September, peaks in early October, and ends in November. During this time, males go through "a period of temporary insanity," writes biologist and author Douglas Chadwick, "chock-full of hormone-pumped gumption and gripped by moosey jealousies, bulls have been known to charge not just any and all rival bulls but passing automobiles and, according to some stories, freight trains." A pair of rutting bulls will face off and dip their antlers from side to side as they circle each other with long, stiff strides. Ears back and manes bristling, the two size each other up. If neither backs down, both start shredding trees and shrubs with their antlers. Periodically they'll take a break from this jousting to browse or graze, but their movements remain jerky and quick, and their eyes stay fixed on their opponent. Both may dig wallows with their front hooves, pass urine into the hole, and roll in it. Wherever moose breed you can find wallows; two wallows 6 to 8 feet apart is probably the site of a big showdown. If a cow is nearby, as is often the case, one of the two may go to her, sniff her rump, and then curl his lip and raise his head high in a gesture that brings traces of the female's scent collected on his upper lip closer to his olfactory receptors. Unless one of the males backs down, the two will approach each other until their antlers meet and begin pushing each other back and forth. Occasionally one will stumble, and the other will jab him with his antlers in the ribs or flank or kick him. Usually the confrontation ends quickly with one bull retreating, although some pairs may tussle for hours or simply stand near each other, pretending to browse while periodically shredding trees or shrubs. The challenge goes on until one of the two leaves, which can take days. But when it is over, the winner returns to his female. If undisturbed, the pair will mate repeatedly for several days. A few months after the rut, moose shed their antlers; most fall between December and February.

Moose are browsers; that is, their primary foods are the twigs and shoots of shrubs and trees (as opposed to grazers, which eat mostly nonwoody plants like grasses and herbs). In Glacier Park, moose favor willow, mountain maple, red-osier dogwood, and alder, although they also eat conifers, aspen and cottonwood saplings, forbs, grasses, and aquatic plants like water lilies, pondweed, mare's tail, bur reed, and mannagrass. They spend most of their time near or in water. Their long legs allow them to wade deep into fens where other animals would have difficulty traveling. They are strong swimmers, too, and dive for aquatic plants to depths of up to 18 feet—they "submerge so completely that not a ripple remained in the water near where they went down...[then] the rump would float to the top and break water before the animal raised its head," according to moose biologist Randolf Peterson. In winter, moose chew off the terminal twigs and branches of shrubs and, to a lesser extent, conifers—branches as large as 0.5 inch in diameter. They eat the black lichen that hangs from trees, a plant high in protein. In summer they abandon the conifers but continue to nip twigs, which they supplement with leaves stripped from thicker branches. Like elk, moose eat aspen bark, especially in the spring. They peel freshly fallen, wind-blown trees or gnaw the bark off standing trees up to 10 feet above the ground.

Some moose in the North Fork migrate seasonally, and others use the same habitat year-round. The latter group stay mostly at lower elevations, below 4,600 feet, in areas where the conifer canopy is relatively open and where there are abundant marshy areas and plenty of willow and other water-loving shrubs. The moose that migrate stay higher in the spring and summer, on average about 1,300 feet higher. There is plenty of good range at lower elevations in the North Fork, but that is where wolves tend to hunt. Migrating cow moose may stay high to avoid predation and protect their calves (in the Isle Royale area of Minnesota, solitary moose select areas with the most nutritious forage, while cows with calves use areas with less nutritious foods but where wolves are absent). In winter North Fork migratory moose move onto low-elevation ranges—valley bottoms or gentle southwest-facing slopes. Some travel as far as 50 miles between their summer and winter ranges.

Moose are, for the most part, solitary animals, except for cows with calves. Cows are extraordinarily protective of their offspring, especially during the first weeks of the calf's life. In Alaska I once watched a mother moose defend her week-old calf against a prolonged attack by a grizzly bear. The bear, a large, tawny-furred adult, sat above the moose on a steep, brushy slope. The calf cowered beneath her mother's legs. Every half hour or so, the bear would charge down the hill on all fours, to within 5 or 10 feet of the pair. The cow, ears back and mane bristling, would rise to her hind legs and charge back at the bear, front hooves flying. The bear, dodging the blows, would turn and retreat, the moose following close behind for several yards before returning to her calf. The standoff lasted for two days before the bear gave up and moved on.

In Glacier Park moose of all ages are preyed upon by grizzly bears and wolves. Calves are also taken by mountain lions, black bears, and coyotes. In the fall moose that cross the North Fork of the Flathead River and leave the park are hunted by humans. In a twenty-one month study of thirty-two radio-collared, adult female moose in the North Fork, two were killed by grizzly bears, one by wolves, and one died of natural causes other than predation. In a follow-up 1993 study, five moose were killed: two by wolves, one by grizzly bears, and two by hunters. From these studies, biologists estimate about 90 percent of adult cow moose in the North Fork survive a given year. Among adult wild ungulates, such a survival rate is high. The survival rate of calves is probably much lower.

Of all the animals that bears and wolves hunt, moose are the largest and most dangerous. They are also among the fastest. And they use an escape strategy other large ungulates do not; when chased, they head for water if it is nearby. When they hunt moose, grizzly bears seem to rely on an element of surprise, often attacking moose in bottomlands where the brush is thick and visibility low. One observer watching a moose in McGee Meadow described how a big grizzly "burst from the edge of a very dense stand of lodgepole pine adjacent to the meadow and charged [the moose] . . . the cow ran, high stepping, into a pond and swam to the other side. The grizzly did not attempt to follow . . . " The bears most successful at moose hunting are those that hunt in family groups, mothers with two or more cubs. Grizzly bears in fact can become quite good at moose hunting. In much of the Canadian Rockies, they kill more moose than wolves take.

When wolves take a moose, they generally do so in winter as a pack of four or more animals (although in Minnesota and Alaska, single wolves have been seen taking down adult moose). Their usual method is to chase the animal and bite it on the rear and the sides; they target the area where the hind legs join the abdomen. A rip in the flesh there can spill the viscera and open arteries and veins, bringing a quick end to the chase. Moose are most vulnerable to attack by wolves during harsh winters when the snow is more than about 2.5 feet deep. Heavy snow forces moose and wolves into the same areas so the two animals encounter each other more frequently. And during a chase through deep snow, wolves enjoy an enormous advantage; they can often run on the surface of the snow, while moose cannot. Moose also find it harder to kick in deep snow, and the refuge of open water is usually absent.

Even with these advantages, wolves in the North Fork seem to select the vulnerable—not necessarily the sick, but the young and the old. In six years of study by the University of Montana's Wolf Ecology Project, researchers found twenty-seven wolf-killed moose. Of the eighteen of those that could be aged, fourteen were two years old or younger; the remaining four were ten years old or older. (Moose generally only live to be ten to twelve years old.)

When there is no snow on the ground, adult moose and wolves are on more equal terms. Moose may even have the advantage. Wolves are slightly slower—their top running speed under optimum conditions is about 35 mph. On firm ground, a cornered moose is free to kick, and its hooves can be deadly—in 1993 the North Fork's Wolf Ecology Project found one of its twenty collared wolves trampled to death, presumably by a moose. Also, wolf packs are less cohesive during summer months, so wolves are more often alone or in small groups. Hence wolves are less inclined to go after healthy adult moose during the months when there is little or no snow on the ground. A substantial but unknown fraction of moose calves, however, are probably taken in the North Fork during their first year.

Moose, Elk, and Deer: A Case of Competition?

In winter, white-tailed deer and elk share the North Fork bottomlands with moose. A small number of mule deer also inhabit the North Fork, and up until a few decades ago, woodland caribou roamed the valley. In the winter all three species—whitetails, elk, and moose—mostly browse woody plants. Because there is only a limited amount of browse available, one might assume that these three members of the deer family compete with each other—that one species, say deer, might consume most or all of the forage in a given area and thereby limit the populations of elk and moose. But that is not the case. Deer, elk, and moose coexist in the North Fork precisely because each exploits a slightly different part of the environment. Each of these species, in fact, inhibits or limits its own population more than it inhibits the populations of the other two. Said another way, the lion's share of the competition is among individuals within a species rather than between individuals of different species.

Whenever similar species inhabit the same area, a dynamic operates to prevent all but one from being exterminated by competition. One of the classic papers on this subject was written in the 1950s by Robert MacArthur, a well-known bird biologist. He studied warblers—the Cape May, the yellow-rumped, the black-throated green, the Blackburnian, and the bay-breasted—five species that occupied northeastern coniferous forests. Prior to his work, many believed these five birds assumed identical roles in the same community—after all, they occupied the same trees, were about the same size and shape, and all ate insects. But this violated one of the fundamental maxims of ecology: Two species with essentially the same profession cannot coexist because one will inevitably edge out the other.

Elk flourish in the North Fork and use slightly different habitat than either moose or deer. (GLACIER NATIONAL PARK)

To see if these warblers had somehow found a way around this rule, MacArthur divided the individual trees they were using into zones and observed how much time each warbler spent feeding in each zone. He also kept track of how and when the birds fed. What he found was that each species of warbler not only had its own part of the tree in which it hunted insects but also that each had its own method of hunting. Whereas one fed near the top and outside portions of a tree, another frequented the lower and inside parts. As one took frequent short flights to catch insects on the wing, another diligently sought its prey among the branches and foliage. Where one moved vertically, another moved in circles. Some appeared nervous and active, others slow and deliberate. MacArthur concluded that each species behaved "in such a way as to be exposed to different kinds of foods." Putting it another way, each bird had its own cupboard. Only by partitioning themselves in this way, only by being specialists in their methods and place of feeding, only by becoming, in a sense, professionals, could these otherwise very similar species coexist in the same area.

So it is with the North Fork's ungulates—deer, elk, and moose. They are able to winter together because, for the most part, they feed in different places, feed in ways that allow them to find different foods, or express different preferences. One of the big factors affecting where each feeds is body design. In winter, the snow in the North Fork can reach 3 or more feet deep. Factors that affect an animal's ability to travel through deep snow, like leg length, dictate to a large extent the parts of the bottomland each species uses. White-tailed deer, for example, stand a little more than 3 feet high at the shoulders—quite a bit lower than elk or moose—and they have difficulty traveling or feeding when the snow gets deeper than 1.5 feet. Consequently, they winter where snows are shallowest, typically beneath stands of old-growth Douglas fir and spruce, trees with dense canopies that intercept falling snow. Elk stand about 5 feet at the shoulders and use areas—mostly lodgepole pine savannas—that have, on average, about 2 feet of snow (although during severe, deep-snow winters, they may be pushed into the same coniferous stands deer use, and during mild winters they may graze the meadows). Moose average almost 6 feet high at the shoulders; they feed wherever the browse is good, usually in brushy fields where snow depths exceed 2.5 feet.

There are other factors that come into play, too, besides leg length. Relative to elk and moose, white-tailed deer have small bodies, so it is harder for them to stay warm. (Big animals have less surface area relative to their mass so they retain heat better than small animals; in other words, a polar bear is like a lot of squirrels huddled together to keep warm.) Deer winter in old-growth spruce communities because, in addition to catching snow, the large trees provide shelter from the wind and warmth—at night, the trunks give off the heat they absorbed during the day from the sun. Moose have a different problem. They seem immune to cold. Their bodies, however, are so large that they have to eat an enormous amount of food every day. They feed where food is abundant and even tolerate deep snows to enjoy a full larder. The moose's enormous upper lip may further distinguish what it eats from what deer and elk consume—much the way variations in beaks separate Darwin's finches. Perhaps the lip better enables moose to strip leaves from branches. Specialization demands special tools.

Because of these differences and certainly others, deer, elk, and moose eat slightly different foods, although there is overlap, especially during severe winters. Deer browse mostly on conifers—one study estimated that 65 to 90 percent of a North Fork white-tail's winter diet is made up of the needles or twigs of spruce, pine, fir, and Douglas fir trees. Their menu also includes a selection of deciduous shrubs like serviceberry, red-osier dogwood, and wild rose and large quantities of a low-growing, hollylike evergreen called Oregon grape. Elk dine on conifers, too, but they eat more grass and deciduous shrubs than deer. Moose concentrate on willow and other deciduous shrubs as well as young aspen and cottonwood trees. Like warblers, the ungulates of the North Fork have divided up their common pantry in such a way that, during all but the most severe winters, there is room for all.

The Hunters of the North Fork

Now broaden this picture of the North Fork's ungulate community to take in the large predators. There are eight of them in the North Fork: wolves (which began recolonizing the valley in the early 1980s), mountain lions, grizzly bears, black bears, humans, coyotes, wolverines, and lynx. All are capable of taking the fawns and calves of deer, elk, and moose. The first five on the list prey on adult ungulates as well. Humans are included because, even though they can't hunt in the park, they can and do hunt the public lands that border the park—everything west of the river, a boundary that poses no barrier to the animals.

Studies have shown that lions are the primary predators of adult white-tailed deer and elk in the North Fork, while wolves are the chief predators of adult moose (even though wolves seem to be selecting white-tailed deer as their main prey). It seems surprising that lions take more deer and elk than wolves. But lions are more capable ungulate killers than wolves. Indeed, wolves profit from lions by stealing from them. They follow lion

A tranquilized North Fork wolf. By placing radio collars on wolves and moose, biologists learn about the relations between these two species. (WENDY CLARK)

tracks and chase the lions off their kills and up trees. Sometimes they even kill the lions, prompting one observer to remark that the two predators are, in many ways, acting like cats and dogs.

It appears that things are still settling out in the North Fork. Wolves were absent from the valley for half a century. During that time, the lion population may have increased because they did not share prey with wolves. Now that wolves have returned, lions may decline, not because wolves are the better hunters but because wolves are able to take animals the lions kill. Lions may also be forced to hunt in more marginal parts of the valley. Time will tell.

A Look at the North Fork Wolves

Given a choice, wolves, here and in other places, seem to prefer deer over either elk or moose, even though an elk or a moose provides anywhere from five to ten times more meat than a deer. Some carnivores, like those of the weasel family, often try to prey on the largest animals that they are capable of killing to get the best return for their effort. Apparently, however, it's more efficient and safer for wolf packs to kill several deer than a single moose or elk. Smaller prey require fewer wolves, involve less risk of injury, and take less energy overall.

Wolves in Glacier spend almost all of their time where deer are most numerous. When they encounter elk or moose tracks on their travel routes, they often ignore them to go after deer. One researcher who has spent more than a decade and a half tracking wolves in the valley told me that a pack will spend the entire winter just moving from one white-tail winter range to another. So it should come as no surprise that deer, mostly adults, make up nearly two-thirds of their winter diet. Elk and moose make up the bulk of the rest, although a survey of kill sites turned up an assortment of other species as well: beavers, porcupines, mountain lions, ruffed grouse, ravens, golden eagles, coyotes, skunks, and meadow voles. (Wolves hunting in the Canadian part of the North Fork tend to have a higher percentage of moose meat in their diet than the wolves in and adjacent to Glacier. That is because the northern part of the drainage has lots of moose and few deer. South of the international border, deer outnumber elk by two to one and moose by about six to one.) In spring, summer, and fall, wolves tend to eat more fawns and calves than adults because the younger animals are so much easier to catch.

Kill sites are not necessarily as gory as they sound. Most carcasses are almost completely consumed within a few days, bones and all, a remarkable feat in and of itself considering the size of some ungulate bones. Often, all that is left by the time the researchers arrive is the stomach and its contents, a little hair, and a patch or two of bloodstained snow or soil. The exception occurs during unusually severe winters when, because of heavy snow, deer flounder in the chase and are easily caught. Severe winters are times of plenty for wolves, and they consume less of each kill then. By contrast, late summer and fall are difficult; young ungulates are large enough to outrun a wolf, and adults are healthy and fit from a summer of browsing and grazing.

A wolf must consume about 10 percent of its body weight in meat each day on average to stay healthy. Wolves in the North Fork average 90 pounds. This means that during one month in winter, when energy demands are highest, a pack of eight to ten wolves in the North Fork will take approximately twenty-two deer, six elk, and a quarter of a moose. Many of those will be young animals, yearlings, fawns, or calves. Almost all will be killed in the park, where the wolves spend better than 95 percent of their time and where human hunting is not allowed.

The number of wolves living in the North Fork fluctuates from year to year, as does the number of packs. For example, in 1993 in the U.S. portion of the North Fork, thirty-nine wolves lived in two packs: The North Camas Pack had ten adults and eight pups; the South Camas Pack thirteen adults and eight pups. In 2000 the population in the U.S. part of the North Fork had dropped to thirteen wolves, but there were three packs. The South Camas Pack had just two adults; the North Camas had four; and a new pack called the Whitefish Pack, which was first known to breed in 1996, had three adults and four pups. Territories in the North Fork had changed, too. By 2001 the Whitefish Pack had displaced the South Camas Pack by moving into the area around and north of Lake McDonald. The two remaining adults of the South Camas Pack, meanwhile, found a home in the Middle Fork of the Flathead, where they raised a litter of pups. That pack was called the Nyack Pack. In 2004 two packs hunted the west side: the Kintla Pack with five wolves just south of the Canadian border and the Whitefish Pack with seven wolves in the central part of the North Fork Valley.

Between 1993 and 2004, the total number of wolves in all of northwestern Montana averaged just under sixty-eight animals. In 1998 the total number dropped to forty-nine, a decline attributed to the unusually severe winter of 1996–97, when deep snows dramatically reduced the number of white-tailed deer. As the deer numbers dropped, ranchers in northwestern

Montana experienced record-high levels of livestock depradations. Wolves then experienced high levels of wolf control actions, and their numbers dropped. Since then, white-tail populations have rebounded. Wolf numbers in northwestern Montana, as one might expect, have bounced back, too, reaching a peak of 130 in the Northwestern Montana recovery area in 2005.

As evidenced by the bad winter of 1996–97, wolves are just one factor affecting ungulate numbers. Weather and disease take a toll, as do half a dozen other predators, including lions, which probably kill more deer and elk than wolves. Plus there is an ever-increasing population of humans in the Flathead area, many of whom hunt in the North Fork. Their land use practices and developments outside of the park affect ungulates just as fires and epidemics of insects do. Indeed, factors that alter the quantity or quality of habitat influence wildlife more profoundly than any predator.

In the ten or fifteen years prior to 1990, the numbers of deer and elk in the North Fork reached all-time highs because logging and a major mountain pine beetle infestation cleared the overstory and increased the amount of browse available. Wolves may have been responsible for a slight downward trend in ungulate populations in the early 1990s. But it was that severe winter that really caused deer and elk populations to drop. Exactly what part a single predator plays in a valley like the North Fork is difficult to pin down. We do know that wolves kill many of Glacier's deer and elk. But deer, elk, and moose evolved with wolves. It's a fair bet the four species will coexist in the North Fork for a long time to come.

Recolonization: A Case Study

"Beasts of waste and desolation" is how Teddy Roosevelt described wolves, and he was normally quite progressive on conservation issues. Until rather recently, Americans generally thought of predators like wolves as evil and destructive. Wolves were killers that plagued our livestock and our game, and it seemed we could do without them. So we tried, destroying them wherever we found them by whatever means. By 1910 only three or four packs with maybe forty or fifty individuals remained in the western United States, and those were all in Glacier. The park was established that year, and

A wolf on a recently killed elk. Wolves generally consume almost the entire animal, including the massive bones. (BRUCE WEIDE)

high on its new managers' agenda was "resolution of the wolf problem." Rangers employed every means at their disposal, from guns to traps to poisons, to extirpate the species. They killed the last few individuals before 1936, and other than an occasional sojourner from central Canada, the species remained absent until the 1980s.

Among the circumstances that allowed wolves to return to the park was an increase in the North Fork's deer and elk populations. Changing public attitudes and the listing, in 1973, of the wolf as an endangered species helped. Canada also gets some credit for relaxing their wolf control program.

Coincidentally, about the time the wolf was listed as an endangered species, the number of sightings on the west side of Glacier Park started to increase. Wolves were trickling out of central Canada into the North Fork one or two at a time. The first litter of pups, seven of them, was reported in 1982 in the Canadian portion of the North Fork. Eventually, these progenitors of most of the wolves in Glacier and the rest of the North Fork came to be known as the Magic Pack. They were given that name for their uncanny ability to elude the team of seasoned biologists so intent on studying them.

The Magic Pack moved south from Canada into Glacier Park in November of 1985 and the following spring had a litter there, this time of five pups, on a flat-topped, heavily wooded knoll at the edge of a small meadow near one of the larger prairies. Those may have been the first wolves to be born in Glacier Park in more than fifty years.

Two years later, the Magic Pack split into the Camas, Sage Creek, and Headwaters packs, each establishing its own territory in such a way that little of the North Fork Valley bottom went unclaimed. By 1992 the three packs had become four: the Headwaters and Spruce Creek packs in the Canadian part of the North Fork, and the North Camas and South Camas packs in Glacier National Park. In the years that followed, those North Fork packs sent out "dispersers"—wolves that struck out on their own to recolonize other areas. North Fork dispersers set up or attempted to set up territories in central Idaho and the Marion, Fortine, Augusta, and Nine-

Wolf tracks pass over an elk antler in the North Fork. (WENDY CLARK)

mile areas of Montana. Apparently, they even found their way as far south as Yellowstone Park—genetic tests showed that a wolf killed just south of there in 1992 was probably a Magic Pack descendent, or at least a close relative. Dispersers have traveled even farther. A young Magic Pack female that left Glacier Park in January of 1987 turned up dead—shot by a farmer—six months later near the Peace River in Alberta. She was 550 air miles north of Glacier when she died.

Wolves are social animals. They live in hierarchical packs with territories that they scent-mark by urinating on tree trunks, bushes, and rocks. Territories may be vigorously defended from intruding wolves. Interlopers are either run off or killed. In some areas, like parts of Alaska, more wolves die for trespass than are killed by moose, humans, disease, or anything else. Wolves in the North Fork, however, showed little interest in defending their territories from the occasional encroachment by a neighboring pack as they recolonized the valley. In fact, in 1986 the Camas and Sage Creek packs were seen socializing. This extraordinary level of tolerance may have occurred because both packs were relatively new to an area that for decades had been without wolves. There were plenty of prey animals, so there was little need for competition. Second, because all the wolves were descended from the Magic Pack, everyone in the North Fork was related and likely familiar. Perhaps, in this circumstance, near cousins were considered "licensed" intruders, the way humans might tolerate their mother-in-law walking into their home unannounced, whereas they would likely be hostile toward a stranger. But that level of familiarity decreased with each new generation born. In 1993 a yearling caught in the "no-man's land" between the North and South Camas packs was killed by one of those packs, the first known incident of wolf-killing-wolf in the park since recolonization started some seven years earlier.

Many visitors to the North Fork have heard the unforgettable howl of a wolf, a long, mournful wail that, in the words of Barry Lopez, "quickly reaches pitch and then tapers, with several harmonics . . . to a tremolo." Howls can travel 10 or more miles, and can change how one thinks about an area of wilderness. Knowing wolves are about makes a place feel untamed, the way it might have felt a hundred years ago. Wolves howl to bring a pack together, to bond a pack prior to a hunt, to warn fellow pack members of an impending danger, to communicate an individual's whereabouts, to warn trespassing wolves, or to pass on over a great distance some other, yet undeciphered message. Because each individual howl can encompass a series of up to twelve harmonics, and because when wolves sing together, they harmonize, rather than all singing on the same note, two or three wolves can sound like a pack of fifteen or twenty. This is advantageous when a pack howls to warn wolves intruding into its territory.

Visitors to Glacier have little reason to fear wolves. There has been only one documented account of a healthy wolf killing a human in North America. This is not to say the animal doesn't deserve your caution and respect, as does any wild animal, but wolves do not pose the same kinds of dangers to hikers and campers that grizzly bears do.

The Two Bears: Evolutionary Adaptations

Both grizzly and black bears are common in the valley, and during the spring and the fall many feed extensively on floodplains and along tributary drainages. Grizzly bears may exist in two distinct populations: bears that rarely leave the floodplains, and others that live in mid-elevation, mountainous habitats—fields of shrubs, avalanche chutes, and hillside meadows, or parks, as they are often called. One grizzly bear study found that roughly 80 percent of spring and fall grizzly bear feeding sites in the North Fork Valley bottom occur on floodplains and along tributaries—even though those areas comprise only about 30 percent of the bottomlands.

Early in the spring, grizzly bears move onto the wet, sometimes flooded meadows along streams and the river bottom. At this time, the protein content of their chief springtime foods—grasses, sedges, and

Grizzly bears dig for the roots of sweetvetch and other plants on the North Fork floodplain, especially in spring and fall. (FRANK TYRO)

herbs—averages from 15 to 25 percent. Twenty-five percent is exactly equal to the amount of protein in the cheddar cheese I carry on day hikes. However, as plants develop and flower, the fiber content of their leaves and stems increases, and bears can't digest foods high in fiber. So, to benefit from all that protein, they have to forage the wet meadow areas of the North Fork bottoms early, while the plants are still young and succulent.

Despite the predominance of vegetation in their diets (vegetable matter makes up 70 to 80 percent of what a bear eats), bears have the digestive system of a carnivore. They do, however, possess a few herbivorous adaptations, modifications that allow them to eat plants without affecting their ability to digest meat. For example, they have long claws, which they use mostly for digging roots, and blunt molars that enable them to grind plant foods (that kind of dentition is lacking in animals that eat only meat). Also their total intestinal length relative to body size is greater than that of other carnivores. But unlike deer and elk, bears lack digestive organs such as a cecum and a rumen that are specialized for digesting vegetative materials, and so they pass food quickly. To get adequate nutrition they have to eat a lot. And because bacterial fermentation plays only a minor role in their digestion, they are unable to digest coarse forage efficiently. As the amount of fiber goes up, even by slight amounts, their ability to digest crude protein and carbohydrates goes down—rapidly.

Plants at an immature stage of development have the highest nutritional levels and the lowest amounts of fiber. Hence, throughout much of their active season, bears forage in areas, such as river and stream bottoms and receding snowbed communities, where plants are young and succulent. After herbs bloom, the protein content of their leaves and stems decreases while the contents of their cell walls—the fiber part—increases. Flowers, however, are just as nutritious and low in fiber as the leaves are when the plants are young. So once mountain plants begin to bloom, bears abandon the leaves and stems and start munching blossoms.

Cow-parsnip, a tall, fast-growing, leafy plant with wide umbels of small white flowers, is a member of the carrot or parsnip family. It is one of the first leafy herbs up in the spring and actually begins growing under the snow, beneath drifts as deep as 2 feet, by using the small amount of light that penetrates the melting snow. If you had visited the North Fork in May or June 200 years ago, you might well have seen Kootenai Indians harvesting the tender, sweet, and pleasantly aromatic leaves and flowerstalks of the plant not far from the bears. Its protein content approaches 30 percent when it is at its prime (pine nuts have about half that). Bears absolutely love it. A researcher once described in his field notes how a camp-robbing black bear that had been captured and penned up in a culvert trap most of the day wasted no time in going after cow-parsnip plants when the trap was finally opened in the Camas Creek drainage: "Upon release, she immediately rushed to the nearest cow-parsnip plant, reached out with front paws pulling the flower umbels and stems to her mouth, and took large bites, chewing with her mouth open and smacking [her] lips loudly. For about ten minutes she ate flower umbels, upper stems, and leaves of cow-parsnip before gradually moving off into a spruce-cottonwood thicket."

Bears, both black and grizzly, can take some credit for cow-parsnip's relatively wide distribution. Scientists have shown that the plants' seeds that pass through the digestive tracts of grizzly bears germinate at a much higher rate than those that simply ripen and drop to the ground. I have seen the evidence for this myself—young cow-parsnip plants sprouting from year-old piles of bear scat. The higher rate of germination may be because gastric juices in the bears' digestive system partially dissolve the seed coat. The same holds true for many other plants they eat.

In the spring, deer and elk use some of the same areas and prefer some of the same plants that grizzly bears favor. One biologist reported seeing deer and elk standing at the edges of North Fork meadows, evidently waiting for grizzly bears to leave so they could enter the meadows to feed. Bears and ungulates both seem to crave the first spring leaves of groundsel.

Black bears eat many of the same river-bottom plants grizzly bears do, but they generally feed in different areas or in the same areas at different times. Unlike their dish-faced, hump-shouldered, crankier cousins, black bears avoid big openings and stay instead near the edges, close to trees.

Black bears evolved to cope with threats, such as large predators (grizzly bears, wolves, and humans) by climbing trees. Their habitat is therefore restricted to mostly forested areas. Grizzlies, on the other hand, are larger and much more pugnacious than black bears. They are likely to stand their ground and confront whatever threatens them or their offspring. They don't need trees to escape. They therefore use both treeless and forested habitats. Although grizzlies prefer areas with good hiding cover, they basically feed where they want.

One food they want is the root of sweetvetch (also known as *Hedysarum*). It is plentiful, palatable, and nutritious, and the grizzly bears in the North Fork make good use of it. But black bears do not. With all the wildlife research that has gone on in the park, with thousands of hours of bear observations, no one has documented black bears eating sweetvetch roots. Perhaps it is because sweetvetch grows in open habitats such as floodplains that lack the escape cover black bears require.

Unlike grizzly bears, which generally den high in the subalpine, black bears den low, many in the valley bottom. They hibernate in shallow depressions and natural caves, beneath the roots of large blown-down trees, and high above the ground in the cavities of standing trees. Grizzly bears never den in trees. Black bears are especially vulnerable during hibernation. Biologists in other areas have written of humans, wolves, domestic dogs, coyotes, grizzly bears, even other black bears killing and eating denned individuals and family groups. It seems only natural then that some black bears would take to hibernating in the trees.

Like bear number 82, a sixteen-and-a-half-year-old female captured and radio-collared in July of 1980. In November of that year, she denned 70 feet above the ground in a cavity atop a big larch. But Harry Carriles, the graduate student tracking her, wasn't sure where she was holing up. Though his transmitter took him to the old larch, his other collared bears had all denned on the ground, so he expected to find her sleeping in a hollow log or depression. He searched all the possibilities and, finding nothing, he decided she had to be in the cavity. So he climbed an adjacent tree a few feet away that would allow him to look into the snag's cavity. The bear apparently heard him, because just as he leaned over to peer into the hole, she stuck her head out, and for a tense moment Harry's nose was about 6 inches from the bear's. Then two cubs stuck their noses out. A friend who watched all this from the ground said that from his perspective the scene was quite amusing. Harry, however, who was 70 feet up, wasn't laughing. That April, the bear emerged with both cubs. Whether she carried them down or they climbed down, Harry doesn't know.

The next year, in October, the same bear and her cubs denned on the ground under a log jam on a side channel of the North Fork. When, a few days later, a man walking his dog happened upon them, the three woke and fled, wandered for a few days, then settled into a cavity near the top of an old cottonwood, where they spent the rest of the winter. Judging by the number of claw marks on large, damaged trees, especially trees with cavities, tree denning by black bears is common in the North Fork. The practice may increase now that wolves have returned to the valley.

Plant Communities Guide

Going-to-the-Sun Road

Because Going-to-the-Sun Road extends from the lowest elevations on both sides of the park up to the Continental Divide, it provides a good sampling of Glacier Park plant communities. About 4 miles from the East Entrance, you enter Two Dog Flats, an important elk winter range. The grasses and herbaceous species found in this small patch of **prairie** are typical of those growing on the foothills in southwestern Alberta, but the community is different from what you would encounter a few miles farther east on the Great Plains. Notice the browse line on the **aspens** surrounding Two Dog Flats. If you walk through those trees, you'll see that many have had some of their bark gnawed off. In winter, elk obtain vitamin K and other nutrients by eating aspen bark.

Through most of the Upper Saint Mary Valley, Going-to-the-Sun Road passes through a **spruce-fir community**, a subalpine forest made up of Engelmann spruce, subalpine fir, Douglas fir, limber pine, and whitebark pine. Above about 6,000 feet (just beyond Siyeh Bend), the trees show increasing signs of stunting caused by strong winds, winter drought, and a short growing season. The trees growing on the most exposed sites are stunted to the point of *krummholz* (a shrublike form). Exposure to severe winds and desiccation of new growth also causes trees at the upper margins of the subalpine to grow in widely spaced islands or ribbons. These dense clumps are usually initiated by a single tree. In the past, **whitebark pine** was often the first tree to pioneer these sites after a fire or some other disturbance. Hardy individuals of that species provided windbreaks that enabled other trees, like subalpine fir and spruce, to take over. But whitebark pine has declined in recent years because of an introduced disease and outbreaks of insects. Also notice how many of the trees near the pass are wind-trained flags; that is, all their branches grow on the leeward side because windward buds and new growth have been blasted off by blowing ice or killed by winter drought.

Logan Pass, 6,640 feet above sea level, lies just below treeline in the subalpine, as evidenced by ribbons and islands of stunted subalpine fir, especially north of the road. The meadows crossed by the boardwalk are subalpine, even though they contain alpine species. Several different grass and herb communities are represented here. **Dry meadows** blanket the gentle slopes and rock ledges (although these may appear wet in early summer when the snow is melting, they quickly dry out). **Wet meadows** border streams and seeps and poorly

Subalpine fir snags in the upper subalpine. Most of these trees were probably killed by fire decades ago. (JOE WEYDT)

drained flat areas. Heath-moss communities of pink and yellow **mountain heather** and *Sphagnum* hug the wettest depressions where water tends to accumulate. Small **fellfield** communities grow near moraines, on scree slopes, and on rock ledges where soils are thin. With so many people visiting Logan Pass, it is not a good idea to leave the boardwalk or designated trail. The growing season is short, and many wildflowers here take a decade or two to mature. Trampling by even a few people will kill sensitive species; it is better to enjoy the plants from the path.

If you want to hike in an **alpine** area, Siyeh and Piegan Passes are good places. Both can be reached on day hikes via a trail that takes off from Going-to-the-Sun Road just before the Jackson Glacier Exhibit. Both are strenuous walks and require some preparation. Free trail maps of the area are available at park visitor centers. Overnight trips into Glacier's backcountry require permits that you can obtain online or from a visitor center or ranger station.

In 1967 a fire burned portions of the Garden and Glacier walls. Young trees now blanket the burn, and in a few more decades it will be difficult for most visitors to tell this area burned at all. In the meantime, the plants and animals that depend on open habitats benefit. (JOE WEYDT)

Beginning about 6.5 miles below Logan Pass, the road passes through an area of spruce-fir forest that burned in 1967 as a result of lightning. The fire covered large areas of both the Garden and Glacier walls. Snags, which provide homes and food for many birds, still stand in the burn. (In the early days of the park, snags like these were cut down after a fire to improve the view for visitors.) A vigorous community of shrubs and young trees—**lodgepole pine**, **western larch**, and **black cottonwood**—now blanket the area and provide habitats for insect, bird, and mammal species that require more open, sun-washed habitats. Compare this forty-year-old-burn with The Loop where, in 2003, the **Trapper Fire** jumped the Going-to-the-Sun Road. **The Loop** is now a wonderful place for visitors to see firsthand the immediate effects of a wildland fire. By creating a mosaic of plant communities, fires help maintain biological diversity in the park.

About 14.5 miles below The Loop, a roadside pull-off and exhibit provides a good view of an **avalanche chute.** This one, on Mount Cannon, is typical of the treeless swaths you see throughout the park. These lush corridors harbor many grizzly bear foods and are favorite foraging areas. Because bears prefer young, succulent plants, they tend to follow the receding snowline upslope through the summer to feed on grasses and herbs that sprout in the snow's wake.

Trail of the Cedars, about 16 miles below the pass, is a 0.5-mile-long handicapped-accessible trail that loops through an **old-growth** stand of **western redcedar, western hemlock,** and **black cotton-**

Cow-parsnip grows in moist areas throughout the park. A favorite bear food, it is high in protein and quite palatable. (JOE WEYDT)

wood. A wet forest characteristic of the Pacific Coast, the **redcedar-hemlock community** occurs no farther east than this part of Glacier National Park. Because the climate is so wet in the lower part of the McDonald Valley, fires are less frequent here than they are just a few miles to the north. This has enabled the forest to grow quite old. The trees along Avalanche Creek are around 500 years old (the stand dates back to 1517). Still, fires that raged in adjacent areas along Lake McDonald and McDonald Creek in centuries past and as recently as 2003 created a complex mosaic of different-aged stands and forest types, and have made the McDonald Valley a rich zone that harbors all but two or three of the park's tree species. Barring further fires and other disturbances, the natural succession that occurs in forests would ordinarily convert those various stands to the kind of redcedar-hemlock community you see thriving along Avalanche Creek. But thanks to global climate change we can no longer predict with any certainty what will happen to those forest stands.

Johns Lake Fen, an example of a *Sphagnum*-**dominated fen,** is only a 0.25-mile-long walk from the Going-to-the-Sun Road. The trailhead takes off just 3.4 miles below Trail of the Cedars and Avalanche Campground. This fen receives most of its nutrients for plant growth from the atmosphere, so it is closer to being a bog than most of the fens or mires in the park. Many of the plants growing here occur only in *Sphagnum* fens, and more than half a dozen are considered rare in Montana or the northern Rocky Mountains. Northern bog lemmings, one of the park's least known mammals, are also found mostly in fens. Watch for moose, too.

The North Fork Valley

Glacier Route 8 (also known as the Camas Road) loops around the east base of the Apgar Mountains, passing right through the area burned by the 2003 **Robert Fire,** a 57,550-acre blaze. An exhibit describes some of the area's fire history—how a 1929 burn consumed the redcedar-hemlock community that once grew here. Notice the big **western larch** trees near the turnout. Their thick, fire-resistant bark spared them from that 1929 blaze. But thick bark was not enough to protect them from the 2003 fire. In the fall, larch needles turn brilliant yellow and drop. In the spring the new foliage that sprouts on larch trees gives portions of the forest a light green color that stands out against the deep forest greens of other trees.

The McGee Meadow turnout affords a good view of one of the North Fork's **wet meadows.** Take a good look so you can do a mental comparison later with the dry meadows that occur farther up the North Fork. Again, because of the traffic through this area, it is better to stay out of the meadow itself, which harbors rare and sensitive plants. The McGee Meadow Fen lies to the southeast.

Heading north, just past the Camas Creek Entrance Station, the Camas Road joins the North Fork county road. A few miles before you reach that junction, you enter the area burned by the 2001 **Moose Fire,** which covered a total of 71,000 acres, about 28,000 of which were in the park. The fire burned mostly lodgepole pine but also some spruce-fir forest and some ponderosa pine stands. Its perimeter overlaps portions of the areas burned by the 1967 **Huckleberry Fire** and the 1994 **Howling Fire**. For about the first 5 miles past the junction, the road stays within the area scorched by the Moose Fire.

A bumpy, gravel thoroughfare, the **North Fork Road** follows the North Fork of the Flathead River to Polebridge and beyond, passing through the 1988 Red Bench Fire just before Polebridge and the 2003 **Wedge Canyon Fire** a few miles south of the Canadian border. Although it

In North Fork forests, spruce, lodgepole pine, western larch, western redcedar, western hemlock, Engelmann spruce, Douglas fir, and subalpine fir flourish. (GLACIER NATIONAL PARK)

remains west of the park, the road passes through many of the same vegetation communities you see across the river, inside Glacier.

On the North Fork of the Flathead River floodplain, the dominant trees are **cottonwood** and **spruce.** There are two species of spruce in the North Fork: white spruce and Engelmann spruce. White spruce or hybrids of the two species generally grow in the valley bottom, while Engelmann spruce or hybrids with strong Engelmann traits thrive on higher slopes. Although from a distance the two species look and feel similar—both have cornflake-like bark, a classic conical evergreen shape, and short, prickly needles—differences exist. The cone scales of white spruce are widest near their tips and rounded and smooth. Cone scales of Engelmann spruce are broadest at their bases and almost pointed at their tips, and their margins are crinkled and papery. Engelmann spruce also has fine hairs on its branches, whereas those of white spruce are bare. As you would expect, the spruce hybrids show a mix of these traits. Farther upslope, **western larch, lodgepole pine, subalpine fir,** and **Engelmann spruce** are dominant. In places, you will see dead trees, most likely killed by fire. A **mountain pine beetle** epidemic killed 170,000 acres of lodgepole in the North Fork in the 1970s and 1980s, but most of those dead trees have fallen down or been consumed by subsequent fires. Like fire, periodic outbreaks of forest insects and diseases are natural occurrences.

About 3 miles south of Polebridge, the road enters the area burned by the 1988 **Red Bench Fire.** The fire consumed 38,000 acres of lodgepole, most of it already killed by mountain pine beetles. The wind-driven flames also took a number of western larch and ponderosa pine trees, trees up to 350 years old and older that had survived up to seven previous fires. Already lodgepole and western larch have reseeded this area. Those trees are coming in strong. A small amount of ponderosa pine is regenerating along the Inside Road and Bowman Lake Road.

Big Prairie can be reached by crossing the North Fork River at Pole-bridge and heading north on Glacier Route 7 (also known as the Inside North Fork Road). Big Prairie is a type of dry grassland described by botanists as fescue/wheatgrass prairie. Because of a rain shadow cast by the Whitefish Range, this part of the North Fork is substantially drier than the McDonald Creek Valley. Thus, species like **sagebrush** and **ponderosa pine** grow here. Look for individual ponderosa pine trees on the margins of the prairie.

The East Side

U.S. Highway 89 and Highway 49 and the Chief Mountain International Highway are all good ways to see the east-side **aspen parklands**—patches of grassland interspersed with aspen groves and conifers. Because of the variety of plant life found here, the parklands support a huge diversity of insects, birds, and mammals. Although these areas lie outside the park on the Blackfeet Indian Reservation, they provide important seasonal habitats for the park's grizzly bears, elk, deer, and wolves. Without these seasonal ranges, those species either couldn't survive or would exist in much lower numbers.

Recommended References

For real plant lovers, Peter Lesica's *Flora of Glacier National Park* published by Oregon State University Press in 2002 is the best reference available on the park's plants. Amateur botanists may find *Wildflowers of Glacier National Park and Surrounding Areas* by Kimball and Lesica (2005) more user-friendly.

Plant Community Sensitivity List

This list shows the sensitivity of high-elevation plant communities to trampling. Because damage often begins with only a few passes, and because rare plants occur in all plant communities, the best rule is to stay on designated trails. Some activities, like climbing, require traveling off trails. In those cases, the best strategy is to stay on rock or snow and to travel in small groups. As a general rule, stay out of moist areas, and when in dry terrain, spread out to avoid creating a trail. If a trail exists, use it, even if it is a goat trail.

These plant communities are listed in order of decreasing sensitivity to trampling:

1. Saturated soil (most sensitive)—mossy streambanks, boggy sites, very wet meadows; characterized by monkeyflowers, sedges, saxifrage, and mosses.

2. Wet ledges—seeping water running over rock; mosses, saxifrage, and plants in crevasses.

3. Unstable talus—scree slopes with sparse vegetation; very susceptible to damage or uprooting.

4. Tundra turf—(dense plant cover) less than 6 inches high, moist until late into the year; dominated by grasses, sedges, and dwarf willow.

5. Heath—low shrubs of heath and heather.

6. Cushion plant—low-growing matlike plants, often on windswept ridges or steep slopes; moss campion, draba, and phlox.

7. Meadow—moist to dry meadows, dominated by relatively robust herbaceous species; asters, fleabane, paintbrush, glacier lily, and grasses and sedges.

8. Krummholz—dwarf or windswept conifer islands.

9. Dry ledges—areas with thin soil, either bedrock outcrops or relatively level alpine cobble (flat, stable rocks with soil between).

10. Stable talus—level or stable talus and boulder fields with high lichen cover and few plants.

7

The McDonald Creek Valley

Of the many streams that issue from Glacier's high country and empty into the North and Middle Forks of the Flathead River, McDonald Creek is unique, as is the valley that holds it. The basin is deeper and wider than that of any other tributary on the west side, and it cradles McDonald Lake, one of the largest lakes in the park. Most important, it is subject to flows of wet Pacific air.

All this—a big, wide valley at a comparatively low elevation, a large lake that moderates both winter and summer temperatures, and a peninsula of mild, moisture-laden air dropping quantities of rain and snow—has made possible forest communities more typ-

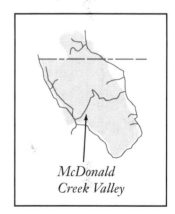

McDonald
Creek Valley

ical of coastal Washington and Oregon than Montana. The wettest of these, the western redcedar–western hemlock forest, lies between the head of Lake McDonald and Avalanche Creek, at elevations ranging from 3,200 feet to 3,500 feet. It is the eastern limit of this forest community's range.

Almost a Rain Forest

Western redcedar and western hemlock support dense canopies over a scant understory that is as shady and cool as it is damp. The shade prevents

Beneath the thick canopies of western redcedar and western hemlock, mosses and liverworts carpet everything on the forest floor, including rocks. (JOE WEYDT)

other kinds of trees from growing and limits the understory to a few shrubs and herbs. Some that tolerate plenty of shade, species like Pacific yew, Virginia grape-fern, oak and lady fern, coolwort-foamflower, equisetum, ocean-spray, enchanter's nightshade, mountain lover, devil's club, queen's cup bead lily, and broad-lipped twayblade, have leaves crowded with chloroplasts, the granules that hold chlorophyll. The greatest diversity occurs in the few scattered islands of sun. Where the shade is heavy and the ground wet, a thick cushion of mosses and liverworts carpet the soil and everything on it, including the exposed rocks and fallen logs. On a hot summer day, these places are green and cool, small, quiet refuges from the sun and the rest of the world. Beneath the densest canopy, nothing grows in the understory, and there the forest seems strangely dark and empty.

The most ancient stands of redcedar and hemlock in the drainage exceed 400 years in age. Western hemlock, the largest of the eighteen species of hemlocks in the world, reaches heights of more than 100 feet. Along the Pacific coast, from southern Alaska to northern California, the tree is common—at one time southeast Alaskan Indians made bread from its reddish cambium layer. In Montana western hemlock is found only in the far northwest corner of the state near Libby and in Glacier Park, where its distribution is centered around McDonald Lake. You can often recognize it from a distance by its drooping tip. Western redcedar, which has a slightly larger but similar range, is a bigger tree. The record redcedar grows in the western part of Olympic National Park and is 21 feet in diameter. Only the giant sequoias, the most massive living things in the world, are larger. In Glacier the biggest redcedars range from 2 to 7 feet in diameter and are probably 500 to 600 years old. You can see some of these giants along the Trail of the Cedars across from the Avalanche Creek Picnic Area.

Western redcedar can reproduce both sexually and vegetatively. Vegetative reproduction comes about when a tree's limbs touch the ground. If the duff is damp, roots may sprout and another tree begins. Saplings also sprout from trees blown over by the wind or from branches that fall out of the canopy. Unlike other conifers, the trunks of western redcedar are fluted, and the bark is fibrous and fissured and ridged lengthwise. It pulls off easily in long narrow strips. Native Americans made baskets, rope, and thatchings for their shelters from the bark. They used it and the pleasant-smelling foliage in their rituals. They carved canoe frames and bowls from the wood. Of the two species, western redcedar and western hemlock, the redcedar prefers the wetter sites and dominates streamsides and ravines—it thrives in areas with high water tables—while western hemlock outnumbers redcedar on the drained slopes. In between, both trees coexist.

A Change in the Forest

When the park was established in 1910, the redcedar-hemlock community covered many more acres of the valley than it does today. All that is left of much of that earlier forest are white, weathered snags, and they sit beneath a thriving but mixed overstory of lodgepole pine, western larch, black cot-

After a fire, seral species move in, as they have in this stand along Lake McDonald. But seral species like lodgepole pine, western larch, western white pine, and spruce shade out their own offspring. More shade-tolerant species move in and eventually dominate the site. (JOE WEYDT)

tonwood, quaking aspen, Douglas fir, western white pine, Engelmann spruce, and subalpine fir (all but three of the park's roughly twenty tree species grow in the valley). At first this may seem puzzling. What happened to the redcedar-hemlock community that this place supported for half a millennia, and how was it replaced by such a heterogeneous mix of trees? Certainly, fire or some other natural disturbance—an avalanche, a flood, a landslide, an ice storm, high winds, disease, an insect outbreak—can change a plant community, but why isn't it replaced by itself, as a community of species best adapted to the site's moisture and temperature conditions?

The answer has to do with a natural process called forest succession, a biological term for the procession of forest communities through time. Although we may think otherwise because our snapshot of the world is so brief, nothing in nature is constant, not continents, not rocks, and certainly not forests. Forests, like many types of natural communities, constantly move through a series of changes or stages, beginning with the pioneer stage and temporarily stabilizing, in the absence of a disturbance like a fire, with what's called climax—the most mature phase of the cycle. The climax state is rarely achieved for very long due to numerous disturbances, the most common being wildland fire. The pioneering communities and those that follow before the site reaches climax are called seral or temporary communities. Each seral community changes the site enough to allow a new community to move in and dominate.

Two kinds of succession are occurring in Glacier National Park: primary and secondary. Primary succession is the kind of vegetational development occurring on recently glaciated areas, such as on the moraines, fresh talus, and scoured bedrock that sits just downslope from the park's receding glaciers. Those sites are colonized first by lichens and mosses. The mosses, along with wind, water, and constant freezing and thawing, slowly break down the rock and build a thin mantle of soil. Once soils have developed, grasses, sedges, wildflowers, shrubs, and even trees move in. Secondary succession refers to the revegetation of previously vegetated areas, such as occurs after a fire or a flood. Typically, the first plants to return to these sites are grasses, shrubs that resprout from old root crowns and rhizomes, and pioneering herbs like fireweed. These are joined by tree species that also specialize in revegetating burns. Within a few years, trees dominate the site, shading out many of the light-loving shrubs and herbs. Ironically, the trees produce enough shade to preclude their own ability to reproduce, because their seedlings need bare soil and lots of sunlight. New species, trees that can tolerate shade, gain a foothold and eventually take over. But, once again, their presence alters the site, ensuring that they, too, will be replaced. The progression continues like this, unless it is disrupted by a fire or some other kind of disturbance, until the trees occupying this site are so shade tolerant and so perfectly adapted to the moisture and temperature conditions that they can reproduce in their own shadow—something the seral species, the ones preceding them, could not do. That ability allows those species to persist on the site indefinitely, barring a disturbance. This climax community will remain unchanged until some disturbance, natural or human-caused, lays it low. Then the process starts over. The pioneer species return and the forest is reborn.

In the past, forest succession was thought to progress in this kind of circular fashion, moving from a pioneering community, through a series of seral communities, to climax, and then back to the pioneering stage again. The climax condition was often thought of as the goal to which all forests were progressing. But in recent decades, forest ecologists have replaced this single-circle model with one that might be described as circles within circles, because it better represents what actually happens in most northern Rocky Mountain forests. Before European settlement, many forest types rarely reached climax conditions because of frequent disturbances—fire, insects, disease, windthrow—all of which were made more widespread by periodic drought. Indeed, some forest types require fire to maintain old-growth conditions. Ponderosa pine is a good example. We've come to realize forests are much more dynamic than we previously imagined.

Getting back to the earlier question I posed—why isn't a community replaced by itself, as a community of species best adapted to the site's moisture and temperature conditions? The answer now becomes apparent. Each community *is* the one best adapted at the particular time it occupies the site. But the site's moisture and temperature conditions are changing as each new community grows and matures. Topography and climate are but two elements in the equation that determines the distribution of living things. Organisms themselves are also central to the equation.

Now, for a specific example, let's return to the redcedar-hemlock forest along McDonald Creek, which is the climax community occupying the wettest, mildest sites in the park. Big fires in such humid settings are rare; they happen only about once every 300 or 400 years. Judging from fire scars on the trees, the last fire to burn through the redcedar-hemlock forest in the lower Avalanche Creek drainage probably occurred in the early 1500s. Imagine how such a fire might happen. In the absence of fire, the forest builds up enormous quantities of fuel—dead and downed wood that most years stays relatively damp. But the region experiences a prolonged drought with summer after summer of scorching temperatures and low

The climax or mature forest of lower Avalanche Creek is a western redcedar–western hemlock community. Mosses, ferns, and shade-tolerant shrubs like thimbleberry thrive in the understory. (JOE WEYDT)

humidity. All that debris dries out. Finally, an August thunderstorm with high winds moves through, and a bolt of lightning hits an old snag atop one of the ridges. The resulting fire burns everything from the forest floor to the tops of the trees (as the Robert Fire did in 2003). All that remains is a 2,000-acre smoldering tangle of charred logs. Even the earth is charcoal-colored. It may take weeks to cool, but as it does, renewal begins.

Fire leaves behind a thick layer of ash, a mineral-rich growing medium, and one of the first plants to take advantage of it is a tall, bright member of the evening primrose family called fireweed. Fireweed, the seeds of which are carried by the tens of millions on the wind, can blanket portions of the burn the following summer, turning them a mallow pink. Other mass bloomers include arnica, showy aster, spirea, lupine, pinegrass (which you won't see blooming any other time), and even wild hollyhock. Mosses, too, are pioneers; they recolonize the wettest sites. Mushrooms appear by the millions. Other herbs appearing that first spring after a burn include large-leaved avens, yellow monkeyflower, bracken fern, pearly everlasting, and sweet-scented bedstraw. Shrubs and deciduous trees sprout from old root crowns and rhizomes, and from wind- and animal-transported seeds—Scouler's willow, thimbleberry, mountain maple and snowbrush, serviceberry and globe huckleberry, cottonwood, aspen, and birch among them. The seeds of some plants, like snowbrush, may stay dormant in the soil for centuries until the heat and sunlight created by wildfires triggers their germination. Species like Bicknell's geranium, dragonhead, red-stem ceanothus, and rock harlequin are rarely seen except in the first few years following a fire. Within five to ten years, woody plants dominate, converting large portions of the burn into chest-high shrubfields that deer, elk, and moose can readily use. Lodgepole pine and western larch saplings, growing as densely in places as hair on a dog's back, poke through. Soon these conifers tower above everything else. Beneath them the shrubs and herbs thin, and because both lodgepole pine and western larch require bare soil and plenty of sunlight to propagate, they thwart their own reproduction, limiting their occupation of the site to a single generation. But the shady habitat they foster is ideal for other species of conifers—Douglas fir, white pine, subalpine fir, Engelmann spruce, western redcedar, and western hemlock. Those long-lived trees take over the stand within eighty to one hundred years and dominate it for centuries. But most of those species, too, shade out their own offspring. Only western hemlock and western redcedar are able to reproduce beneath such a dense canopy— hemlock through seeds, redcedar vegetatively (cedar seedlings require lots of light, but vegetatively generated offspring do not). As the old Douglas fir, western white pine, and spruce trees gradually die and create openings in the canopy, the hemlock and redcedar respond with a spurt of growth (relatively speaking) to fill the opening. Eventually they become the dominant trees of the canopy *and* the only saplings in the understory. Once again, the redcedar-hemlock forest, like the mythical phoenix of ancient Egypt, has risen, and it has only taken 500 years.

So the heterogeneous mix of lodgepole pine, western larch, black cottonwood, quaking aspen, Douglas fir, western white pine, Engelmann spruce, and subalpine fir that now occupies much of the McDonald Valley is in that never-ending cycle called forest succession. Will the site once again host a redcedar-hemlock community similar to that found along Avalanche Creek? In the past it probably would have, but now climate change is making that possibility unlikely.

Who Cares about Checkerspots?

The fire that consumed the original old-growth forest was destructive, but it was also renewing. Wildland fires, however frequent and of whatever severity, promote diversity. When allowed to burn naturally, they create a mosaic, a patchwork of communities—meadows, shrubfields, young forests, medium-age forests, old-growth forests—that together provide homes for a greater diversity of organisms (more habitats mean more

One of Glacier's Yellowstone checkerspot butterflies. This little orange, cream, and black nectar drinker lays its eggs on the leaves of only those black twinberry bushes that grow in full sun; hence fires are essential to its survival. (CRAIG ODEGARD)

species). For example, forage for ungulates is almost nonexistent in an old-growth redcedar-hemlock forest. But periodic fires in that climax community can create rich pockets of forage—meadows and shrubfield habitats that elk and moose must have. Grizzly bears benefit in similar ways. And fires favor not only the larger, more familiar animals but also Glacier's birds, small mammals, butterflies, beetles, bumblebees, dragonflies, mollusks, even fungi. Fire for them is both natural and necessary. Most would probably disappear from the park in the absence of fire.

Take, as just one example, one of Glacier's small, inconspicuous butterflies, the Yellowstone checkerspot. The species occurs only in the northern Rocky Mountains. It lives in small populations of fewer than thirty individuals, populations often separated from one another by 30 or 40 miles. The park has five such populations. One main reason for the checkerspot's patchy distribution is that females are picky about where they lay their eggs. Not only do they need a black twinberry bush (which is not unusual; the life cycles of many butterflies are tied to a single species of plant), but the bush has to be growing in a sunny spot. This latter restriction limits the species to moist areas in the early stages of plant succession—wet meadows along streamsides and in canyon bottoms where black twinberry grows in full sunlight. Without fire, succession follows its course. Trees encroach on sun-washed places and shade the twinberry plants, making them unsuitable for checkerspot egg-laying. Like many organisms in the park, checkerspot butterflies depend on fire. After sixty years of fire suppression, their populations declined.

If checkerspots are hurting, it is a good bet other fire-dependent species are, too, which is why the Park Service is managing fire and, whenever it is safe, allowing it to play a more natural role in the park. One of the reasons Glacier Park is such a fantastic place to visit is because it harbors diversity and because it is, for the most part, an intact biological system—most of what was here a century or two ago remains. The natural lacework in this park has not begun to unravel to the extent it has elsewhere. Organisms still interact as they have for millennia. As such, Glacier Park has an aesthetic value few other places have. Equally important, it offers opportunities to learn about how intact natural systems work, how a tree depends on a fungus or how subterranean stoneflies recycle nutrients that fertilize plants eaten by grizzly bears. What we learn here can help us restore what we've lost elsewhere.

In his book *Biophilia,* Edward O. Wilson of Harvard has argued that humans possess an innate love for living things and that that love manifests itself as a tendency or need "to focus on life and life-like processes." Wilson, and many others, believe this proclivity may be hereditary. If it is, then the loss of plants and animals from our world will, inevitably, impoverish our spirit. Each incremental loss, a checkerspot butterfly here, a grizzly bear there, subtracts something of aesthetic and emotional value from the human experience and lessens the chances for human fulfillment. Imagine the extreme, a world where the only bits of nature that remain are things we have either tamed or altered, a world where the only "natural things" a child knows are cows, parakeets, and cultivated or genetically engineered plants.

There are also utilitarian arguments for preserving the diversity of life found in a place like Glacier. By preserving species, even checkerspot butterflies, we, as humans, stand a better chance of improving our agriculture, medicine, industry, and who knows what else. The remarkable cancer-fighting drug taxol was first derived from Pacific yew, a shrubby evergreen that does quite well in the redcedar-hemlock forest along McDonald Creek. Taxol blocks cell division in a manner unlike that of any other drug yet discovered and is a broad-spectrum tumor fighter that shows promise against colon, lung, breast, prostate, and pancreatic cancers as well as leukemia. And taxol is just one example—half of all prescription drugs in use today were originally derived from plants. By preserving gene pools, we preserve opportunities for addressing unforeseen problems of the future, those that will confront our own children. No generation has the right to steal portions of the earth's richness from the generations to come.

The Fungi Makes the Forest

One of the peculiarities of the redcedar-hemlock forest is the unusual abundance of large, fallen logs crisscrossing the forest floors. They persist because decomposition in cool, damp, northern coniferous forests is quite

Old logs and soils in the redcedar-hemlock forest nurture a variety of fungi, which in turn form mutually beneficial associations with surrounding trees and shrubs. (GLACIER NATIONAL PARK)

slow, slower than in both temperate deciduous forests or tropical evergreen forests. A big log sitting on the ground above Lake McDonald can take a century or two to decompose. Because there are so many downed logs and because they take so long to be recycled into soil, legions of organisms have become specialized to a life on top of or within them. Most are insects and fungi, but the list also includes several plants and small mammals. Beetles, both larvae and adults, are the first to move in. Tunneling through but otherwise ignoring the outer bark, their goal is the nutrient-rich cambium and sapwood layers. Among these deadwood-eaters are the long-horned beetles, whose antennae are sometimes twice the length of their bodies; slender pinhole borers and ambrosia beetles that cut holes all the way into the heartwood and then turn around to graze the fungi that quickly colonize the tunnel; engraver beetles that excavate patterned galleries, each species with its own pattern; and shy, fast-running, metallic wood-boring beetles, whose larvae are better known as flat-headed borers. This crew ushers in the fungi—most beetles carry the spores with them—and provides a way for dozens of other creatures to enter the fallen log as well—amoebae, mites, ants, millipedes, spiders, and, eventually, small mammals and salamanders. Their work makes it easier for plant roots to tap into the log.

In the denser parts of the forest, newly downed trees are about the only places western hemlocks can get a start because everywhere else the ground is coated with a thick cushion of moss. A single "nurse log" can provide a home for hundreds of hemlock seedlings. The rotting, fungus-infested, insect-riddled wood of these logs soaks up water like a sponge and stays damp, exactly what young western hemlocks need. Hemlock seedlings cannot tolerate even short periods without water. Sometimes toppled trees that get hung up in the canopy sprout dozens of small western hemlock trees, saplings perched 10 to 20 feet above the ground. Other plants, too, like woodnymph, spreading wood-fern, and twisted stalk, grow best on downed trees.

Besides providing a moist place to put down roots, fallen logs are chock-full of fungi, many of which are able to form symbiotic associations with plant roots. Fungi are more apparent after a good rain, especially in the fall, when mushrooms appear by the thousands on logs and the ground around them. The mushrooms themselves are only the fruit of various fungi, the cap and stem part of a much larger organism. Invisible, unless you dig into a piece of decaying wood, are the mycelia, webs of minuscule white threads called hyphae that spread everywhere through the logs and the duff of the forest floor like fine netting, secreting digestive enzymes that break down the wood into absorbable nutrients. This "rot" gives the wood its characteristic amber color and sweet, earthy smell—the telltale signs of decay. Fungi reclaim and recycle centuries of nutrients stored up in fallen trees back into the forest.

The mycelia also attach themselves to the roots of living trees and shrubs and some herbs, where they form sheaths. Each species of fungus attaches to a specific plant or group of plants. Like little spears, the hyphae of the fungi penetrate the spaces between the cells of the plants' rootlets. But these are benevolent entries; the fungi and plants benefit each other. The combinations of root and fungi are called mycorrhizae, and all the conifers, hemlocks included, have them. Mycorrhizal roots increase the ability of the trees and shrubs to take up water and absorb nutrients such as nitrogen and phosphorus—growth-stimulating compounds that are otherwise mostly lost to higher plants. Mycorrhizal fungi also protect plants from soilborne diseases. The fungus benefits by absorbing carbohydrates from the roots.

Mycorrhizal and nonmycorrhizal roots are part of every healthy tree in the forest. Mycorrhizal roots are pale and translucent and grow in paired, equal branches. Nonmycorrhizal roots are dark and opaque and composed of a central taproot with small branches. By starting growth in decaying logs, hemlocks are assured of an association with their companion fungus— and normal growth, for a hemlock seedling, or the seedlings of any other conifer for that matter, cannot compete without mycorrhizae. Similarly, mycorrhizal fungi cannot exist without their tree and shrub hosts. Among the common, better-known groups of mushrooms that form these associations are the amanitas, the boletes, the russulas or milk mushrooms, and the chanterelles. You are likely to see many of these growing in the redcedar-hemlock community if you are there at the right time of year.

In the redcedar-hemlock forest, you might also look for fungi on living trees. One kind of fruiting body that is hard to miss are conks. A conk is a hard, sometimes leathery, sometimes woody, shelflike structure that grows on both living and dead trees. One kind, often seen attached to live hemlocks, is the hoof-shaped Indian paint fungus, the flesh of which is a bright cinnamon to rusty red color. As its name implies, Indian paint fungus was mixed with bear grease by Native Americans and used as a dye and face paint. The Indian paint conk's presence means the host has a serious case of heart rot.

Other plants you may come across in this forest are several ghostly pale members of the orchid and wintergreen families. These plants can live in even the shadiest parts of the forest because they have forsaken photosynthesis in favor of taking the food they need from their mycorrhizal relations with fungi. They include four coral-root orchids—the spotted, the striped, the yellow, and the western—and three members of the wintergreen or heath family—pinedrops, pinesap, and Indian pipe. All lack chlorophyll, so

Pinedrops grow without chlorophyll by tapping into an ongoing mutualism between conifers and fungi. They grow up to 3 feet high. (GLACIER NATIONAL PARK)

none is green. Rather, their colors range from waxy white to pale pink, yellow, brown, or orange. These primitive-appearing plants were once called saprophytes (from the Greek *sapros*, for "rotten"), because it was thought they obtained all their nourishment from dead and decaying vegetation. But now we realize they get their food from fungi, some of the same mycorrhizal fungi that form associations with conifers, so they have been renamed mycotrophs, or fungus feeders. Consider, for example, pinedrops, which grows only under conifers and looks something like a primitive, orange-colored spear of asparagus when it is young. As the plant develops, its stalk turns reddish brown and bears dozens of small, light yellow, egg-shaped flowers that dangle like bells from short stalks. The energy to produce this growth comes from adjacent trees via mycorrhizal fungi. In other words, pinedrops and the other mycotrophs tap into an ongoing symbiotic relationship between conifers and soil fungi. The mycorrhizal fungus that serves as a bridge between the two also benefits. It receives energy-rich carbohydrates from the tree and growth-stimulating substances from the pinedrops plant. The whole affair is an example of three-way mutualism—a complicated triple partnership in which all participants contribute and benefit.

It is strange to think that so much of the forest, everything from the smallest flowers to the most giant trees, owes its livelihood to the gossamer-thin strands of fungi growing in the soil and duff, an association unknown a few decades ago. Here's another reason for preserving biological diversity: Sometimes you don't know what you've got till it's gone.

Creepers, Swifts, and Chickadees— Some Birds of the Old Growth

If plants have adapted to the shade of the redcedar-hemlock forest in different ways—either by manufacturing large concentrations of chlorophyll or by becoming mycotrophs and parasites—so have animals. Most that thrive deep in the forest, in communities like those along McDonald Creek, are darker in color than their counterparts living in open habitats. Their deep browns and blacks make them more difficult to see and therefore less likely to become a meal for visually oriented predators. Compare, for example, the golden color of the Richardson ground squirrel, which lives in grasslands, with the dark red and brown of the forest-dwelling red squirrel. Some of the birds, namely the warblers and woodpeckers, use a different camouflage strategy. Their bold markings are designed to blend with the dappled patterns of light and shadow created by the dense forest canopy, while at the same time serving to attract members of the opposite sex.

Among the birds well adapted to life in the old-growth forest communities of the McDonald Valley are Vaux's swifts, barred owls, pileated woodpeckers, chestnut-backed chickadees, brown creepers, winter wrens, Hammond's flycatchers, golden-crowned kinglets, Swainson's and varied thrushes, Townsend's warblers, and red- and white-winged crossbills.

Glacier's chestnut-backed chickadees are an example of a Pacific Coast species at the very eastern edge of its distribution. Like the redcedar and hemlock trees, they are here only because moist Pacific air reaches this far east. Glacier Park and the surrounding area is the only place in the United States where all four northwestern species of chickadees overlap: the chestnut-backed, the mountain, the black-capped, and the boreal. Like its three cousins, the chestnut-backed nests in the cavities of snags, usually those pounded out by woodpeckers. These they line with snatches of animal fur, feathers, and moss, a cushion for the six to nine eggs (small and white with pretty reddish brown spots) laid by the females each spring. Chickadees eat both animal and plant material. About a third of what a chestnut-backed chickadee eats is vegetable—seeds, buds, and fruit. The other two-thirds of their diet consists primarily of insects.

Here in the park, chestnut-backed chickadees and mountain chickadees occur in the same habitats, and both species have similar diets. But research in redcedar-hemlock communities on the coast has determined that when the two occur together, the chestnut-backed feeds in the top half of conifers and the mountain in the lower half. Yet when mountain chickadees occur alone, they feed throughout the crown. Summer and winter, chestnut-backed chickadees form flocks with other chickadees, nuthatches, brown creepers, ruby-crowned kinglets, downy woodpeckers, and juncos.

A mountain chickadee returns to its nest hole, beak coated with aphids. Chestnut-backed and mountain chickadees feed in the same trees, but each feeds in a different part of the canopy; chestnut-backs take the top half, while mountain chickadees patrol the lower half. (GLACIER NATIONAL PARK)

Several theories have been proposed to explain why different species flock together. One of these says that by grouping together, birds can better avoid predators, and this benefit alone more than makes up for whatever food individuals might sacrifice to others in the flock. This theory is based on the assumption that each species of bird offers something unique to the flock in the way of predator detection—keen eyesight, for example, or a flighty, easy-to-spook disposition. Some research has shown that downy woodpeckers rely on chickadees to alert them to dangers when in mixed flocks.

A second theory argues that mixed-species flocking could actually improve the foraging efficiency of each species. With more birds searching for food sources, chances are better for finding them. When several species feed together, each has an opportunity to learn about new food sources from the others; a chickadee, for example, might sample seeds being eaten by juncos. And finally, the competition in a mixed flock is probably less than in a single-species flock of equal size because each species has distinct food preferences that relate to its bill size and specialized foraging techniques.

The brown creeper travels in winter flocks with chestnut-backed chickadees and exploits the same habitats in summer. Creepers glean insects and spiders from bark with their long, thin, curved bill, whereas chickadees hunt the foliage. Creepers look for food by spiraling up the trunks of large-diameter trees. When they stop to catch a moth or spider, they use the stiff points of their long tail feathers as props, like woodpeckers. They are drab, inconspicuous little birds—brown with a subtle white streaking, a cryptic blend that matches the bark. Indeed, when pursued by a hawk or a shrike, they flee to a tree trunk, land, spread their wings, flatten their bodies tight against the tree, and do not move until the threat is gone. The bird seems to simply disappear.

Not only do these bark gleaners take on the appearance of bark, but they also nest there. The preferred nest site for a creeper is a big western white pine snag that has died recently enough to still have bark on it. The breeding pair locates their hammock-style nest between a slab of sloughing bark and the dead wood. In recent years, however, brown creepers have had to make do with other species of snags—mostly Douglas fir and hemlock—because western white pine, once common in the McDonald Valley, has been devastated by the white pine blister rust, a disease introduced from Europe. Appropriate nesting sites now more than any other single factor limit Glacier Park's population of brown creepers.

Two other birds of the McDonald Valley, both swifts, fascinate me. Vaux's and black swifts, like chestnut-backed chickadees, are at the eastern edge of their range in Glacier Park. Swifts look and forage like swallows. Both swift and swallow have long, pointed, and slightly curved wings. Both are elegant flyers. Both feed almost exclusively on flying insects and occupy similar habitats. They are so much alike that for years ornithologists grouped them together, believing that swifts and swallows had descended from a common and recent ancestor. But now we know, thanks to a closer look at their anatomy and DNA, that the two families are widely separated. The swifts' closest relatives are hummingbirds. Swallows' nearest cousins are bushtits and kinglets—two songbirds. The similarity between swifts and swallows is not the result of descent from a common ancestor but is an example of evolutionary convergence, two or more unrelated organisms evolving similar structures, profiles, and habitats because they exploit similar resources.

Swifts are great fliers—strong, fast, agile. They need to be; just about everything they do, they do in the air. Whatever they eat—mosquitoes, gnats, flies, small beetles—they catch on the wing. The twigs they use to build their nests, they break off as they swoop through the trees. They mate in flight, a pair coming together from opposite directions, joining and then tumbling together, heads over tails, for hundreds of feet. They even bathe as they soar; swooping low, they dip their bodies into a stream or lake and then, as they rise, flip their tails to splash the water across their backs. Not surprisingly, swifts' feet are poorly developed. So small are those appendages that, if downed with a damaged wing, a swift can scarcely crawl. Aside from nighttime roosting, brooding a nest of eggs, and feeding young, flight is all they know.

Like their hummingbird cousins, swifts have high rates of metabolism and correspondingly high energy demands. They have to eat all day long,

Packed tight as sardines, Vaux's swifts stay close for warmth. They hang by their claws, which are strong and well developed. Their feet, however, are quite weak. (EVELYN L. BULL)

every day, or starve to death, which can pose a problem: what to do when heavy rains or other inclement weather keeps them in their roosts, sometimes for days on end? Their solution—which is the same as that of many animals, especially mammals—is to shut their engines down. Swifts, like hummingbirds, have the ability to enter a state of torpor or dormancy, in which they temporarily let their body temperature plummet until it approaches that of the surrounding air. Declines of as much as 50°F have been reported. During times when food is scarce, swifts may become torpid for two or three hours a night, or, in the case of an extended period of stormy weather, they may shut down for several days. Swifts avoid northern winters by migrating to Central and South America.

Torpor has its drawbacks, however. An unconscious bird is easy prey. Also, to wake from torpidity, swifts have to expend large amounts of energy getting their body temperature back to normal. Once they take to the air, they must find food soon or collapse from starvation.

Both Vaux's and black swifts summer in the McDonald Valley near Avalanche Creek, where the two species' nesting and roosting habitats are as different as day and night. Vaux's swifts soar for insects high above the valley's old-growth forest but roost and nest in large, hollow snags and broken-topped trees. Roosting is a period of inactivity analogous to mammalian sleep, and after the breeding season, Vaux's swifts roost in flocks of hundreds. In the McDonald Valley, prior to their migration, you may see dozens, perhaps hundreds, of them pouring out of the evening sky into a single tree to roost for the night. If you could look inside the broken tree, you would see the birds lined up like sardines, attached to the walls of the cavity by their claws, which, unlike the other parts of their feet, are strong and well developed. The same kinds of hollow-topped trees serve as nest sites for Vaux's swifts. The birds stick their semicircular, twig and conifer-needle nests to the vertical sides of the hollow with gluelike saliva. (The famed Chinese delicacy, bird's nest soup, is made from swift nests and gets its flavor from this sticky saliva.) Adults feeding young carry boluses of food in their mouths back to the nest. Each parent, it has been estimated, delivers more than 5,000 small insects a day to its nestlings.

A flock of Vaux's swifts spiral down into the cavity of a broken-top snag to roost at dusk.
(EVELYN L. BULL)

Black swifts can also be seen feeding over McDonald and Avalanche Creeks almost any summer evening, but their preference in nest sites resembles that of dippers more than Vaux's swifts. Out of moss, fern, and algae, they too construct saucer-shaped nests, but they locate them on cliffs behind high, inaccessible, and heavily shaded waterfalls. Four or five breeding pairs of black swifts will occupy a site. They exhibit what is called site tenacity, returning to the same cataracts, even the same rocks, each breeding season for generations. Black swifts probably have nested on cliffs behind some waterfalls for centuries, perhaps longer.

Fungus-Eating Voles and Ever-Pregnant Fishers—the Mammals of the Old Growth

As swifts soar above the trees of Glacier Park's redcedar-hemlock community, a host of mammals set about their business within the forest. Red-backed voles, a half dozen bats, flying squirrels, pine martens, and black bears are especially at home under the heavy canopy of an old-growth forest. Others, like grizzly bears, elk, and moose, are driven elsewhere by the limited forage—to the edges of meadows or in burns or even beneath mature stands of Douglas fir and larch, where there is more of a shrub and herb understory.

One species apparently dependent on old growth is the boreal red-backed vole, a blunt-nosed, small-eared, short-tailed mouse that, as you might guess, has a red back (although with a blue-gray tinge). Their specific habitat within the redcedar-hemlock community seems to be downed trees—the same fallen logs that play host to so many fungi and hemlock seedlings. Red-backed voles flourish in such shady places where almost nothing green grows because they feed primarily on the fungi growing on and around these logs. They are the only mammal in North America that thrives on fungi. In this capacity, red-backed voles seem to be important dispersers of mycorrhizal fungus spores, in the same way grizzly bears disperse cow-parsnip seeds. Because the forest depends on mycorrhizal fungi, these little rodents can be seen to carry more than their share of the world on their shoulders.

Buckskin-colored oyster mushrooms sprout from dead cottonwoods and are eaten by red squirrels, flying squirrels, mice, and red-backed voles. (GLACIER NATIONAL PARK)

If you take a late evening or nighttime walk on the Trail of the Cedars, you will probably see bats, possibly as many as five or six different species. The park has little brown bats, big brown bats, long-eared bats, long-legged bats, silver-haired bats, and hoary bats. All use the coniferous forest. But bats are not the only mammals soaring through the trees of the McDonald Valley at night. The northern flying squirrel, the park's only nocturnal squirrel, is here, too, gliding from tree to tree in search of food—lichens, barks, insects, bird eggs, and fungi. Loose, fur-covered folds of skin that stretch between their front and hind legs serve as gliding wings, and a fat, soft, bushy tail acts as a rudder. With this combination, a flying squirrel can cover 50 yards or more in a single flight. But because they sleep during the day, few who visit the park will ever see a flying squirrel gliding by. Which is unfortunate, for they are beautiful creatures. I once had a cat that would catch one from time to time, a sad ending for such a shy and lovely creature. Nothing feels softer than the satiny coat of a flying squirrel. And their large, dark eyes are fetching. Northern flying squirrels do not hibernate and are unique among small mammals in that, during the long winter, they feed almost exclusively on epiphytic lichens (lichens that grow on trees and other plants). In stormy weather they make cozy little shelters out of abandoned birds' nests by capping them with roofs of lichens and leaves and then curling up inside. To bear and rear their young, they make their own nests, as many birds do, in cavities made by woodpeckers.

So who is the stalker in the darkness of redcedar and hemlock? The pine marten is one predator that thrives here, devouring red-backed voles, Vaux's swifts, chestnut-backed chickadees, and northern flying squirrels. These dark, slender-bodied, kitten-size members of the weasel family are one of the few predators of this forest community that regularly hunts all of the above and a good deal more. Quick and skillful hunters, martens are able to catch and eat a variety of small mammals and birds. They also eat insects, berries, and seeds. One study found the martens in Glacier National Park regularly consume some forty-two different foods. Avid tree climbers, they spend most of their time in the forest canopy, where they probe nooks and cavities for birds and rodents and mark their territories by rubbing chin and anal scent glands across branches. Marten populations in northwestern Montana have for the most part recovered from the all-out trapping that went on in the last part of the nineteenth century and the early part of this century.

Martens, in turn, are hunted, though only occasionally, by a much rarer member of the weasel family, the fisher, a secretive, graceful predator that looks and acts like a large version of the marten. In addition to a meal of marten, the fisher eats porcupines, snowshoe hares, squirrels, mice, voles, white-tailed deer fawns, birds, insects, and fruit. Like martens, fishers were trapped heavily into the 1920s, and, easily caught, they were all but exterminated from northwestern Montana. In a bid to restore the animal to some of its original range, the state released thirty-six of the animals in 1959–60 into three areas of western Montana. More recent reintroductions were made in the Cabinet Mountains between 1988 and 1991. A few fishers have been seen in both the North Fork and Middle Fork of the Flathead since then.

Both fishers and martens are sexually dimorphic, which is to say males are markedly different from females. In this case the difference is one of size; males are, on average, twice the weight of females. One theory for this dimorphism argues that size differences allow the sexes to concentrate on different prey and that this division reduces competition between the sexes. The underlying assumption here is that individual fishers and martens usually go after the largest prey that they can efficiently capture and kill. If this is true, then males probably focus on animals like squirrels and hares and porcupines, prey too big for females to kill easily. Meanwhile, females pursue smaller quarry, like red-backed voles, into hollows and burrows too small for males to enter. Another possible cause of the size difference is the competition that occurs between males before and during reproduction. Male fishers and martens are highly territorial and compete with each other for access to females during the breeding season. The biggest males are usually the best fighters, and therefore they have been the most successful at passing on their genes. Both theories may be correct.

Fishers and martens, like an odd assortment of other creatures—bears (both black and grizzly), seals, walruses, roe deer, armadillos, and certain bats—practice a sort of gestation called delayed implantation. Once a female becomes pregnant, the development of the embryo is put on hold. Fishers, for example, mate around the middle of April. The fertilized egg develops for about fifteen days as it travels to the uterus. But once it arrives, it does not implant itself in the uterine wall and continue with development, as happens in most other mammals. Instead, the early embryo, or blastocyst, floats free in the uterus, its development suspended, for the next ten months. Not until the following spring, when the days begin to grow longer, does implantation take place. At that point, embryonic development resumes, and gestation is completed in about thirty days. In early April the kits are born. Over the next few weeks, the mother spends little time away from them, but she does manage, within the first ten days, to slip away long enough to breed again. That event may take two or three hours. Except for no more than ten days, adult female fishers are pregnant all the time.

No one yet has come up with a very good explanation for the function of such a lapse. Perhaps there is an optimum time for breeding and an optimum time for birthing. Perhaps only by uncoupling those two events in time could both occur during their most favorable season.

As their population continues to recover, fishers will play a greater part in the park's old-growth forests. But it may take another human generation or two before their numbers rebound enough to allow them to assume the role they once had.

8

Glacier's Subalpine

Although two-thirds of the park is covered with trees, trees or forests are not mainly what I come to Glacier to see, or what I remember once I leave. When hiking or driving in the park, I enjoy the wooded places, but I always seem to be merely traveling through these areas on my way into or out of the treeless high country. Unobstructed views are easiest to find above treeline, and Glacier is probably most loved for its heart-stopping views. To ignore the forests, however, is to ignore the lion's share of the park, a mistake for anyone interested in natural history.

Most of the low-elevation forests that cover parts of Glacier's east side, and that blanket the North Fork Valley bottom and the McDonald Valley, lie below 4,000 feet. They are only a small portion of the park's woodlands. Above them (but below the alpine) on both sides of the Continental Divide lies the subalpine zone, with its extensive forests of lodgepole pine, western larch, Douglas fir, Engelmann spruce, subalpine fir, whitebark pine, and alpine larch. These forest communities that cover the flanks of the mountains make up most of the park.

The Lower Subalpine

You can divide the roughly 3,000 feet of the subalpine zone into the lower subalpine, the upper subalpine, and treeline. The lower subalpine, the widest of these three subzones, is also the mildest and has the longest growing sea-

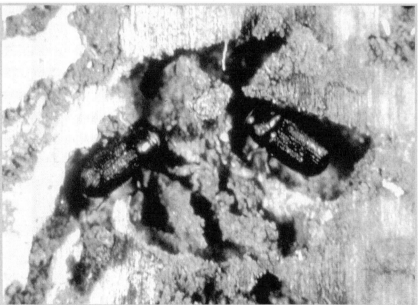

Lodgepole pine often sprouts thick as the hair on a dog's back after a fire, top. After seven or eight decades, the trees in these stands become susceptible to epidemics of mountain pine beetles, above. The beetles girdle the trees and kill them, promoting severe fire-danger conditions. (GLACIER NATIONAL PARK)

son. It extends from 4,000 feet to between 5,500 and 6,500 feet. Climax stands here and in the upper subalpine are dominated by subalpine fir. But because of past fires, climax stands are widely spaced in the subalpine. Thin-barked, low-branching, and with a sticky resin that ignites like kerosene, subalpine fir burns more easily than other conifers. Lewis and Clark reported in their journals how Nez Perce Indians in Montana's Bitterroot Mountains lit individual trees as a kind of fireworks display. Subalpine fir also forms dense stands. When a fire does catch, it stands a good chance of becoming catastrophic for the existing community. Catastrophic fires not only incinerate the trees and understory but they also consume all the duff on the forest floor and can cook the organic material incorporated 4 inches into the soil. According to fire scars on 400- to 700-year-old larch trees in the lower subalpine, this kind of stand-replacing fire happens about once every 185 years. As a consequence, lower subalpine forests are complicated mosaics of subalpine fir and seral species—western larch, lodgepole, Engelmann spruce, Douglas fir, and smaller amounts of western white pine.

On the west side of the park, dominant trees in seral communities are lodgepole pine and western larch. Both are superbly adapted to fire—but in different ways. Western larch, one of the few deciduous conifers in North America, is the most fire resistant of all the conifers growing in the northern Rockies. The lower trunk of a mature larch tree is covered with up to 6 inches of bark, an insulating layer of corklike material that protects the sap layer or cambium from scorching. The bark itself doesn't easily burn because, unlike the bark of most other conifers, it lacks resin. Larch trees also have a relatively fireproof foliage and a tendency to prune themselves of low branches. Both qualities make it less likely that fires will spread into the canopy. Even if a fire does manage to get into a larch crown, the tree stands a good chance of recovering because the species replaces its needles every year, so defoliation is less traumatic than for the evergreen conifers that renew their foliage over a two- or three-year cycle.

Not only does western larch resist fires well but it is also one of the first trees to become established after a burn. Larch seeds germinate best on soils laid bare by a blaze, and the seedlings require full sun. Larch seeds are small and light, about 150,000 to a pound, and have relatively large wings. They travel long distances on a good wind. The big trees that survive fires or those growing on the edges of burns act as seed trees. Fire, in fact, could be called western larch's best friend. The species must have it to propagate.

The same is true of lodgepole. Lodgepole, because of its thin, resiny bark, is only moderately fire resistant. The species is short-lived and dominates stands for only 100 to 150 years, at best. Unlike larch, its fire strategy is not to survive the flames but to create conditions that actually promote fires. Lodgepole is expert at regenerating itself on burned-over landscapes. It can reseed itself so densely after a burn that a person has difficulty squeezing through the young stand. Trees can be so thick that after fifty or sixty years they all but stop growing and become susceptible to all sorts of maladies—mountain pine beetle epidemics, dwarf mistletoe infestations, blowdown, heavy snow breakage, death from competition. The net effect is a forest floor crisscrossed with dead wood, which almost guarantees another stand-replacing fire, usually within a few decades. And that's good—if you're a lodgepole. Good because many of the lodgepoles bear serotinous (closed) cones. These cones, sealed shut with resin, open only when temperatures exceed 113°F. The adaptation allows the species to spew enormous quantities of its highly viable seed onto the soil immediately after a fire. If those seeds fall on an ashbed where the sun shines, many will survive. Lodgepole seedlings grow fast, so a new stand can replace an old one in a matter of twenty to thirty years. If fires are frequent enough, this sequence of lodgepole-fire-lodgepole will proceed indefinitely.

To see this dynamic in action, we need only look at what has been happening in the North Fork over the last few decades. Before 1972 much of that valley's lower subalpine zone was blanketed by a thick, almost continuous stand of aging lodgepole mixed with larch. The expansiveness and homogeneity of the stand had been aided by almost sixty years of the park's fire suppression policies. The lodgepole was past its prime, densely stocked, and ripe for an epidemic. And one came—in the form of a deadly, rapidly spreading infestation of mountain pine beetles. For nearly a decade these shiny, black, wood-munching insects fed on the tender cambium layer of the lodgepole. You could hear them chewing beneath the bark as they excavated their tree-girdling galleries or look up and see dozens of them flying through the air. The woodpecker population boomed. The beetles left in their wake 170,000 acres of standing and falling dead timber, a tangle of wood that over the next few summers dried to a tinder. The forest had become the biological equivalent of a powder keg. All that was needed to set it off was a single lightning strike. That strike came late in the dry summer of 1988, the summer of the great Yellowstone fires. Driven by fierce winds, the resulting conflagration, the Red Bench Fire, consumed 38,000 acres. You could call it a win for both lodgepole and larch, which quickly reseeded the burn. Today those trees are coming on strong, and thanks to the fire, their dominance is guaranteed for at least another generation or until another fire sweeps through.

I mentioned earlier that fire suppression had played a part in this story. The park's records indicate that between 1930 and 1987, ninety-five fires had been promptly suppressed in the Red Bench burn area. Had those fires been allowed to burn, they probably would have created a different kind of forest in the North Fork. Extensive stands of mature lodgepole would have been replaced by a patchwork of young and old stands. Because young lodgepole is not susceptible to mountain pine beetle infestations, the epidemic would have been less severe. Fewer beetle-killed trees would have meant less fuel. And less fuel would have meant a smaller Red Bench Fire. By suppressing fires, we only ensure that eventually larger and higher-severity fires will occur. That's why the Park Service now manages some lightning-caused fires in the park as long as they do not threaten human lives or property or as long as conditions are not too dry. Since the Red Bench Fire in 1988, there have been other major blazes in the North Fork—the 1994 Howling and Starvation Creek Fires, the 1999 Anaconda Fire, the 2000 Parke Peak Fire, the 2001 Moose Fire, and the 2003 Robert, Wedge Canyon, and Wolf Gun Fires. While the size and severity of these fires was almost certainly greater than it would have been without a century of suppression, the burns have helped to restore the park's naturalness.

The Upper Subalpine and Treeline

Hike above about 6,000 feet but stay below treeline, and you will be in the upper subalpine zone, above the cold limits of western larch, western white pine, and Douglas fir. Subalpine fir is the most common tree here, joined by two longer-lived species: Engelmann spruce on moist sites and white-bark pine on sunny, dry sites. Beneath the canopy you will see menziesia or fool's huckleberry, black elderberry, thimbleberry, pink and yellow mountain heather, tall huckleberry, grouse whortleberry, cow-parsnip, beargrass, meadowrue, arrowleaf groundsel, mountain arnica, and smooth woodrush.

Fire plays a different role in the upper subalpine than it does in the lower. Here the terrain is broken and rocky, trees are more widely spaced, and the ground is snowbound much of the year. In addition, temperatures are cooler and the climate wetter than in the lower subalpine. For these reasons, wildfires are infrequent here, even though lightning strikes are common. And when a blaze does start, it is usually limited to a few dozen acres. Exceptions are expansive, wind-driven crown fires that start at lower elevations during extremely dry years and burn upslope into the upper subalpine. Those fires can, on occasion, incinerate hundreds or even thousands of acres of high-elevation forests, forests that can take centuries to recover because the upper subalpine is a marginal place for trees; the growing season is cool and short, the winters harsh. The result is that wildfires in the upper subalpine often create meadows that persist for decades, even centuries. Given enough time, whitebark pine is often first to colonize these sites, eventually followed by subalpine fir growing in the shelter of the whitebark.

Go higher still, and you break out of the continuous forest into that famous transition zone known as treeline, where trees—subalpine fir, Engelmann spruce, and whitebark pine—take on wind- and frost-stunted, shrubby forms, called krummholz. Beyond it lies tundra.

Alpine larch also grows at treeline in Glacier. Unlike other treeline conifers, however, alpine larch seldom grows in krummholz form, occurs in only a dozen or so places in the park, and forms nearly pure stands that can extend well above the upper limits of other trees. Alpine larch is one of

Fires that start in the lower subalpine and spread into the upper subalpine can burn hundreds or thousands of acres of high-elevation forest. (GLACIER NATIONAL PARK)

the least common conifers in Glacier. It grows off the beaten path, so few visitors ever see it. The only stands along trails are in Preston Park and near Boulder Pass—neither area sees many people.

"What elevation is treeline?" is a question often asked by people traveling through Glacier. The answer varies depending on where you are. In some places, such as along Going-to-the-Sun-Road, treeline may dip as low as 5,700 feet, while elsewhere, such as on the north side of Grizzly Mountain, it extends up to 8,000 feet. The particular level depends on a number of related factors, most of which fall under the general headings of climate and topography.

Surprisingly, winter temperatures have little to do with how high these trees can ascend on a mountain—conifers grow in parts of Alaska and Siberia, for example, where winter temperatures have been known to drop below -80°F. Summer warmth, or more precisely, the length of the growing season, is critical. Trees cannot grow above the elevation at which temperatures are consistently too cold to support their metabolic processes during the brief, two-month-long summer growing season. In Glacier Park that uppermost limit is reached on the most favorable slopes at anywhere from 7,500 to 8,000 feet. East Flattop Mountain and Scenic Point are two places where treeline is highest.

Treeline is usually lower, however, and wind is a major reason. It would be hard to exaggerate the severity of the winds that hammer portions of Glacier's mountains in the winter. Wintertime wind speeds average 20 mph in the park. During storms, which are frequent, the average goes up to 40 mph. That's the average, however. Passes, which funnel air, and exposed ridges, where winds blow unobstructed, experience higher gales. During the dozens of blizzards that occur each winter, gusts in these places often exceed 100 mph. But the force of the wind by itself is not what damages most trees at upper treeline, although it will snap branches, break trunks, and rip foliage. Rather, particles of ice and desiccation, in concert with the wind, damage and deform the hardiest of trees or prune them into krummholz. Sudden dry winds steal moisture from a tree's needles faster

Throughout Glacier Park, avalanches are so common that in many places they have lowered the elevation of treeline. (GLACIER NATIONAL PARK)

than the tree's frozen trunk and roots can replace it, and wind-borne particles bruise and tatter foliage. While I have not experienced desiccation, I do know what it feels like to be blasted by ice.

One February, I and two others waited out a severe, five-day blizzard in a tent atop a mountain divide just south of the park. At one point we tunneled through the 5-foot-high drifts that covered our tent to peer out into the storm. Whiteout is a perfect description of what faced us when we emerged. Not only could we not see, but we could not breathe. The heavy, I'm guessing 70 mph, gusts seemed to steal the air right out of our mouths and noses. But the blowing ice pellets and snow crystals that pummeled our faces were even more terrible than the feeling of suffocation. They stung so badly that we did not attempt to crawl out and stand. At treeline, ice blasting takes its heaviest toll on trees by wounding new growth, causing needles and buds to desiccate and die. Consequently, trees growing on high ridges often have branches only on their leeward side, and windward slopes are often treeless, while adjacent protected sites are blanketed with krummholz or support scattered trees.

Wind also deposits snowdrifts, and when snow gets too deep, deep enough that it is mid- to late summer before the drifts melt, it shortens the growing season. Enough windblown snow collects in the basin just below Grinnell Glacier, for instance, to depress treeline to 6,100 feet. Surrounding ridges collect less snow and support trees at elevations 500 to 1,000 feet higher.

Avalanches also affect how high trees grow in the park. From just about anywhere you can look up and see the treeless swaths or fans cleared by snowslides. There are more avalanche chutes in Glacier than in most other parts of the northern Rockies because the terrain is so steep. In fact, snowslides are prevalent enough to have lowered the elevation of treeline throughout the park. The places where treeline communities and forests are highest are usually convex ridge spurs or gradual slopes, landforms too gentle to generate avalanches. Some mountains in the park, such as Snowslip on the south end, are striped with dozens of these herb- and shrub-filled chutes. Surprisingly, it is not the crush of the snow that does the most damage to trees. Rather, cyclone-strength winds that move in advance of the cascading snow most often topple and flatten timber. Winds generated by hundreds of tons of snow racing downhill approach speeds of 130 mph.

Tree line in the park is also influenced by the preponderance of rock above 6,000 feet. Thanks to ice-age glaciation, a good percentage of the upper subalpine is nothing but rock, solid bedrock without any mantle of soil at all, where trees simply cannot grow. The talus on most high-elevation slopes prevents all trees but alpine larch from getting a start. And because the terrain is so steep, rock slides are frequent.

Fires also lower treeline, to a lesser degree than other disturbances. Much of the Logan Pass area, for example, including the area bisected by the boardwalk, was probably once densely forested with subalpine fir krummholz. Perhaps as long ago as several centuries, a lightning fire destroyed most if not all of those trees. The stunted forest became a meadow filled with alpine plants. Eventually, a few subalpine fir trees reestablished themselves on the site and grew large enough to create windbreaks that protected other seedlings, the crowns accumulating snow during winter that later in the summer provided critical moisture for the young trees (because poorly developed subalpine soils do not hold enough moisture otherwise). Over the course of a century or two those trees, which grew in dwarfed and krummholz forms, increased and formed the bands and scattered islands of stunted trees we see today. The meadows on Logan Pass are a temporary phenomenon, created by fire. One day trees will replace them.

Without viable seed, trees are slow to reestablish themselves in a burned area or an avalanche chute at treeline. Krummholz produces little or no seed; the environmental conditions are simply too harsh. Most trees at treeline have to get their start from seed carried by wind or animals from upper subalpine forests half a mile or more away, or they spread vegetatively from existing trees. The lower branches of subalpine fir, Engelmann spruce, and, to a much lesser extent, whitebark pine, are able to take root and become "new trees" when pressed against moist ground. Of the seedlings that do get a start in a place like Logan Pass, few survive because the growing conditions are so harsh, and those that do can take centuries to grow to tree size. At treeline, alpine larch seedlings only an inch high are sometimes five to ten years old. John Muir counted 426 rings on a treeline whitebark pine tree with a trunk only 6 inches in diameter. Of that tree he wrote: "one of its supple branchlets, hardly an eighth of an inch in diameter inside the bark, is seventy-five years old, and so filled with oily balsam, so well seasoned by storms, that we may tie it in knots like a whipcord." Although this particular whitebark did not grow in Glacier, it grew in conditions similar to those found at treeline throughout the park. It can take up to 500 years—as long as it's been since Columbus first set foot on this continent—for some upper subalpine or treeline sites to fully recover from disturbances such as fires or avalanches. Other kinds of disturbances can have even longer lasting effects. Consider, for example, what has happened to the park's whitebark pine.

The Sad Tale of a Grand Old Tree

Near Boulder Pass, on the south side of a ridge some 6,000 feet above sea level, a magnificent old whitebark pine snag stands, its roots still clutching a fractured knob of yellow dolomite. The tree is stout, its trunk better than 4.5 feet in diameter. Its branches, exposed to the strong winds that blow on these ridgetops, are crooked and twisted, all bent in the same easterly direction. The tree is ancient. When it died in about 1986, it was 900 to 1,000 years old.

With the exception of aspen clones, no other living thing in the park gets that old. The feat is even more impressive considering whitebark pines occupy some of the harshest sites, sites where no other trees grow. They do well, for example, on windy ridges and south-facing slopes near treeline, where winter gales can reach hurricane force and temperatures can drop to 30° or 40° below zero, where summers are short and cool, and soils, if they exist at all, are thin, rocky, and infertile. This tree grew large under those conditions and survived nearly a millennium. And it did not die of old age.

Around 1910, humans began suppressing fires in the park. Lodgepole pine stands in the North Fork Valley matured, and mature lodgepole—

trees more than eighty years old—are susceptible to mountain pine beetle epidemics. In the 1970s an epidemic killed lodgepole pine on some 170,000 acres in the North Fork alone. By the 1980s, the infestation had moved upslope into stands of whitebark pine, where it destroyed another 15,000 acres of trees. The grandfather tree near Boulder Pass died in 1986, just one year before the epidemic ended.

Whitebark pine, once abundant in the park, is now rapidly declining, and the mountain pine beetle is only one reason. Fifty or sixty years ago you could find healthy whitebark pine trees almost anywhere in the subalpine above 5,500 feet. Some estimate the tree occupied more than one-fifth of the park, mostly at elevations above 5,800 feet. Young and middle-aged whitebark pines grew in seral stands in the lower and upper subalpine, and ancient whitebarks, like the one on Boulder Pass, stood like sentinels atop most of the dry, sunny slopes and ridges, their 3- and 4-foot-diameter trunks polished to a rosy sheen by centuries of ice-blasting. At treeline, whitebark formed much of the krummholz: islands of stunted trees growing thick enough in places to be nearly impenetrable. Yet today, many of those trees are dead. A rust fungus introduced from Europe is responsible for much of this damage, although mountain pine beetles killed many of the older trees that had been weakened by the fungus. Decades of fire suppression may have also taken a toll because subalpine fir, which increases in the absence of fire, can encroach on dying whitebark stands and shade out new seedlings. This has happened elsewhere in the Northwest, although it is unclear to what extent it is happening in Glacier.

The fungal disease, called white pine blister rust, attacks white pines, of which there are more than a dozen species worldwide. It enters the trees through the breathing pores, or stomata, of their needles and moves from there into the vascular tissue of the stem, where it grows until it disrupts the tree's ability to transport water and nutrients. Young whitebark pines die within a few years of becoming infected. Older trees may survive, but most end up losing their cone-bearing tops, effectively sterilizing them. It is rare now to see a cone on a whitebark pine tree in Glacier. In fact, it is estimated that nearly half the whitebark pine trees in the park are dead. Of the living trees, 78 percent are infected with rust, and more than a quarter of their cone-bearing crowns are now dead.

Before the onset of the disease, many animals, including nutcrackers, jays, grouse, squirrels, and grizzly bears, gathered to feed on the pine's nuts. Indians, too, made annual excursions into the high country to harvest whitebark pine nuts. In a wonderful book about his early years, Bud Cheff, a retired Montana outfitter, describes several of the trips he took with bands of Pend d'Oreille Indians in the 1930s: "The nuts were an important food [for Indian people] . . . In the days that I went on the trips with the Indians, the trees were loaded with cones. The small trees would be bent over with the weight of [them] and it took no time at all to pick two or three packhorse loads." The Indians would take the cones home, remove and dry the nuts, and then "dole them out to the children and grown-ups, just like we would today with candy."

White pine blister rust was accidentally imported from Europe in 1910 when a ship unloaded a French cargo of infected eastern white pine seedlings at Point Grey, British Columbia. No doubt, the nurserymen never considered they might spread a disease. Throughout Europe and Asia, white pine blister rust is not a problem. All the white pines growing there evolved with the disease and developed a natural resistance to it. But North American white pines, with no history of exposure to the rust, were highly susceptible. And whitebark pine is the most susceptible of all, as much as ten times more so than any other tree. Within thirteen years, blister rust had spread throughout much of the pine's range in the Pacific Northwest. It had also taken a heavy toll on much of the western white pine and limber pine in the region.

To complete its life cycle, the fungus needs an alternate host. To spread, it has to move from a pine tree to a currant or gooseberry bush (plants of the genus *Ribes*) or a paintbrush or lousewort plant (both members of the figwort family) and then back to a pine again. It also requires a relatively moist climate, similar to that found throughout much of Glacier Park. In the middle part of this century, foresters, believing they could stop white pine blister rust by removing the intermediate host, set out to eradicate currant and gooseberry bushes from forests (at that time, they did not realize that paintbrush and lousewort were also alternate hosts). In Glacier Park alone, crews poisoned or pulled and grubbed out over four and a half million *Ribes* plants—Indian currants, stinking currants, alpine prickly currants, sticky currants, white-stem gooseberries, and swamp-gooseberries. The effort proved futile. Not only were the bushes too hardy, too numerous, and too widely scattered, but paintbrush and lousewort are far more common than *Ribes* near most whitebark stands. Seeing little success, the Park Service ended its gooseberry eradication program in 1965.

Now efforts to control white pine blister rust are beginning to focus on identifying and propagating trees showing resistance to the disease. In the 1990s biologists began looking for trees with full, healthy, cone-producing crowns among stands heavily hit by the blister rust. When they found one, they protected the cones in metal, bird-proof cages. Later they returned to collect the seeds, which they planted in a nursery. Then, between 2000 and 2002 they planted the first 5,300 of those whitebark pine seedlings in the wild—one hundred each in recent burns on Grinnell Point and Dutch Ridge and 5,100 atop Flattop Mountain in the 1998 Kootenai burn. Monitoring results have shown that 38 percent of the young trees have survived three to four years after planting, and 90 percent of those were in healthy condition. This strategy holds great promise, but it is excruciatingly slow because whitebark pine is such a slow-growing tree. It will take at least several human generations to know if this experiment will succeed.

The damage caused by the blister rust will not be limited to the trees because whitebark pine is a keystone species. Like the woodpeckers described earlier, which are important because they excavate holes used by other animals, whitebark pine affects the population levels of other plants and animals far out of proportion to its own numbers. Whitebark is a pioneer species that produces nutritious seeds that attract and support a diversity of birds and mammals. Whenever you have a keystone species in decline, you have the potential for upending entire ecological communities, and that seems to be exactly what's happening right now in the upper

At one time, whitebark pine pioneered upper subalpine ridges like this. Even then, it took as long as five centuries for a forest to become established on such a site. Without whitebark pine it will probably take much longer. (GLACIER NATIONAL PARK)

subalpine and treeline zones of Glacier Park. The waning of whitebark pine has affected everything from subalpine fir to grizzly bears.

Much of the dwarf and krummholz subalpine fir growing at or near treeline, for instance, owes its existence to whitebark pine because whitebark pine pioneers high-elevation sites after fires and avalanches. The whitebark affords protection and increases the amount of moisture available to seedling subalpine fir. Once established, the firs are able to reproduce vegetatively and create an expanding krummholz island. Spared another fire or avalanche, these islands eventually expand to form sizeable patches of forest cover. Thus, whitebark pine may be a critical link in the successional process that turns treeline meadows filled with alpine plants into dense copses of subalpine fir and Engelmann spruce. The decline of whitebark may disrupt this entire process or, at the very least, slow it markedly.

Another species that has already felt the loss of this long-lived, pioneering tree is the Clark's nutcracker, a relative of the crow that, because of its black, white, and gray markings, looks a little like a mockingbird. Raucous (their call is a harsh *kra-a-a-a-a*) and crowlike in flight and body form, nutcrackers once dwelled year-round in the upper subalpine, where they fed heavily on the nuts of whitebark pine. The two species, in fact, nutcracker and whitebark, evolved together, each influencing the evolution of the other.

Until a few decades ago, Clark's nutcrackers spent late summer and fall harvesting whitebark pine nuts. The nuts, which are a little smaller than pea size, are locked in plump purple cones attached to the upper branches of the trees. To get at them, the birds perched on the branches and pecked large holes in the sides of the cones. Some they ate fresh, but most they hid in caches. When the whitebark cone crop became depleted in October, the birds turned to seeds from limber and ponderosa pine, which they cached as well. Finally, they revisited some of their whitebark cache sites, collected the seeds, and then re-cached them over a much larger area. The first cache probably served to get the seed out of the tree and into the ground, away from other seed eaters, the second to disperse the seed over a wide area to minimize cache raiding by mice and voles. Between mid-August and the end of October, a single nutcracker would hide anywhere from 35,000 to 98,000 whitebark pine seeds in as many as 25,000 cache sites. From winter to midsummer they returned to these hidden food stores to feed. A single nutcracker might recover about a thousand of its caches a year, for a total of about 4,000 seeds. The balance of the nuts remained in the ground where they stood a good chance of germinating and becoming trees.

Picky about where and how they cache their seeds, nutcrackers not only bury them at exactly the right depth for germination—about an inch below the surface—but also on the kinds of sites whitebark has specialized in pioneering—burns, meadow edges, rocky outcrops, and areas at or just above treeline. The birds prefer south-facing or windblown slopes, probably because those sites are snow-free in winter and spring. It just so happens that southern, windy exposures also favor whitebark pine germination and growth because they are relatively dry and warm. Other animals—grouse, ravens, jays, woodpeckers, sapsuckers, chickadees, nuthatches, crossbills, grosbeaks, finches, mice, voles, chipmunks, squirrels, black bears, grizzly bears, and humans—eat whitebark pine nuts when they are available, but

Whitebark pines that sprout from nutcracker seed caches often grow in clusters; several trees sprouting from the same cache become fused at their bases. (USDA FOREST SERVICE)

A Clark's nutcracker sits on a whitebark pine bough. (DIANA F. TOMBACK)

none caches them in places so favorable to the growth of the tree or at depths appropriate for optimum germination and seedling development. Whitebark seeds are not dispersed by wind because the nuts, which are wingless and heavy to begin with, stay locked inside a cone until an animal frees them. Hence, whitebark pines are almost entirely dependent on Clark's nutcrackers for their reproduction.

This dependence has profoundly altered the biology of the tree. Whitebark pine seeds are large and heavy because trees with big, weighty seeds have been more successful at gaining the attention of nutcrackers and have thus been favored over trees with smaller seeds. And unlike the cones of most conifers, those of whitebark remain closed even when ripe because a cone that retains its nuts increases the foraging efficiency of the seed-dispersing nutcrackers.

But the nut-stashing habits of this raucous bird have affected more than just the pine's cones and seeds. The places where whitebark pine grows, its population structure, even its primary growth form have been influenced by the habits of nutcrackers. For instance, whitebark pine trees often have multiple trunks. But what may appear to be a single tree with several stems is more likely a cluster of two or more trees fused together at or just above the base, each trunk having originated from a seed that sprouted from a multi-seed nutcracker cache. Wind-dispersed conifers seldom show this kind of clustering. And whereas among wind-dispersed conifers, adjacent trees are often related, the genetic relations between neighboring whitebark clusters verge on random, thanks to the caching habits of nutcrackers. Also, nut-crackers distribute seeds over a broad range of elevations and at distances of up to 14 miles from the parent tree, helping whitebark to expand its range and to colonize burns and avalanche chutes. Seeds buried at or above the treeline help to maintain whitebark pine at its maximum elevational limits.

The birds, too, developed adaptations that have improved their ability to take advantage of whitebark pine nuts. They have long, stout, pointed bills enabling them to open whitebark pine cones and extract the seeds. Unlike many other birds, their mandibles are strong enough to crack the tough hull that coats the seeds. Their bills are also ideal for thrusting the seeds into the soil and just the right length to ensure those seeds are planted deep enough for good germination. In addition, nutcrackers have special pouches under their tongues, saclike extensions of the floor of their mouths absent in other jays. These pouches allow them to carry a hundred or more seeds at a time. This burden can weigh almost a quarter of a pound; hence nutcrackers are also strong fliers. And thanks to the thousands of nutritious whitebark pine nuts that they store, they don't have to migrate from their mountain homes in the winter. With food caches, they are able to breed as early as February, months before other seed-eating birds mate. Nutcrackers feed both their young and their fledglings regurgitated pine nuts recovered from their caches. When whitebark pine seeds are unavailable, the birds use several other species of conifer seeds, but they prefer those of whitebark because they are large and easy to harvest and because they keep. Seeds last up to several years in the ground.

Not too long ago, ornithologists believed that Clark's nutcrackers relied more on luck than memory when it came to relocating hidden food caches. They theorized that the birds simply made their caches in certain types of areas and then rediscovered the buried nuts later by randomly probing the ground as they foraged in those same areas. But they were puzzled by how successful the birds were at finding caches. Better than two out of three times that a nutcracker stuck its beak into the ground, it came up with a nut. Often, that nut had been planted as long as two to six months earlier. Were they somehow smelling their caches, or could they see their old bill marks in the soil, or did something else operate? Through experiments with nutcrackers in aviaries, it has been demonstrated that the birds rely on their memories to find hidden caches rather than luck or smell or visual cues. They do it much the way we would, by using landmarks such as rocks and trees as reference points. To prove this, scientists let the birds plant their seeds, then they move things around in the aviary. The birds search for their caches where the landmarks indicate they should be. If a bird plants a seed 6 inches from the tip of a large rectangular rock, and that rock is moved 3 feet to the right, the nutcracker searches a spot exactly 3 feet to the right of where it had actually planted the seed. If the rock is moved 8 feet to the left, the bird searches there. When you consider a Clark's nutcracker may have as many as 25,000 seed caches, with some seeds cached twice, its powers of memory stand out as quite remarkable.

But now the nutcracker's world has changed as whitebark pine nuts have all but disappeared from the park. In the past, during years when the seeds of whitebark pine and other conifers have been scarce, nutcrackers fled from their subalpine habitats in huge numbers in search of other foods—the seeds of other pines, berries, insects. Some years, in fact, when the cone crop has failed, Clark's nutcrackers have been found hundreds of miles outside of their normal range. So they are flexible when need be, able to exploit other foods. Traditionally in Glacier Park, they preferentially harvested and stored whitebark pine seeds before turning to limber pine and other trees. Now, with the decline of whitebark pine and limber pine—the rust has infected 90 percent and killed a third of the park's limber pine trees—they will have to rely mostly on the seeds of ponderosa pine, Douglas fir, and other conifers. Although the change has meant a dramatic decline in their population, there is hope the birds are flexible enough to survive.

Who Else Is Feeling the Pinch?

Other animals will suffer with the decline of whitebark as well, although none has co-evolved with the pine to the extent that the nutcracker has and is as dependent on it. Blue grouse eat the buds and needles and roost in the foliage, which provides protection from the cold and cover from predators. Mountain bluebirds and northern flickers are cavity nesters that favor the hollows of whitebark snags over those of other subalpine trees. Like nutcrackers, however, most animals are attracted to whitebark for its long-keeping, nutritious nuts. While conifer seeds of all kinds make up the bulk of the diets of both red- and white-winged crossbills, they feed heavily on whitebark nuts when they are available. Crossbills have stout bills that cross at the tips, a design especially adapted for prying seeds from pine, fir, and spruce cones. Unlike nutcrackers, however, crossbills are nomadic and move in large flocks from one area to another in search of good seed crops. Their diets are more varied as well. Along with a staple of conifer seeds, crossbills eat maple and birch buds, mountain ash berries, and other fruits and seeds. They also do not cache pine seeds, at least not in the ground. To get through cold subalpine nights, especially during winter, these slightly-bigger-than-sparrow-size seed-eaters have found an altogether different place for storing nuts—their necks. Both species of crossbills have a pouch about halfway down the neck. Only crossbills, the common redpoll, and perhaps a few other finches have such an adaptation. Late in the day, especially during severe weather, they fill this pocket with seeds and retreat to a sheltered place in the trees, where they fluff out their feathers to keep warm and roost. Periodically, they awake and draw on their supply of stored seeds, so as to ensure themselves a source of energy for the long, cold nights, and daytime periods of bad weather. While both nutcrackers and crossbills have evolved seed-holding pouches, the structures—one beneath the tongue and the other in the neck—serve different functions. Yet both accomplish the same goal—that of allowing the birds a means of hoarding food so they can survive the harsh winters.

To a lesser extent, whitebark pine nuts fed Steller's jays, pine grosbeaks, mountain chickadees, and redbreasted nuthatches, but the beaks of these birds are not designed specifically for feeding on whitebark pine cones; thus all four generally limit their foraging to cones already opened by nutcrackers or squirrels. Of the four, only Steller's jays cache nuts. Seeds stored by Steller's jays, however, seldom grow into trees because jays don't plant them in the ground. Instead, they hide them in the crotches of trees, under the lichen that grows on branches, and in the witch's-brooms of dwarf mistletoe, places they revisit when other foods are scarce.

The only other animal that cached whitebark pine nuts in the ground and in numbers similar to those of the Clark's nutcracker is the red squirrel. Red squirrels are year-round residents of all the coniferous forests of the park and rely on conifer seeds to see them through the winter, for unlike ground squirrels, they do not hibernate. Although they take a variety of seeds in their diet, they prefer mixed stands with plenty of whitebark, apparently because the tree offers large seeds that are better than three-quarters fat. So although red squirrels, like nutcrackers, are not dependent on whitebark pine, the decline of the tree has meant a decline in their numbers in areas where whitebark was once plentiful.

Not surprisingly, squirrels and nutcrackers have altogether different styles of harvesting and caching conifer seeds. Rather than chewing a hole in a cone while it is still attached to the tree, a squirrel will cut the cone loose with its teeth and let it drop to the forest floor. They do this all day long, sometimes several days in a row, before climbing down to collect their harvest and stashing it in their middens. They then return to the canopy for more. Squirrels cease their cone harvest around the middle of September to begin the work of extracting seeds at their middens. In what seems an incredibly tedious and inefficient process, a squirrel will pick up a stashed cone, chew at the scales until it removes a single seed, then carry that seed in its mouth several yards to a 2- to 6-inch-deep hole that it has previously excavated in the ground. After depositing the seed in the hole, it hurries back to the midden for another. After placing about thirty seeds in the hole, the squirrel covers it and digs another. These buried caches, along with dried mushrooms, make up all of the squirrel's winter food stores. The midden itself is but an interim storage site and a collection of

A squirrel midden in a whitebark pine forest. Squirrels use middens as short-term storage sites for cones. They also extract the seeds from the cones at their middens. The seeds are then cached in holes dug elsewhere. (USDA FOREST SERVICE)

cone debris. Middens, which are typically used for years, if not decades, can be anywhere from 1 to 30 square yards in size. Not many whitebark pines sprout from either middens or caches; usually the seeds are planted too deeply to germinate.

Back when whitebark was abundant, nutcrackers were occasionally seen taking whitebark pine cones from atop squirrel middens. Today the squirrels chatter fiercely and may chase after nutcrackers and other seed-eating birds that linger within their territory. Bears, too, excite the squirrels. During good whitebark cone crop years, both black and grizzly bears would visit whitebark forests specifically to raid squirrel middens and caches. They ate a good number of squirrels in the process.

During the most productive cone years prior to the whitebark pine's decline, outfitter Bud Cheff used to see grizzly bears feeding exclusively on pine nuts from August to October. Bud has described to me how fifty years ago he and his Indian friends could often hear the bears chomping whitebark cones before they could actually see them. Sometimes they would top a ridge where they knew the cone collecting would be good, only to confront a troop of as many as five or six roly-poly bears that had beaten them to it. Roly-poly is Bud's adjective; he is adamant that bears were fatter in the days when whitebark nuts were plentiful, which makes sense when you consider that few other autumn bear foods are as high in fats as whitebark pine nuts.

Grizzly bears are not good tree climbers, so once they stripped the dwarf trees of their cones, they turned to raiding squirrel middens, a profitable venture. In a good whitebark cone year, a single squirrel could gather a number of cones estimated to contain better than 800,000 seeds. Although some grizzly bears would eat entire cones (the fleshy pulp of which also has some food value), most were remarkably adept at eating only the seeds. The bears would use their claws to strip away the cone scales, dump out the seeds, and then lap them up with their tongues. At the height of the whitebark season, when they were eating nothing but nuts, their spoor usually contained only broken seed coats and occasional squirrel parts. No cone scales.

And whitebark pine nuts were not just a fall food for grizzly bears in the park. In the spring, grizzlies started feeding on them as soon as they emerged from their dens. They were able to locate and excavate cone caches under at least 6 feet of snow.

Black bears spent much of their autumn in the trees eating cones, as well. Two or three decades ago it was common for black bears in Glacier Park to lose all the hair on their front legs each fall: Pitch would collect there when the bears climbed the pines, and it would gather dirt and other debris. Eventually, the whole mess would peel away, taking all the hair with it.

How valuable whitebark pine was to Glacier's grizzly bears is clear. One biologist has been quoted as saying that whenever the seeds were available, grizzly bears fed on them exclusively until there were no more to be had. In a bumper year the bears ate the seeds from August through autumn, and there was still enough to feed them the next spring. How the tree's demise will affect bear numbers in Glacier over the long term is not as clear. In Yellowstone National Park, where many trees still produce cones, female bears that consume large numbers of whitebark nuts have relatively higher reproductive rates. They also begin reproducing at a significantly younger age and wean their cubs earlier. Researchers reported in 2003 that during years of abundant cone availability, roughly 70 percent of the grizzly bears in Yellowstone derived half of their protein from pine nuts. In poor cone crop years, bear conflicts with humans escalate dramatically; the numbers of "troublesome" bears that had to be trapped and moved were six times higher in bad cone years. And because of these conflicts, two times as many adult female and three times as many male Yellowstone grizzlies died during years when the nuts were not available.

Bears in Glacier Park once congregated in whitebark forests in the fall, just as they once gathered to feed on beached whales along the California coast or in oak forests to feed on acorns. Autumn foods are crucial to grizzly survival. Pregnant females that do not gain the necessary pounds in the fall face the possibility of aborting their young, and some adults, male or female, may die in the den for lack of nourishment. Since the decline of whitebark pine, the park's grizzly bears have had to rely on berries and roots to put on autumn pounds, neither of which is anywhere near as fat-rich as pine nuts. In the spring, too, when emaciated bears emerged from their dens, the nuts provided critical calories. Thus, losing this high-elevation food source has been the equivalent of subtracting a large slice of first-rate grizzly bear habitat from the park.

Grizzly bears can ill afford such a loss. In the lower forty-eight states, the species is listed as threatened under the Endangered Species Act. Biologists estimate that approximately 300 bears live in Glacier and the immediate surrounding area. Something most people are unaware of is that early in this century, Glacier's grizzly bear population was at much lower levels; market hunting, trapping, sport shooting, and park-run predator control programs had taken their toll. The species has been rebounding ever since, slowly filling up under-used habitat. It has taken better than eighty years because grizzlies reproduce at a very slow rate. But with whitebark pine now in decline, Glacier will support fewer bears than it would have otherwise. Fewer bears per square mile affects a host of other species, from ungulates to ground squirrels to cow-parsnip. And without pine nuts to fatten on in the fall, grizzlies may be more likely to get into trouble with park visitors, as they have in Yellowstone.

The loss of a single plant or animal can send ripples through an entire ecosystem, but the decline of a keystone species like whitebark pine can have the effect of a tsunami, causing major fluctuations in the populations of dozens of plants and animals.

Huckleberry Fields Forever

Avalanche chutes, another kind of grizzly bear habitat in the park, are never in short supply. These long, treeless corridors are loaded with many of the foods bears prefer: arrowleaf groundsel, cow-parsnip, biscuit-root, dandelion, strawberry, sweet cicely, angelica, licorice-root, stinging nettle. And because snowslides reach from valley bottoms to mountain tops, the plants ripen at different times as the snowline recedes upslope. As a general rule of thumb, every 100-foot gain in elevation delays the plants about one day. So, for example, cow-parsnip blooms at the summit of Rogers Peak about

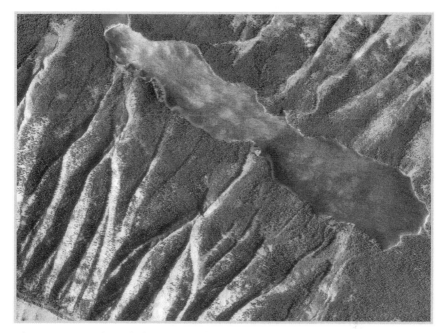

Like many areas in the park, the mountain slopes above Trout Lake are covered with avalanche chutes. Bears forage in the chutes all summer long. (NATIONAL AGRICULTURAL IMAGE PROGRAM)

a month after it flowers at the peak's base, some 3,300 feet lower. The silver-tips simply follow the melting snowfront upward and forage the nutrient-rich plants sprouting in its wake. Bears gain little nutrition from foods high in fiber, and the older a plant gets, the more fiber it produces. Many grizzly bears therefore concentrate their mid- and late-summer foraging in the snowbed communities of avalanche chutes, which at almost any time during the summer harbor the youngest and most succulent plants to be found anywhere in the park.

Avalanche chutes contain a variety of vegetation types. They can be brushy, choked with 10-foot-high stands of alder, menziesia, and willow from top to bottom; or they can be open and lush with wet, waist-high herbs, plants like meadowrue, beargrass, groundsel, and cow-parsnip; or relatively dry and sparsely vegetated with mostly low-growing grasses and hardy alpine wildflowers. Some hold intermittent or continuously flowing streams and are full of water-loving plants like brook saxifrage, sweet-scented bedstraw, monkeyflower, and streambank butterweed. Others are almost monocultures, beargrass or sedges throughout. Most are an amalgam. Thus, in addition to so many fine herbaceous foods, grizzly bears find plenty of other good things to eat in avalanche chutes: grasses, sedges, rushes, equisetum, roots like those of sweetvetch, corms of glacier lilies, ground squirrels, marmots, ants, ground-nesting wasps, and fruit—huckleberries, bearberries, serviceberries, mountain ash fruits, currants, and gooseberries. Bears also bed down in snowslides and use them as travel corridors.

Huckleberries, one of the plants most closely associated with grizzly bears, grow not so much in the treeless centers of avalanche chutes as along the timbered margins and within the narrow stringers of trees sometimes found in chutes. The bushes are also found in a variety of other habitats from below the lower subalpine to above treeline. There are six species—blue huckleberry, tall huckleberry, dwarf huckleberry, velvet-leaved huckleberry, dwarf billberry, and grouse whortleberry—often as many as four or five growing in the same patch. While bears eat them all, they concentrate on the first two, blue and tall huckleberry. "Hucks" come ripe from July through mid-September, when the last of the herbs flower and mature and the bears need to accumulate fat for winter. Since the loss of whitebark pine, hucks have become the principal late-summer food of both grizzly and black bears, at least during most years. I add that qualifier because huckleberry production can vary from year to year; many summers, the bushes produce poorly.

Weather is a major influence on huckleberry crops. A late cold front or snowstorm, for example, can damage blossoms or hinder pollinators and leave the plants with nothing but dry, white fruits. Another factor affecting production is fire. It seems huckleberry bushes need to burn at least every few decades to be very fertile—the heavy shade beneath closed canopies inhibits flower formation and keeps fruit from ripening. Even areas with lots of bushes produce few berries if they go more than fifty years without burning. During bad huckleberry years, bears are forced to move into stream bottoms and wet areas, where they feed on hawthorn berries, buffalo berries, and serviceberries. Without a good fall diet of hucks, however, bears don't gain the weight they need. Pregnant females can end up producing fewer cubs, and some bears, especially older, more frail individuals, may not make it through the winter. Unlike pine nuts, huckleberries are low in both fat and protein but high in carbohydrates or sugar. The sugar puts the fat on.

A huckleberry hot spot for both grizzly bears and black bears is the Apgar Range just north of West Glacier. The shrubfields of those low mountains support such an abundance of huckleberry bushes that large numbers of bears congregate there in the latter part of the summer and into the fall. Arriving as soon as the berries begin to ripen, both black bears and grizzlies feed at first at lower and mid-elevations. Black bears, however, avoid the more productive, higher-elevation huckleberry fields that come ripe a little later in the season. Those higher areas are more sparsely wooded and are heavily used by grizzly bears. Because of competition between the two species, black bears of the park enjoy a shorter huckleberry season than grizzlies.

As you might expect, black bears generally come out on the losing end when the two species come in contact, especially around food. One observer recorded such an event near McGee Meadow in 1969. A large, reddish brown, adult silvertip came upon a big black bear feeding on a deer carcass. The grizzly chased the black bear away, then picked up the deer in its jaws and dragged it to its own cache site about 0.5 mile north of the meadow. The bear cleared a circle of about 10 feet around the carcass, scraping the ground clean and piling the cleared debris atop the deer. Near the cache were six grizzly bear scats, each having a volume of about a gallon. There was no evidence of a fight between the bears. The scats in this instance probably served as territorial markers, a warning that might have read: *"I'm a big bear and this is my meat!"* At certain times, grizzlies are in direct competition with their smaller and less aggressive cousins. Black bears avoiding prime huckleberry patches used by grizzlies is such a situation, and probably a far more significant one in the life of the bears than the occasional encounter over meat.

There is one other way in which grizzly bears may express their dominance in the subalpine. "Bear trees" are often seen scattered throughout huckleberry country. Used as rubbing posts by both grizzly and black bears year after year, many are scarred with claw and teeth marks, some of those marks 10 feet or more above the ground. All these trees have their bark rubbed smooth, and many have grooves and snatches of hair caught here and there. No one knows exactly what part bear trees play in the life of bears. Some biologists believe the trees serve as measuring posts, a way for bears, especially male bears during mating season, to express dominance, each animal rubbing to leave its scent, some clawing and chewing the trunk as high as possible to advertise their size and potential rank within a given area. Other biologists think they are simply scratching posts with no territorial significance. All summer long, bears are plagued by insects and, it seems, have an urge to scratch.

Another kind of bear tree may also catch your eye. Throughout the subalpine, especially the lower subalpine, small pockets of young, vigorous larch, pine, spruce, and fir have their bark peeled off, pulled from the bottom up to heights of 8 feet. Usually, the shredded ribbons of bark still hang from the tops of the peeled areas. These trees supply food for bears. Once they strip the bark, the bears use their incisors to shave away the sweet, vitamin-rich cambium layer, their teeth leaving vertical grooves in the tender sapwood. Most of the trees survive; only one in ten is killed. Indians also ate the cambium of conifers, cutting large pieces of inner bark from big ponderosa pines in the North Fork. Many of those "Indian-scarred trees" are still there, alive and well. Indians may have learned that sapwood was edible by watching bears. Perhaps they discovered the edibility of cow-parsnip and dozens of other food plants similarly.

Fire Guide

Because fire plays such an important role in the park, I have included brief descriptions of the park's fire regimes and definitions of a couple key terms used by park managers to describe fire.

Fire Regimes

The term **fire regime** refers to the kind of fire that typically occurs in an area over a long period of time and the effects that that particular type of burning has on the vegetation. Fire regimes are described by the size of the typical fire, the burn's pattern on the landscape, the season in which the fires generally occur, how often the fires occur (on average), and the severity and intensity of the fires. The term **severity** is a measure (low, moderate, high, or very high) of the immediate effects of fire on the ecosystem, especially plants, while the term **intensity** can be defined simply as the flame length of the typical fire. In Glacier Park, managers recognize three main fire regimes:

An **understory fire regime** has a fire frequency of less than thirty-five years. Fires are generally of low severity and low intensity because they typically burn on the surface of the ground. Most larger trees survive these fires and many species in the understory fire regime are adapted to fire and/or dependent on it. Big Prairie is an example of an understory fire regime.

The **stand-replacement fire regime** can have a fire frequency of between 35 and 100 years or greater than 200 years. An example of the former would be an even-age lodgepole pine stand in the North Fork; an example of the latter a mixed conifer stand (subalpine fir, spruce, and pine forests) on north slopes or elevations above approximately 5,000 feet. West Flattop and much of the east side of the park have a stand-replacement fire regime.

Fire severity and intensity are generally high, and the fires kill most if not all of the trees, although size and severity can vary somewhat with topography, fuels, and burning conditions.

The **mixed-severity fire regime** has a fire frequency of between thirty-five and one hundred-plus years. The fires range from low and moderate severity to partial stand replacement. Examples include mixed stands of lodgepole, ponderosa, Douglas fir, aspen, larch, spruce, subalpine fir, and whitebark pine in the North and Middle Fork Valleys. The mixed-severity fire regime is generally characterized by many small stands with various structures. It is often rich in diversity.

Fire and the Distribution of Animals

Fire not only shapes the distribution of plants. It has a huge effect on the distribution of most of the park's wildlife species, too. Take birds, for example. Some species are consistently more abundant in burned forests, others in unburned forests, while a third group shows little or no preference. In general, woodpeckers and aerial foragers favor burned forests while foliage-gleaning species prefer unburned forests. Burn severity also plays a role. Bird species frequently found in stand-replacement burns are typically less common in understory burns, and the species commonly seen in unburned forests generally decrease in abundance as burn severity increases. Recent research on bird use of burned and unburned areas in the northern Rockies found the following pattern:

More Abundant in Burns	Mixed Response to Burns	More Abundant in Unburned Forests
Three-toed Woodpecker	Mourning Dove	Steller's Jay
Black-backed Woodpecker	Common Nighthawk	Plumbeous/Cassin's Vireo
Olive-sided Flycatcher	Cassin's Finch	Warbling Vireo
Mountain Bluebird	Pine Siskin	Gray Jay
Western Wood-Pewee	Chipping Sparrow	Ruby-crowned Kinglet
Hairy Woodpecker	Dark-eyed Junco	Brown Creeper
House Wren	American Robin	Red-breasted Nuthatch
Tree Swallow	Townsend's Solitaire	Hermit Thrush
Northern Flicker	Hammond's Flycatcher	Mountain Chickadee
	Clark's Nutcracker	Golden-crowned Kinglet
	Red-naped Sapsucker	Townsend's Warbler
	Western Tanager	Swainson's Thrush
	White-breasted Nuthatch	Varied Thrush
	Evening Grosbeak	
	Pygmy Nuthatch	
	Williamson's Sapsucker	
	Red Crossbill	
	Yellow-rumped Warbler	

The results show again one of the key reasons why fire is important in the park: It ensures diversity of plants and animals, and diversity is one of Glacier's hallmarks.

9

The Alpine

Stretched out on this soft cushion of tundra, I feel very close to the sky. I am lying in the sun on the lee side of a giant, lichen-covered boulder to escape a cold wind that has been cutting right through my heavy wool sweater and undergarments. It is August, and though the air is cold, the sun is intense, and I feel comfortably warm in this sheltered place. In fact, I begin to worry about sunburn. And for good reason. Up here, at well over 9,000 feet, the air is thin, and the atmosphere filters the sun less than at lower elevations. Here the air is clean and dry. Neither pollution nor humidity blunt the sun's rays very much. As a consequence, almost twice as much ultraviolet radiation, the invisible rays responsible for sunburn, pours down here than at sea level. I can feel it burning the cells of my face.

A patch of snow lingers nearby, but it's almost too bright to look at, for not only is the invisible part of the spectrum more intense here but there is also more visible light, almost 20 percent more than on an ocean beach. I squint to protect my eyes and then turn away from the glaring snow to focus on the enormous peaks all around, brilliant and sharp in the light. I roll over onto my side and am greeted by an arctic bellflower poking through a tuft of grass. Its single, delicate, lavender-blue flower seems too small to invite the insect pollinators it needs to reproduce. But just then I notice a tiny fly, minuscule even in comparison to the flower, pushing its way out from between the stamens. After pausing for a moment on the anthers, this midget nectar-drinker takes flight, quickly disappearing into the wind, perhaps carrying a grain or two of pollen with it. It seems odd that an insect manages to move in such cold air. Perhaps it hesitated on the flower's anthers for the same reason I am pressed up against this rock; perhaps, like me, it was pausing to collect enough of the sun's warmth to see it to its next goal.

Six inches away from the bellflower, a slightly larger but distinctly more squatty plant has forced itself up from a circle of blue-green rock. Bursting with sunny, bright yellow, star-shaped flowers, this is lance-leaved stonecrop. It prefers dry areas. The fat, fleshy leaves, which form dime-size rosettes at its base, suggest as much. I pierce one with my fingernail, and it bleeds a thick mucilaginous sap, water the plant was storing as insurance against drought. I notice the leaf surface is waxy, a surface designed to lock in moisture. Even the compact growth form of the leaves, a basal rosette, is a defense against desiccation; the plant keeps its leaves tight and close to the ground. At this elevation, many plants have adaptations like these. Even though much of Glacier's alpine receives more than 100 inches of precipitation a year, the environment for plants is often quite dry, particularly on the east side. Moisture may be unavailable to plants for as much as eight to nine months a year. Winter snow, of course, goes unabsorbed, and summers are often without significant precipitation. Add to that the desiccating effects of the wind, especially the chinooks, and the increased level of solar radiation. It is no wonder that alpine plants have evolved some of the same characteristics desert plants have.

Nearby I spot a rather rare plant: Arctic rock-jasmine, also called sweet-flowered androsace. I stretch to smell the blossoms and decide the appellation fits. This remarkably tiny member of the primrose family stands just over 0.5 inch high and has leaves clustered into minute rosettes not unlike those of stonecrop, except they are smaller. Its cream and yellow, forget-me-not–like flowers are about the size of Lincoln's head on a penny. Looking around, I see that all the plants here are small; none grows taller than a few inches. Many have leaves at or barely above ground level. Small stature is another character of many high-elevation plants. By stay-

Most of the area above treeline in Glacier is too rocky and snowbound to support lush communities of alpine plants. (GLACIER NATIONAL PARK)

ing close to the ground, leaves, stems, and flowers escape most of the pruning and drying effects of the wind, while at the same time keeping warm. Thanks to the heat absorbed by rocks and soil, temperatures at ground level are much warmer than those just a foot or two higher, part of the reason I, too, am snuggled so close to the ground. Also, a low-growing plant need not invest as much energy in tissue production, and the precious water it absorbs from the soil has only a short distance to travel before it reaches every leaf and blossom.

Inspecting the rock-jasmine, I notice that its stalk is covered with a thick coat of long, soft hairs. The leaves, too, are hairy, as are the leaves of many alpine plants. In this environment, hairiness serves several purposes. Perhaps most importantly, it diffuses the intense alpine light, which at certain times of the year is strong enough to damage sensitive cells such as those that form the stomata, or breathing pores, of a plant. Hairs also trap precious warmth close to the surface of the plant and allow it to carry on metabolic and reproductive functions at lower temperatures than it could otherwise, activities like photosynthesis, flowering, and seed production. And hairs serve to reduce the amount of water lost through transpiration and to protect the plant against desiccation. Aridity is truly a factor to be reckoned with up here. I pull out my water bottle and take a long drink before rising to face the wind and finish my hike across this tundra landscape.

Cushions and Mats and the Color Red: Survival in the Alpine

When I think of alpine tundra, I think of remote, wild places, of time spent alone in the high mountains, of wildflowers, marmots, goats, and grizzlies. The word *alpine* derives from the Alps but is now used to describe the higher regions of all mountainous areas, while tundra comes to us from Russia, where it means a treeless place. In English, tundra refers to the plants or the plant communities that grow beyond the trees, either at high elevations or in the Arctic (those are the two main types of tundra: arctic, which requires permafrost; and alpine, which does not and which occurs above treeline). So, as a vegetation zone, the alpine tundra portion of Glacier Park is that uppermost band of plant life that stretches from treeline to the point where perpetual snowfields and solid rock make plant growth impossible. And though Glacier's mountain tundra is similar in many ways, such as in the species of plants it supports, to tundra found in other parts of the world, it is also unusual. That is because the glaciers of the last ice age have robbed this place of wide, rolling terrains—the broad, flower-spangled alpine landscapes many people are familiar with from travel brochures and *The Sound of Music*. Except in places like Yellow Mountain and East Flattop Mountain, Glacier's alpine vegetation is not extensive, even though approximately 335,000 acres of the park lie above treeline. The terrain is simply too steep, rocky, and snowbound. And most of the tundra here is sparse and grows on talus and scree slopes or on dry, windswept ridges blown free of snow much of the winter. Lush meadows strewn with alpine wildflowers seen in other high mountain ranges exist only in small isolated pockets in the park.

Scree, an unstable accumulation of fist-to-thumb-size rock fragments;

and talus, a similar accumulation of larger rock pieces, are tough environments for plants. It is difficult for them to become established because of the lack of exposed soil; those that do take root find it difficult to endure because the sharp-edged rocks are constantly shifting, migrating downslope. Consequently, the kinds of plants that grow on scree slopes and talus slides generally have root systems specifically designed to resist uprooting. Most possess either thick taproots that go deep into the underlying soil or intricate tangles of fine, clinging roots or rhizomes that form dense, shallow, underground nets. The milk vetches—alpine, Bourgeau's, bent-flowered, Indian, field, arctic—and yellow sweetvetch fall into the latter category. These members of the pea family send out extended meshes of subsurface rhizomes, which are not roots but horizontal stems. The strategy seems to be to send forth enough earth-hugging lifelines so that even if a large number of them are torn by shifting or falling rocks, recovery is possible. Rhizomes are also able to produce new shoots; thus, rhizome-anchored plants can reproduce without investing the energy required to produce seeds. Thick, flexible taproots, such as those put down by the succulent-leaved alpine springbeauty, are yet another means of staying put while everything else is moving. But instead of clutching the earth with a wide net, these plants attach themselves with a single, resilient tether. Others don't try to stay in one place but migrate downslope with the scree, none the worse for the ride.

One plant that seems almost restricted to life on scree, specifically scree formed from the red argillites of the Grinnell and Snowslip formations, is the pygmy poppy, also known as the alpine glacier poppy. This little, orange-flowered beauty is an endemic, which means it grows only one place in the world, Glacier and Waterton Parks and one or two neighboring peaks. The plant may have evolved from a separate species, one that was once widespread in the alpine but is now extinct or far removed.

The broad top of East Flattop Mountain, which lies just north of Saint Mary Lake, is a good place to experience Glacier's tundra. Except for its expansiveness, the tundra on East Flattop is typical of that found in other areas of the park. This tundra is a fellfield. The term comes from the Gaelic word for stone and refers to a tundra that is 35 to 50 percent bare rock. A fellfield is shaped by almost constant wind and thin, rocky soils. It supports mostly extensive mats of a woody shrub called alpine dryad, interspersed with cushion plants, mosses, and lichens.

The term cushion plant refers not to a species of plant but to a distinctive growth form taken by many different species of perennials: phlox, snow cinquefoil, cushion-buckwheat, carpet pink, sandworts, forget-me-nots, Douglasia, and purple saxifrage, to name a few. Cushioning is one of the most common growth forms in the alpine. Cushion plants look like plump, round pillows. Compact, close to the ground, and hemispherically shaped, wind flows easily over them, like water rushing over rounded river stones. Indeed, from a distance it is easy to imagine a field of cushion plants as a riverbed. While this streamlining minimizes the plants' exposure to the wind, it maximizes the amount of leaf surface exposed for photosynthesis and creates a microclimate effect within the cushion. Both the temperature and humidity inside that umbrella of foliage stay consistently higher than on the outside. Cushions are especially good at conserving moisture. The short, densely packed growth form catches and holds blowing soil and also traps leaves and dead branches that fall from the plant itself. This organic mulch then helps to absorb and hold water beneath the cushion where it is shielded from drying winds.

But even with the favorable microclimate they create, cushion plants grow slowly. A cushion of carpet pink, a relatively fast-growing alpine species, may take five years to grow 0.5 inch high and an additional twenty years to top 7 inches, assuming there are no competing plants nearby. Such a plant may be ten years old before flowering and twenty before flowering profusely. One reason the plant grows so slow is that it invests much of its energy into its root system. Many have 4- to 5-foot-long taproots, which anchor the plant against the wind and ensure a constant source of moisture. Carpet pink plants can grow to be 350 years old.

Mats are another growth form common in the alpine. As the name suggests, a mat plant spreads itself over the surface of the ground like a carpet. Within it, each branch sends down roots; thus the plant anchors

A cushion of carpet pink. These plants can grow to be 350 years old.
(GLACIER NATIONAL PARK)

itself and is able to extract nutrients and water over a wide area, often many square feet. On East Flattop, alpine dryad forms extensive mats, some of which are a century or more in age. A dryad mat not only accumulates soil by catching blowing particles and trapping its own organic debris as cushions do, but it also enriches the soil by fixing nitrogen, an element in short supply in the young soils of fellfields. Our atmosphere is three-quarters nitrogen by weight, but atmospheric nitrogen is generally unavailable to plants and animals; only certain cyanobacteria and bacteria can use it. Through a process called nitrogen fixing, those primitive organisms convert nitrogen gas into an organic form that higher plants and animals can use. Alpine dryad and legumes like sweetvetch have nitrogen-fixing bacteria associated with their roots. Thus wherever they grow, they enrich the soil.

Like whitebark pine, cushion and mat plants are pioneers. On stony, windswept fellfields, they build the soil and provide shelter for other plants with more vulnerable growth forms. It is not uncommon to see shoots of a black alpine sedge sprouting from a cushion of carpet pink or tufts of bluegrass poking through a thick mat of alpine dryad. Those tall invaders, which are often shallow rooted, use cushions and mats as anchors and take advantage of the moisture and warmth they offer. Eventually, after many centuries of soil building, the grasses and sedges will grow thick enough and tall enough to push out the pioneers that nurtured them. And though it may take millennia, the fellfield will eventually be transformed from a dry, rocky place into a lush alpine meadow or turf, all due in large measure to the tenacity of the hardy cushion and mat plants.

Relative to the human clock, many things in the alpine, like soil development and plant succession, take a long time because the growing season is so short, the soils so meager, the climate so cold and dry. Tundra plants, well adapted to these circumstances, operate on entirely different schedules than plants growing in the lowlands. Most are perennials; the alpine season is just too abbreviated for annuals, which must produce all their parts—stems, leaves, flowers, fruit, and seed—within a single season. There are of course exceptions, fast-growing annuals that do well at high elevations, plants able to go from seed to seed in the span of a few cool weeks. Woods whitlow-wort, northern eyebright, and four-parted gentian are examples. And while perennials may take a decade or more to reach maturity, they too are sprinters, racing through the short, alpine growing season. Many start growing beneath the snow and flower within a week after poking through it. Purple saxifrage takes only one to three days to bloom once it emerges from the snow. Some, like mountain pasqueflower, bloom before their leaves unfold, burning sugars stored the preceding season. Because seed ripening takes so long and requires the warmth of mid-summer, early flowering is a must for most alpine plants. Thus, in June and early July, bright spring blossoms in islands of yellow, orange, red, and blue form a patchwork along with slow-melting drifts of snow, especially on fell-fields and scree and talus slopes.

The color red is abundant in Glacier's alpine in the spring, more so in stems and foliage than blossoms. Anthocyanins, the same pigments that render beets and apples red, also color the stems and leaves of many alpine plants, especially early in the season. Like passive solar heaters, plant cells with abundant anthocyanins convert light rays to heat energy and thereby increase a plant's cold hardiness. Thanks to their burgundy and red-colored leaves, some alpine species such as alpine sorrel are able to photosynthesize at temperatures as low as 11°F. The reds tend to fade, however, as days lengthen, summer temperatures warm, and anthocyanins are replaced by green chlorophyll.

Another survival strategy of alpine plants is the ability of the seeds of some species to remain viable for long periods. In the Yukon, for example, seeds of lupine taken from "permanently" frozen lemming burrows germi-nated within forty-eight hours when placed on damp paper and kept at the proper temperature. Based on the level of soil from which they were removed, it is believed the seeds were at least 10,000 years old. There are other equally amazing, scientifically verified accounts of delayed germina-tion. Just how many years that germ of alpine life can endure locked within its seed remains a question.

The Meadows

Alpine meadows nurture a different kind of tundra than that of the fellfields. They have fewer cushion plants, and their flowers tend to bloom later in the season. In a meadow, soils are deeper, winds milder, and moisture more abundant, so there are fewer physical demands placed on the plants. The tundra is diverse enough to have layers: at the bottom, mosses and lichens; above those, a carpet of tiny to medium-size flowers; on top, a canopy of thin-leaved grasses and sedges. All these plants, while still adapted to a life at high altitudes, embrace fewer of the modifications common to the pioneers of the fellfield: succulent, hairy, thick-skinned leaves, for instance.

Near Logan Pass, gentle, south-facing slopes watered by snowmelt support some of the lushest alpine meadows in the park, green patches of wet tundra. These sites, characterized by relatively mild microclimates and exceptionally damp soils, are unusual in that they nurture a large number of arctic species, plants that, in Glacier, are at or near the southern limits of their ranges. One is northern eyebright, a tiny, white-flowered, water-loving annual that also grows in Scandinavia, Greenland, and northern Maine. Three-flowered rush, another water-lover, grows in the Arctic and Logan Pass and a few widely scattered alpine locations south of the park. Little false-asphodel is found in the Arctic, British Columbia, and Glacier.

The wet tundra of the Logan Pass area found above treeline also supports Montana's only carnivorous alpine plant, the common butterwort. Its rosette of soft, fleshy leaves contains thousands of tiny glands that exude a slimy substance attractive to insects. The genus name, *Pinguicula*, means "greasy little one." Small flies and other organisms land on the leaves, become entrapped in the slime, die, and are digested by enzymes. In July and August the plant bears bright purple, violet-like flowers on single, leafless stems. The rest of the year, the insect-eating leaves are all that is visible.

These wet tundra communities are amazingly diverse, harboring dozens of vascular plants, mosses, and lichens. In Glacier many of these plants are found only in the wet meadows within a few miles of Logan Pass; a number are found nowhere else in the northern Rockies, though they may be common in the Arctic. What is it about these Logan Pass sites that allows the persistence of so many rare species? All the sites have several factors in common. First, they occur on gentle, south-facing slopes at the edge of precipitous headwalls. This combination prevents deep snows from accumulating and allows for early snowmelt and a longer growing season. Second, wet tundra communities are above treeline where summer temperatures generally stay cool. Third, the areas are watered by runoff from perennial snowfields. The Logan Pass area appears to be the only place in the park where all these factors, which are typical of the Arctic, come together. Hence Glacier's wet tundra communities might be considered disjunct examples of arctic tundra.

Birds of the Alpine

Alpine birds have developed special modifications to cope with the rigors of life above treeline, just as alpine plants have. Of the 250-plus birds found in the park, the male white-tailed ptarmigan is the only one that spends both winter and summer in the alpine. Females migrate just down-slope into the willow and alder thickets of the upper subalpine for the winter. The size of a bantam chicken and ground-dwelling, both male and female ptarmigans spend as much as eight to nine months of the year on snow. To get around, they have evolved the avian equivalent of snowshoes, a layer of stiff feathers on both the tops and bottoms of their feet. The adaptation, unique in the bird world, increases the amount of surface area contacting the snow by as much as 400 percent. Thus, ptarmigans can walk on the snow where other birds of the same weight would only plow through it. Feathered feet and legs also preserve heat, another energy saver. *Lagopus*, the generic name for the species, means "hare-footed" in Greek.

The word *ptarmigan,* however, comes to us from the Gaelic where it could mean either "mountaineer" or "white game." Both descriptions fit, the former for obvious reasons, the latter because ptarmigan turn snow white in winter, a perfect camouflage. In summer the ptarmigan's plumage is a speckled mix of tundra colors: olivaceous gray, brown, black, buff. And in between, when snowdrifts lace the alpine, the birds are piebald, literally half white and half brown, once again, camouflaged. During spring and fall, they

As white as snow in winter, a ptarmigan will burrow into the snow to keep warm at night. (GLACIER NATIONAL PARK)

spend most of their time at the edges of snowdrifts, where they are hardest to see. A big, ground-oriented bird that lives on open ridges and slopes is extremely vulnerable to predation; hence selection has favored the ptarmigan with cryptic plumage. So good is the bird's ability to blend with its background that often only its movements give it away. So ptarmigans move slowly and tend to sit tight when threatened. In fact, females on a nest sit so tightly they can often be touched before they'll flush. Once, on a hike over Piegan Pass, I almost put my foot on a nesting hen. She exploded off the nest an instant before I touched her. Startled, I flew in the other direction. She landed a short distance away and immediately began feigning a broken wing, as sandpipers and many other ground nesters will. It is not surprising that I failed to see her; female ptarmigans delay nesting until they have completely finished molting. Also, they are meticulous nest-keepers, going so far as to eat their own feathers to keep their nests as inconspicuous as possible.

Aside from feathers, ptarmigans find plenty to eat in the alpine. Meals include leaves, buds, flowers, seeds, berries, and, to a lesser extent, insects.

Ptarmigans are especially fond of willows, and the tiny alpine willows that grow in the park—the arctic, the snow, and the rock willow—make up the bulk of their diet. In the winter, ptarmigans form single-sex flocks and browse twig tips and buds. When they have had their fill, they burrow beneath the snow to stay warm, insulated by snow and feathers.

White-tailed ptarmigan, like Canada geese, generally mate for life. How the mates locate each other in spring after spending the winter apart, no one knows for sure.

The water pipit prefers meadows and marshes over fellfields. According to my bird book, the word *pipit* is Latin and simply means "to chirp," although the bird's call, which sounds like *pippit*, could also be the source of the name. Unlike ptarmigans, which live year-round in the park, water pipits are only summer residents; they spend their winters in El Salvador, Guatemala, and Honduras. And whereas ptarmigans are plant eaters, pipits thrive on insects and other small organisms, terrestrial and aquatic. They'll pluck black flies, mosquitoes, butterfly larvae, moths, ladybugs, beetles, wasps, grasshoppers, spiders, and millipedes from snow or vegetation and wade the shallow margins of ponds and marshes for snails and the larvae of caddisflies and other aquatic insects. Sparrow-size birds, pipits stride rather than hop their way across the tundra, tails bobbing and swinging all the way.

Other birds you may spot in the alpine include white-crowned sparrows, horned larks, rosy finches, pine siskins, Townsend's solitaires, Clark's nutcrackers, Steller's jays, calliope hummingbirds, blue grouse, white-throated swifts, spotted sandpipers, ravens, golden eagles, merlins, gyrfalcons, and prairie falcons. This list is much smaller than that of any other vegetation zone in the park, and only the first three on it nest consistently in the alpine.

I once had a roommate who loved birds and often spent his weekends and days off driving long distances to see new species. He had not seen a rosy finch, a bird that breeds and nests in the rocks above treeline and winters in the subalpine. He was handicapped, so it was difficult for him to get into the high country. But one fall, on a trip to Glacier, we stopped along the Going-to-the-Sun Road, and a small flock of rosy finches lit on the cliffs above us. In every Christmas card he has sent since, he recalls that moment. Rosy finches are a treat to see, with their plump brown bodies, their rose-colored wings, rumps, and bellies, and little gray caps. In spring and summer, their alpine diet includes both insects and plant matter. In fall and winter, however, they eat only the seeds of grasses and herbs. Rosy finches are tame, gregarious little birds. Small flocks of them will often feed on rock faces only a few feet away from hikers or climbers. In winter huge flocks of rosy finches, numbering up to a thousand birds, will roost together in sheltered locations. Interestingly, the males typically outnumber the females by six to one, a ratio that holds true year-round. Whatever the explanation for such a strong gender imbalance, it makes for plenty of battling come breeding time.

Male rosy finches court by slowly raising and lowering their rose-colored wings. Once a male has won a female, the pair builds a bulky, cup-shaped nest of moss, grass, lichen, goat hair, and ptarmigan feathers in a rock crevice near the top of a mountain. Nutcrackers occasionally rob finch nests of their eggs.

To Sleep or Not to Sleep

The mammals of the alpine come in all sizes and have a variety of ways of coping with the cool, short summers and long winters at high altitudes. Some, like ground squirrels and marmots, survive the deep snows and chill of winter by hibernating. Others, like pikas, are active all year.

Pikas, which live in colonies, look like squirrels without tails but are classified with rabbits and hares in the order Lagomorpha. Like their rabbit and hare cousins, pikas have two pairs of upper incisors. Rodents, by contrast, have just one. Pikas and rabbits also possess a scrotum that sits in front of the penis rather than behind it, a trait shared only by marsupials. Gone are the long rabbit ears, however. Their hind legs are decidedly unrabbit-like, too, being not much longer than their front legs. Obviously, this lagomorph is not a leaper.

The pika lives in rockslides and boulder fields, where hopping wouldn't do much good. Instead, it dives into the rock piles to escape most predators. On the way it issues an alarm call, a single, sharp *eep!* that you will almost certainly hear if you pass near a rock pile in Glacier's alpine. It has a ventriloquial quality, sounding more distant than it really is. Predation pressures have affected pika behavior in other ways, too. In fact, all the members of the rabbit family have evolved the unusual habit of gorging themselves on vegetation, then retreating to a secure place, where they defecate. In that safe location, they re-ingest the pellets at their leisure, extracting from them the balance of the nutrients.

Pikas also show specific adaptations to a life in the dry, cold alpine. For example, they do not urinate; instead they "deposit" what are almost solid crystals of uric acid. This trait saves moisture. And pikas have fur on the soles of their feet, a feature like the ptarmigan's feathery snowshoes, except the pika's furred soles are designed to provide traction for dashes over wet and icy rocks, as well as some extra warmth.

Pikas survive the frigid alpine winters not by hibernating but by putting up hay. Late in the summer, these little farmers begin clipping greens—grasses, sedges, and herbs—and carrying them crosswise in their mouths

Pikas are members of the rabbit family that live in alpine rock piles. Awake all winter, they get by on grasses and sedges that they dry and store throughout the summer. (GLACIER NATIONAL PARK)

Hoary marmots hibernate in the winter, so all summer long they concentrate on putting on fat by eating as much as they can and by lounging in the sun on boulders.
(GLACIER NATIONAL PARK)

back to their rock piles. There they spread them out to cure in the sun. When it rains, they scramble about, hauling the little piles into sheltered places beneath boulders and such, for as every farmer knows, wet hay stands a good chance of molding. After the piles cure, the pikas store them in "haystacks" deep within their rock piles, nine months' worth of winter food that allows them to stay active the entire year. Lest there be any doubt how hard these guys work, a single 5-ounce pika will put up some 30 pounds of dry hay.

But if the alpine has its industrious little farmers, it also has its couch potatoes. Hoary marmots pass their summers either stretched out in the sun or eating. Both activities get them in shape for the rest of the year, which they spend sleeping, or more accurately, hibernating. The alpine version of the woodchuck, hoary marmots are large members of the squirrel family. They weigh as much as 30 pounds, much of it fat. Summer portliness is a requisite of hibernation; animals that sleep through the winter get by entirely on what they can store in the form of lipids. And they have to store plenty in Glacier because the alpine winters often last eight months or longer. Many hoary marmots have probably perished during hibernation, either by freezing or starving. But who knows how global climate change will affect this and other hibernators in the decades to come.

Hoary marmots put on their winter reserves by grazing grasses and sedges and tundra delicacies like mountain sorrel, stonecrop, dryad, alpine fireweed, thistle, and dandelion. With pikas as neighbors, they often live in the boulder fields that surround alpine meadows and fellfields. Lounging on flat rocks or shambling through the tundra after wildflowers, occasionally wrestling with their compatriots, hoary marmots seem to have few worries in the world; the biggest of them, at least in the summer, is likely predation. Most predators probably consider a marmot a real prize, a storehouse of fat. So, like pikas, these alpine rock dwellers are on constant alert. They are quick to dive into their boulder piles, but not before piping a warning to relatives and neighbors of the potential danger, be it eagle, cougar, bobcat, lynx, coyote, grizzly, wolverine, wolf, or human. Except instead of "eeping" like pikas, marmots whistle their alarm. It is a far-reaching and piercing call that can be heard for a mile or more across the tundra.

Other rodents of the alpine include Columbian ground squirrels, golden-mantled ground squirrels, least chipmunks, pocket gophers, western jumping mice, deer mice, heather voles, and water voles. Of these, only ground squirrels and western jumping mice are true hibernators; that is, they sleep all winter long while they burn body fat, like their larger cousins, the marmots. The temperature of hibernators drops to near 32°F, and breathing and heart rates slow to a crawl. Least chipmunks are not true hibernators. They spend their winters dozing, but their sleep is comparatively light, their metabolism only slightly depressed. They wake periodically to dine on food stores cached the summer before, so stored body reserves play a relatively minor part in their winter survival. This winter condition is described as a state of torpor or dormancy. Alpine mice and voles are less lethargic. They are active all year; winter finds them scampering along runways or in shallow burrows beneath the snow. All these creatures, from ground squirrel to jumping mouse, play a part in turning, aerating, fertilizing, and generally improving soil in fellfields and meadows. Their activities speed the slow process of alpine succession. Burrows and diggings also allow the soil to absorb and hold water, a tremendous boost to plants, especially on dry fellfields.

Bears, perhaps the most famous winter sleepers of all, are also not true hibernators, although many people, including biologists, use that term to describe them. Their brand of winter lethargy actually falls somewhere between that of least chipmunks and marmots. Bears do not cache food but rely on body stores. Their temperature drops about 8° to 10°F, and their heart rate slows from 40 to 50 beats per minute to 8 to 12. Once in the den, they refrain from urinating and defecating and may sleep for as long as seven months. But grizzly bears and probably black bears have been known to wake from this winter dormancy and travel. It is possible to see fresh grizzly tracks in any winter month in Glacier, and in Yellowstone National Park grizzlies occasionally run down elk in midwinter. Bears seem more flexible than the true hibernators.

Most grizzly bears sleep all winter, but bears emerge even in the coldest months. Although winter sightings are rare, grizzlies have been spotted every month of the year in Glacier. (GLACIER NATIONAL PARK)

As a rule, Grizzly bears den at treeline or in the alpine. Unlike black bears, they excavate their sleeping quarters. Generally they choose sites on leeward slopes, away from prevailing winds, a place where enough snow will accumulate to cover and insulate the entrance. The den is a tunnel dug horizontally into a gentle or moderate slope that terminates in a chamber just large enough to hold the bear. Because females give birth in the den and sleep with their cubs during the following winter, their sleeping chambers may be slightly larger. I visited one den that struck me as too small for the 560-pound animal that had occupied it a few months earlier. The floor of the sleeping chamber was carpeted with a 12-inch-deep bed of dried moss and grass, and from the way it was compressed on one side, I could make out the bear's sleeping form.

Grizzly bears move enormous quantities of earth in their den-digging and in their excavations for roots, bulbs, corms, and burrowing animals, and many plant species benefit. Glacier lilies colonizing dig areas, for example, are larger and produce more seeds than plants in undisturbed areas. Just how much earth do the bears move? One conservative estimate put the volume of Glacier Park stone and soil churned by grizzly bears at 4.8 million cubic feet every century. For comparison, a single avalanche, depending on several variables, might move about 175 cubic feet of earth. The park's grizzly bears move so much earth that geographers believe they are one of the dominant earth-moving forces in the alpine, shapers of both the vegetation and the terrain.

A Buggy Diet

Grizzly bears spend a fair amount of time in the alpine, especially in late summer. In mid-July they begin congregating near the summits of many of the peaks on talus slopes and boulder slides, places that appear to be nothing more than great fields of loose and broken rock perched at the angle of repose, places that seem too barren to support grizzlies. But on those high peaks, under all that rock, army cutworm moths escape the intense summer heat of the plains. They have migrated there from eastern Montana and the Dakotas. Millions of them feed bears from mid-July to mid-September.

Those that escape the bears leave before the snow flies and return to their winter homes on the Great Plains up to 600 miles away.

When the moths first arrive in Glacier in mid-June, they are, by weight, roughly one-third protein and one-third fat. They spend their days under the talus but emerge at night to feed on the nectar of alpine flowers in fellfields and meadows. By fall, when they leave, they are almost 80 percent fat. The bears are there because the moths have as much nutrition as venison—venison has about 7.6 calories per gram, the moths 7.9. But moths are more abundant than deer and easier to catch. The bears face uphill, firmly plant their hind paws, and rake rock downslope, sometimes moving boulders half the size of a Volkswagen, to expose blankets of the gray-winged, thick-bodied moths resting in the cool shadows of the rock. Some fly, most scurry a little. The bears lick them up. During peak feeding periods when moths are abundant, bears eat an estimated 40,000 moths per day. That's equal to about 20,000 calories.

While huckleberries are the bears' staple late-summer food, some prefer moths when they are available. During a good moth year, ten or more bears may use a single peak harboring moths, and plenty of peaks fit that bill. But not all bears visit the peaks. There are probably two kinds of grizzlies in Glacier: Lowland bears leave their high-elevation dens and migrate into the valley bottoms where they stay until autumn. High-country bears leave their dens, migrate into the lowlands, and stay through the spring. In June they move back into the high country, where they remain until fall, a few returning to the lowlands perhaps for berries in August and September, depending on the state of the huckleberry crop. The lowland grizzlies rely mostly on huckleberries and herbs in late summer and fall, whereas those with a high-country orientation eat moths, at least during good moth years. In off years, they too would depend on hucks, but they forage for them at higher elevations.

Some years ladybug beetles also congregate on peaks and may be eaten by bears. Unlike moths, which are in the alpine to escape the summer heat of the plains, ladybugs come to hibernate. Arriving in September and departing in June, they overwinter in the alpine, apparently to escape the cold of the prairies. Ironically, the lee side of mountaintops offer a form of protection low-elevation prairies often lack: a heavy, insulating snow cover. Ladybug aggregations can be so large that a person can collect gallons of them in a matter of hours, and the bears do the same when ladybugs are present. So here's to the continent's largest, most fearsome predator, the grizzly bear, who will climb the highest peaks to prey on . . . ladybugs.

Much of the time grizzly bears spend in the alpine is devoted to eating, but food is not their only interest. Some mountaineers have observed bears on peaks licking rocks bearing salts like magnesium chloride. High-altitude bear scats sometimes contain nothing but salt-rich mineral matter. The peaks may also provide a refuge from the heat and insect pests of lower elevations. Climbers have seen grizzlies draped over snowbanks, perhaps to cool off. One biologist wrote of a dark bear floating in one of Glacier's alpine lakes on a hot afternoon, "blowing bubbles through its submerged snout and then pricking them with its 4-inch-long claws." Others have described grizzlies climbing up and sliding down steep-pitched snowfields. I have seen cubs doing the same, and I have watched a mother grizzly gamboling about with her offspring in a boulder field at 10,000 feet. So even though these winter sleepers feel a strong need to put on summer pounds, they still find time for what could only be described as the ursine equivalent of play and relaxation.

Alpine Ungulates

Deer and elk summer in high-elevation basins, but the time they spend on tundra is short relative to that of two other ungulates—mountain goats and bighorn sheep. Because both species occupy rocky alpine habitats, many visitors confuse them. But in appearance they are quite different. Mountain goats are shaggy, bearded, snow white beasts with relatively short legs, deep chests, and prominent, well-developed shoulders. The horns of both males and females are nearly smooth, coal black, and daggerlike in design. Bighorn sheep, on the other hand, have short coats and are brown to buff in color, except for their large, white rump patch. They are also longer legged and heavier than goats. Their horns are heavier, too, lighter colored, blunt-tipped, and ridged. On rams they form massive curls used in butting battles against other males. Those on females resemble goat horns only in their length.

Like deer and elk, goats and sheep occupy different habitats and eat different foods. In summer, bighorn sheep use a composite of areas—meadows, fellfields, and mid-elevation grassy slopes bordered by cliffs and ledges. In the snow months they live in the windswept parts of valleys or on bordering south- and southwest-facing ridges where forage is blown free of snow and there is plenty of sun. Sheep are not adept at pawing through deep snow for their dinner, which explains why you see them almost exclusively on the east side, where winters are relatively dry and windy. Although fairly general in the terrain they use, bighorn sheep concentrate their diet on grasses, sedges, and herbs.

Mountain goats are not true goats at all, but members of a group of animals called rupicaprids, or rock goats, that includes the Asian goral and the European chamois. They occupy cliff faces year-round. As a rule, the terrain they prefer is rockier, steeper, and generally higher than the sort used by sheep. Even though mountain goats may move downslope into the subalpine in winter, they avoid heavy forests and seldom stray too far from cliffs, their refuge of safety. Their diet, unlike their haunt, is far more general. They eat everything sheep eat, as well as mosses, lichens, trees, and shrubs.

The two species behave differently as well. Sheep are gregarious. Their summer herds, which are made up of ewes, lambs, yearlings, and two-year-olds, average about ten animals. Winter herds, which include the rams, number to one hundred. Goats are semi-gregarious. More cantankerous, they live as solitary individuals or in small interchanging bands, males seldom associating with females and subadults outside the rutting season. Their average year-round group size is only two to three. During the rut, bighorn sheep rams butt heads to determine dominance. Rearing up on hind legs, heads tilted, chins tucked, they lunge at each other at speeds of more than 20 mph. The crack of heads and horns can be heard as far as a mile away. Mountain goat billies, with their relatively thin skulls and deadly, daggerlike horns, spar differently. With females in heat, a pair of equal-size billies will stamp around each other and then often resort to more threatening behavior, making stiletto-like thrusts and short, rapier slashes with their horns. Although billies seldom draw blood in these circumstances, they have been known to maim or kill opponents.

Because mountain goats favor cliff faces and ledges for foraging, bedding, and traveling, their body form is well adapted to a life on the rocks, much more so than sheep. Their center of gravity is low, and the distance between their front and rear legs is considerably shorter than in other ungulates. They have enormous shoulders, which they use to pull themselves up seemingly impossible precipices and for pawing through snow. And they have the ultimate in slip-resistant footwear. The pads of their hooves bear a textured, rubbery surface for gripping wet or icy rock. Mountain goat hair is rough and resists sliding should the animal fall on its side or scoot downhill on its rump. While the influence of predators is the primary shaper in the design of most ungulates, mountain goats appear to be shaped more by terrain. Indeed, more mountain goats die from falls than are killed by predators.

My favorite goat climbing story comes from the classic book *A Beast the Color of Winter*, by Douglas Chadwick. He had been watching a goat edge its way along a thin ledge that tapered down to almost nothing. When the goat had finally gone as far as it could, there was not enough room to turn around. So, Chadwick writes, "after some tentative foot shuffling the mountaineer braced its front hooves on the ledge and slowly raised the rear of its body off the ground. Clenching my hands tighter and tighter on the binoculars, I watched the beast lift its hindquarters higher and higher and begin to roll them straight over its head. The rear hooves touched the wall here and there for an instant, yet what the creature had effectively carried off by the time it was finished was a compete slow-motion cartwheel, or, technically, what gymnasts call a rollover. I put down my binoculars and remembered to breathe, and this mountain goat, an averaged-sized billy, strolled off in the direction from which it had come."

Some 2,000 goats live in the park. Many visitors see them at Logan Pass, where, incidentally, there are also bighorn sheep. They are also seen at Sperry-Gunsight Pass and at Goat Lick on the Middle Fork of the Flathead River near Walton. At Goat Lick they come down from their alpine haunts to lick the Belt rocks, which are high in sodium, calcium, magnesium, and potassium—sodium, it's thought, is the big draw. Visitors have seen as many as seventy-three goats at one time at this lick.

In the 1920s and then again in the 1930s, most of Glacier's bighorn sheep died from a pneumonia-causing parasite known as the lungworm. During the first outbreak, the population of the Many Glacier herd fell from eighty-six to forty animals. During the second, ten years later, the herd dropped from sixty-nine sheep to seventeen. A third epidemic hit in the winter of 1983–84 and killed most of the large rams in herds all the way from Waterton to Saint Mary. The females, too, were affected; they produced no lambs the following spring. Since then, however, the population has rebounded. Aside from these periodic outbreaks of disease, the condition of winter range regulates the herd, and it has deteriorated due to fire suppression. Wild sheep are somewhat fire dependent. By removing trees, fire improves the growth and diversity of the plants sheep favor. Maps from the 1920s and '30s show sheep winter range in areas that are now overgrown with conifers. Sheep no longer use them. Subtract winter range, and you subtract sheep. Conversely, if a natural fire were to burn the range, it just might bring about an increase in the population.

10

Lakes and Streams

Organisms in the park relate to each other in surprising ways. One of the more remarkable partnerships involves grizzly bears and stoneflies.

Near where Nyack Creek empties into the Middle Fork of the Flathead River, the willow, alder, birch, and black cottonwood grow so high and lush that it is difficult to get a view of the valley from the bank. You have to brave the cold rushing water and slick cobble bottom of the river to see

The Middle Fork of the Flathead River in the fall at low water. (GLACIER NATIONAL PARK)

what lies up or downstream. If you were to wade out knee deep into the river to gain this vantage, you would notice first that you were standing in the middle of a broad, long floodplain, most of which is overgrown with a tangle of river-bottom vegetation. You would discover that upstream, about 1.5 miles from where you stand, the canyon narrows, and, as the mountains press closer, the broadleaf riparian vegetation gives way to the same conifers that grow on the mountainsides. If you turned to look downstream, you would see the pattern repeated in the distance. The canyon narrows, the converging bedrock squeezes the gravel floodplain and pinches off the diversity of river-bottom plant life. If you fly over the Middle Fork, you will see one floodplain like this after another, each separated from the next by a narrow canyon, like beads on a string.

We tend to think floods are the main force shaping floodplains and the plant communities that grow on them. But water does not just flow over the surface of the floodplain. As the river leaves the narrow part of the canyon, as much as 20 percent of its water penetrates the porous gravels of the river bottom and begins to flow underground, beneath the bed of the river. Downstream, near the bottom of the floodplain, where the canyon begins to constrict again, there is a great upwelling of water forced by the encroaching underlying bedrock. Spring brooks suddenly appear, and overflow channels begin to flow as far as 0.25 mile away from the actual bed of the river. The downstream end is wetter, soggy in places, and the vegetation more lush with water-loving succulents like wild onion, horsetail, meadowrue, wintergreen, and nettle. And the air has a swampy smell.

A menagerie of insects and other organisms flourish within the Nyack floodplain. Wells drilled deep into the gravel are full of creatures. They include midge and mayfly larvae, riffle beetles, and water mites. But most dramatic are inch-long cream and ivory stonefly larvae that thrive 15 to 20 feet beneath the ground, up to 0.5 mile from the river channel. These ghosts spend up to three years hidden below the floodplain before emerging on the river as adults, where they live for a few weeks. Thus, they spend most of their lives in darkness, confined to the narrow cracks and crevices of the saturated gravels.

Subterranean stoneflies, like these of the Nyack floodplain, are at the top of a food web that releases nutrients for the rich plant communities growing along the river. (JACK A. STANFORD)

These particular species of stoneflies are part of a large community of strange creatures that spend their entire life cycles submerged in floodplain gravels. Among them are primitive worms known as archiannelids, crustaceans called bathynellids that look like little pincerless lobsters, and 0.5-inch-long blind shrimplike creatures called amphipods. All are prey for the much larger stoneflies. These subterranean floodplain communities were discovered on the Nyack just within the last two decades. Since then, we have learned that all mountain rivers have them. To date, researchers working in the Nyack have identified more than eighty different creatures that live deep in the floodplain, more than half of them hitherto unknown (that is, they are entirely new to science).

At the base of this web of life is a subterranean film of fungi and bacteria that coats the alluvial gravels. This film, grazed by the higher organisms, survives by consuming dissolved organic matter—a soup resulting from the decomposition of leaves, twigs, algae, insects, fish—the remnants of everything that lives and dies in a river like the Middle Fork. The processing of all this material as it moves through the subsurface gravels releases large amounts of previously unavailable nutrients, especially reactive phosphorus and nitrates (the former is the limiting nutrient on the floodplain). The result is that the waters of the Middle Fork, which would otherwise be quite infertile, become charged with nutrients. They emerge on the floodplain surface in the form of springs, sometimes several hundred yards away from the river, where they fertilize the riparian zone. Aerial photographs show clearly that the most productive, vigorous plant communities on the floodplain occur where there are upwellings. Studies show that temperatures are more moderate, which causes physical and chemical conditions to be less variable over time.

And that brings us to grizzly bears.

Emaciated grizzly bears emerge from their high-country dens early in the spring and within a few weeks move to low-elevation riparian areas like the Nyack floodplain. In fact, most of the grizzly bears in the park spend a good portion of their first six weeks or so after leaving their hibernation sites on a floodplain; some bears spend their entire summer there. Not only are these wet bottoms free of snow early in the spring but they also harbor a smorgasbord of the foods that bears prefer. Gray and purple sweetvetch, dandelion, clover, equisetum, wild onion, strawberry, butterweed, angelica, and spring beauty are all favorites. The bears feast.

They return later in the summer to graze, dig sweet-root, onion, and bog orchid, and eat gooseberries, raspberries, buffalo berries, and the fruit of hawthorn, devil's club, and honeysuckle, especially during years when the huckleberry crop fails, something that has happened regularly in the past two decades. Cutthroat trout spawn in spring brooks and overflow channels because the constant upwelling of nutrient-laden waters is an ideal nursery for young trout, and the bears are there, too, up to their bellies, splashing through the spawning beds, chasing and catching fat trout.

It is an exuberance of life nourished and in large measure shaped by organisms that live and die in darkness, phantoms that just a decade or two ago we did not know existed.

Deep in the Nyack floodplain, stoneflies search dark crevices for amphipods and bathynellids like mountaintop bears moving talus. Indirectly, these stoneflies feed bears. The lesson of the Nyack floodplain is that there are no solo performances. The spring amblings of bears, the lush growth of floodplain plants, the patient work of crustaceans and stoneflies, the upwellings of rivers—all are strands in the lacework we call nature.

Life in the Water

Unlike much of the West, Glacier is blessed with water. If the 561 streams that tumble from its mountains were placed end to end, they would stretch from West Glacier to Akron, Ohio. Nestled in its mountains and valleys are 762 lakes. Those waters cover some 30,000 acres. The park also has glaciers, tarns, beaver ponds, fens, bogs, marshes, springs, and assorted other wetlands, an enormous diversity of water habitats that provide homes for an equally diverse range of algae, vascular plants, crustaceans, mollusks, insects, fish, amphibians, birds, and mammals.

Let's consider just the insects. Every stream and lake in Glacier has an amazing variety of them: stoneflies, caddisflies, mayflies, dragonflies, springtails, water beetles, water boatmen, water striders, flies, gnats, midges, mosquitoes. Most are aquatic during their immature or larval stages and terrestrial as adults. Many are specialized for a life within a certain kind of water environment. Fly larvae found in rapids, for example, have flattened bodies and attach themselves to rocks with suction discs to keep from washing downstream. Of the caddisflies, one variety living in fast water attaches itself to rocks with a tether of silk. Stonefly larvae living in slower riffles, runs, and pools are heavier bodied and free ranging. They hold on with stout legs.

As winged adults, stoneflies live along the shores of steams, where the males attract females by beating their abdomens against stones. The females thump out their own rhythmic drum sounds in response, then find a male and mate.

Among the most common aquatic insects in Glacier's lakes and streams are caddisflies. Many are weavers and builders. Of the weavers, some of the larvae spin long, narrow nets in the shape of pockets; others

Aquatic insects living in streams are usually quite specialized. Some live only in falls, others in riffles, others in pools. Many prefer a particular side of the rock. For example, some fly larvae live only in very fast water on the upstream side of stones. (JOE WEYDT)

make trumpet-shaped nets; and some attach their meshwork between two or more fixed supports. Periodically they survey these nets for anything edible swept in by the current. Usually they wait near the net opening, ready to pounce on larger prey that might otherwise escape. In Glacier several closely related species share the same rocks. They avoid competition with each other by spinning nets of different mesh sizes or by constructing their nets at different times of the year.

Case-making caddisflies are builders with an altogether different lifestyle. Their soft, caterpillar-like bodies sheathed in portable pebble and twig cases, they move about laboriously on the bottoms of lakes and streams where they forage for dead and living plant material. Each species builds a case of a different design, but most are made from leaf or twig fragments, sand, or tiny rock pieces cemented together with silk into a cylindrical shape. When the larvae is ready to pupate, it anchors this structure to an underwater rock or log, pulls a twig or pebble over the opening, and seals it shut with silk. When, finally, it emerges and crawls out of the stream as an adult, the caddisfly looks and behaves much like a moth. The two orders of insects—Trichoptera and Lepidoptera—are, in fact, related.

Active mostly at night, adult caddisflies feed on nectar. During the day, they hide in the damp undergrowth along streambanks or beneath boulders and logs. Many become meals for fish, birds, bats, shrews, and other small mammals. The larvae are an important fish food. Many an angler, upon opening the belly of a cutthroat trout, has found it packed with the stone or twig cases of caddisfly larvae.

A Salamander, a Toad, and Four Frogs

Only a few amphibians live in Glacier Park because it is so cold. Long-toed salamanders, with their single, almost neon yellow-green stripe, conceal themselves beneath logs and rocks along many of the lower-elevation lakes and streams west of the divide. Boreal toads, chunky and warty, are active both day and night from the valley bottoms to the alpine. Their diet consists of insects, worms, slugs, snails, rodents, and even other toads. When they themselves are threatened, say by a coyote or bear, they secrete a foul-tasting, sticky white poison from a large, kidney-shaped gland that sits just behind each eye. When faced with drought, the toads dig burrows with their powerful front legs. Sometimes they simply claim the tunnels of mice and voles. I have heard boreal toads peeping at elevations as high as 7,000 feet. They sound very much like a clutch of baby ptarmigans. One visitor saw a toad at 8,000 feet on Mount Brown. Boreal toads are becoming harder to find, however, because they are disappearing throughout much of their range. Spotted frogs, with their gray to light brown speckled bodies, can be found at the marshy edges of ponds and lakes and along slow-moving streams in the park to mid-elevations. Unlike leopard frogs, which they resemble, spotted frogs have rear legs that are colored orange-red on the underside. They mate in early spring, while there is still ice rimming the edges of most ponds, their mating call a rapid, low-pitched croak. Pacific tree frogs live in the park, too, but only at the lowest elevations, in the Lake McDonald area primarily. In spring you can hear them singing out their familiar, high-pitched "ribbets" as they perch on slick boulders or cling to shrubs and herbs with their suction-cup–like toes. Boreal chorus frogs also call the park home (though first confirmed in the park only as recently as 2001), and like Pacific tree frogs they, too, are restricted to just a few places—Railroad Creek and perhaps the Red Eagle drainage.

The only other amphibian found here is the tailed frog, one of the most primitive frogs in the world. Its closest relative is found 8,000 miles away on the North Island of New Zealand. Among its primitive characteristics, the ones shared with ancient fossil frogs, is a relatively heavy skeleton. The species has nine vertebrae, two pairs of ossified ribs, and a prepubis bone. Except for the three related New Zealand species, all other frogs in the world have seven vertebrae, no ribs, and no prepubis bone. The theory is that evolution favored frogs with a reduced and therefore lighter frame to facilitate leaping. Tailed frogs have also retained tail-wagging muscles, which other frogs have lost. These, it should be noted, have nothing to do with the male's false "tail," for which the creature has been given its common name. That structure is a penislike extension of the cloaca, and, unlike true amphibian tails, it plays no role in locomotion. Rather, the tailed frog's tail-wagging muscles are vestigial, from a time when adults had true tails like salamanders. Judging by the fossil record, frogs lost their tails long ago, probably because tails hindered jumping.

Whereas some consider this species "primitive," it might be more accurate to say it has simply remained in a successful form—one that has withstood the test of time—for tailed frogs lay claim to waters where there are no other frogs: high, cold, fast-moving streams. They lack vocal sacs and ear membranes; apparently the roar of the turbulent water has made those structures unnecessary. Their lungs are greatly reduced as well because tailed frogs conduct much of their respiration through their highly vascularized skin, which they can do in these well-oxygenated waters.

Their method of breeding is unique among frogs, too. The short, pear-shaped "tail" borne by males is really a cloaca turned inside out, and is considered a forerunner of the reptilian penis. Like a penis, it becomes hard

Tailed frogs, one of the most primitive frogs in the world, are common in many of Glacier's highest, coldest, and swiftest streams, especially tributaries of the Middle Fork of the Flathead River. (JOE WEYDT)

and is inserted into the female; internal fertilization keeps sperm from washing downstream. In almost all other species of frog, the males simply spew their sperm over the eggs as they are being laid.

Unlike the tadpoles of other frogs, tailed frog tadpoles lack external gills, again because they do not need them in oxygen-rich streams. They have huge, suckerlike mouths that take up half the lower surface of their bodies. The structure enables them to cling tightly to rocks even in the most raging torrents. Their bodies are slate gray in color, their tails stout, much more robust than those of other tadpoles. Because temperatures are so cool here, they take three full years to develop into adults.

When, finally, tailed frogs do emerge as small-bodied and big-eyed adults, all signs of the sucking disc are gone, and their delicate-looking, inch-long bodies have turned slightly lumpy and taken on a rust to olive green dappling, each individual's specific color closely matching the rocks on which it lives. Like tadpoles, adults develop slowly. It takes up to seven to eight years for one to become sexually mature. Adults spend their whole lives within the stream's spray zone. Hiding beneath logs and rocks by day, they emerge at night to feed on ticks, snails, mites, spiders, centipedes, millipedes, insects, and various crustaceans. These they catch in a decidedly unfroglike manner. Because their tongues attach to the backs of their mouths rather than the fronts, they can't flip them out to catch their prey as other frogs can. Instead, tailed frogs hunt like salamanders, snapping up their quarry at close quarters.

The only other vertebrates harbored by Glacier's clear, cold waters are fish. Twenty-four species, seventeen of which are native, live in the park. Among them are members of the trout, sculpin, minnow, sucker, pike, and codfish families. Of these, the trout family is the largest, with ten representatives, of which just five are indigenous: westslope cutthroat trout, bull trout, lake trout, mountain whitefish, and pygmy whitefish. Lake trout, though introduced into lakes throughout Glacier, were originally found only in the Hudson Bay drainage in the northeast corner of the park.

Cutthroats: One of the Natives

On June 13, 1805, Silas Goodrich, one of the youngest members of the Lewis and Clark Expedition, caught half a dozen cutthroat trout with a hook and line from the Great Falls of the Missouri River. In his journal that day, Captain Meriwether Lewis wrote: "These trout are from sixteen to twenty-three inches in length, precisely resemble our mountain or speckled trout in form and the position of their fins, but the specks on these are of a deep black instead of the red or goald of those common in the U' States. These are furnished with long teeth on the pallet and tongue and have generally a small dash of red on each side behind the front ventral fins; the flesh is of a pale yellowish red, or when in good order, of a rose red." The description is the first we have of the westslope subspecies, the only cutthroat trout native to Glacier Park. Later that night, Lewis added another entry: "The fare was really sumptuous this evening: buffaloe's hump, tongues and marrowbones. Fine trout parched meal, pepper and salt, and a good appetite, the last is not considered the least of the luxuries."

Westslope cutthroat trout, named for their primary area of distribution and for what Lewis described as a "small dash of red" beneath the gills, were the dominant fish on the west side of Glacier Park prior to the days of fish stocking. They even occurred in a few places on the east side in the Hudson Bay drainage. Restricted by waterfalls and other natural barriers, westslope cutthroat never made it into the high country, though they were abundant in most of the low- to mid-elevation lakes and streams. Cerulean Lake, at 4,660 feet, is the highest elevation water where they occur naturally.

Several different life histories are represented in the westslope cutthroat trout populations that live in the park. Some spend their adult lives in large lakes outside of Glacier Park and migrate upstream into tributaries within the park to spawn. After spawning, they return to their home lake. Others live their entire lives in rivers and streams and seldom, if ever, enter lakes. They may migrate out of the park into the North and Middle Forks, or they may remain in or near their natal drainage for life. Still other westslope cutthroats live in lakes within the park and only leave briefly to spawn in adjacent inlet and outlet streams. They then return to a nearby lake in the same drainage. These "lake-adapted" cutthroats may be genetically distinct from those that migrate in and out of the park. In spite of their different life histories, all three populations become sexually mature at age three or four (occasionally five), although their respective sizes at maturity vary. Migratory adults may exceed 14 inches, while nonmigratory adults are typically under 10. All spawn in the spring, from May through July depending on elevation, when water temperatures reach about 50°F. During spawning, all build gravel nests, called redds, at the heads of riffles or the tails of pools.

Female cutthroats are the nest builders; the males stand by to chase off other males or predatory fish. To construct a redd, the female turns on her side and repeatedly flips her body, each time moving gravel and raising a small cloud of silt and fine rock that washes downstream. Working like this for several hours, she digs a 4- to 6-inch depression in the riverbed. Then, joined by the male, she settles into this hollow. As their bodies quiver and bump, the female pushes her anal fin against the bottom of the nest and lays her first batch of eggs, the male's sperm fertilizing them as they emerge. After depositing 300 or 400 eggs, the female moves just upstream and excavates a second hollow. The gravels she throws up from it wash downstream and bury the eggs in the first. When this second redd is finished, the pair deposits and fertilizes another several hundred eggs, then moves upstream to excavate a third hole. In this manner, they lay, fertilize, and bury some 1,200 eggs, although the actual number of eggs varies depending on the size of the fish. They will stay near the redd for a week or so, presumably resting, then migrate back to their home lake or stream.

Depending upon water temperatures, westslope cutthroat eggs hatch from thirty to sixty days after being laid. The young, called alevins, remain buried in their spawning gravels for up to two weeks, nourished by their still-attached yolk sacs. Once they emerge into the stream, mortality is high. Competition, disease, and predators will claim 99 percent of them by the end of the first year. Eighty percent of the survivors will die over the next three years. A heavy toll, but then, only two of the pair's many hundreds of offspring need survive for the population to remain stable.

Unlike bull trout or other subspecies of cutthroat, westslope cutthroat are typically not fish eaters. Caddisflies, mayflies, blackflies, and plankton usually make up the bulk of their diet. One June evening, as I sat on the bank of Bowman Creek with my three-year-old daughter, dozens of mayflies suddenly began emerging from the water. Almost immediately, fish started rising. The insects accumulated. They drifted by the hundreds over the smooth riffles, their wings drying along the way. More trout rose. As the insects took to the air, so did the fish. The stream churned with activity. Moments later, nighthawks arrived, perhaps a dozen of them. One after another they swooped down from a rose-colored sky into the clouds of mayflies hanging above the creek. The canyon boomed with the sound of air moving through feathers. Our quiet moment had, in a matter of minutes, become an explosion of life, a primeval flurry of insect, fish, and bird. We watched until the light faded.

The Problem with Imports

Yellowstone cutthroat trout, rainbow trout, brook trout, kokanee salmon, Lake Superior whitefish, and grayling have all been introduced to the park or have invaded it from connecting streams and rivers. For decades, the Park Service, the Great Northern Railway, and individuals planted millions of nonnative fingerlings, fry, and eggs into almost any water that was considered fishable. The idea was to attract tourists, most of whom fished. In the early days there was a hatchery at East Glacier, and in 1947 another was built at Creston; both were dedicated to raising fish for the park. Not until the 1940s and '50s did biologists begin to question whether introducing nonnative species might threaten native fish or destroy unique aquatic communities. And it wasn't until 1971 that Glacier National Park stopped its stocking program altogether. Still, nonnative fish continue to enter the park by way of the North and Middle Forks of the Flathead River.

Perhaps it's because we are terrestrial organisms that we find it difficult to appreciate the problems associated with fish stocking. For example,

Kokanee salmon, not native to Glacier Park, were introduced to some park lakes, where at times they competed with native westslope cutthroat trout. But in recent years, Kokanee populations in the park have crashed. (GLACIER NATIONAL PARK)

would anyone agree with a plan to plow up native plants in the foothill grassland communities of the North Fork in order to replace them with alfalfa and Kentucky bluegrass? How many would prefer to see European chamois grazing alongside mountain goats or Tibetan black bears mixing with grizzly bears? Indeed, aside from the philosophical conflicts, we have known for a long time that even the most well-intentioned introductions can wreak havoc on native communities. The National Park Service's Organic Act of 1916 has as one of its basic tenets the preservation of indigenous plants and animals. Sixty years of fish stocking, however, has made that mandate difficult to meet.

Introduced fish can bring in diseases and parasites. They can hybridize or compete with native stocks, or alter habitats in such a way that makes them unsuitable for natives. They can change plankton and aquatic insect communities, disrupt food chains, and prey on the eggs, fry, and even adults of native fish. In the worst cases they can eliminate indigenous species and initiate chain reactions that affect dozens of organisms and take centuries to settle out.

All of this disruption has occurred in Glacier Park's aquatic communities as a consequence of fish stocking. Rainbow trout and Yellowstone cutthroat trout planted in some drainages have hybridized with and displaced indigenous trout populations. Lake trout, introduced to several of the lakes on the west side, prey on and compete with native bull trout to the extent that the native is now uncommon in Lake McDonald and Kintla, Bowman, and Logging Lakes. Bull trout may even disappear from those lakes. Eastern brook trout, introduced to the Middle Fork of the Flathead, hybridize with bull trout. More important, because eastern brook trout become sexually mature at a young age, are short-lived, and tend to reproduce in overwhelming numbers, they could ultimately eliminate bull trout from the drainage. That has happened under similar circumstances elsewhere in Montana. Brook trout and lake trout introductions along with habitat destruction caused by logging and other developments have imperiled the bull trout over most of its range, and the fish is now designated as threatened under the federal Endangered Species Act. In Glacier Park fishing for bulls is prohibited; any bull trout accidentally caught must be han-dled with extreme care and immediately released.

Westslope cutthroat trout have also suffered. Park biologists estimate that lake populations of westslope cutthroat are imperiled by nonnative species through 84 percent of their original range. This figure is based on acres, as opposed to the number of waters they occupy. Healthy and genet-ically unaltered populations of native westslope cutthroat trout persist in fifteen of the park's lakes, all in the Middle and North Forks of the Flat-head River drainage. They escaped hybridization, even though almost all of the lakes where they live were repeatedly stocked with rainbow trout (*Oncorhynchus mykiss*) and/or Yellowstone cutthroat trout (*O. clarki bou-vieri*); both can interbreed with westslope cutthroat (*O. clarki lewisi*).

To learn how they managed such a feat, you could place a small west-slope cutthroat trout in an aquarium with a bull trout (if the bull trout would fit), and watch what happens. Chances are, when the westslope cut-throat sees the bull trout, it will dart for cover. But if you put a small, hatchery-reared rainbow or Yellowstone cutthroat trout in that same aquar-ium, it would likely sit there until the bull trout gobbled it up. Because westslope cutthroat trout evolved with bull trout, they possess an innate fear of this most aggressive fish predator. They know instinctively bull trout mean trouble, and they waste no time fleeing. The hatchery fish generally lack this trait. And in Yellowstone Park, where Yellowstone cutthroats come from, it is safe, even advantageous, to migrate from streams into lakes within a day or two after being born and to stay there for the next year or two. But in Glacier Park, when planted Yellowstone cutthroat moved into lakes as juveniles, they immediately became food for bull trout and north-ern pike minnow; few survived to breed. The park's native cutthroat trout escape that kind of predation by staying in their natal streams until they are at least two years old and large enough to avoid being eaten by bull trout. And while stream-dwelling bull trout still take a toll on young westslope cutthroat trout, that toll is considerably lower than it would be in a lake.

Yellowstone cutthroat also encountered a new tapeworm in the park, one with a distinctly different life cycle than the tapeworm found in the

Westslope cutthroat trout are found only in lakes below 4,700 feet. Most of the higher lakes, such as Old Man Lake at 6,400 feet, were originally barren of fish because of winter kill and obstacles like waterfalls that prevented fish from reaching them. (JOCK PRIBNOW)

Yellowstone drainage. The parasite poses little trouble for the park's indigenous trout because they evolved with it. But it probably caused serious problems for the nonnative Yellowstone cutthroat and likely accounted for substantial mortality, taking much of what the bull trout missed.

Yellowstone cutthroat may also be more prone to migrate than westslope cutthroat, and some of the stocked fish probably left the park via the North Fork or Middle Fork. Biologists, however, believe the two big reasons Yellowstone cutthroat fared so poorly on the west side are bull trout and the tapeworm. They point out the only waters where the nonnative was able to establish itself were lakes previously barren of fish. It succeeded there only because both bull trout and the parasite were absent.

In short, nonnative cutthroat failed to become established or to hybridize with natives to any significant degree because they were poorly adapted to the park's environment. Today, it is rainbow trout that pose most of the hybridization threat for the park's westslope cutthroat trout. But let's imagine that by chance, some Yellowstone cutthroat trout had been able to hybridize, that they had been able to pass their genes into the native population. It is possible that, by so doing, they would have rendered the native cutthroat less fit, less able to survive rapacious bull trout or parasitic tapeworms, or more inclined to migrate out of the park. Stocking, like Russian roulette, is risky business, even when dealing with closely related subspecies. As it happens, lake-adapted populations of westslope cutthroat trout outside of Glacier Park have been all but destroyed by a combination of nonnative introductions and habitat loss. It is estimated that, partly as a result of hybridization, genetically pure westslope cutthroat trout populations are present now in only about 2.5 percent of their historic range. Thus, Glacier Park is this fish's largest and one of its only remaining strongholds, one of the subspecies' last hopes for survival, a sad state of affairs for what is considered to be the first trout to have populated the upper Columbia River Basin.

The park's cutthroat face at least one other challenge. Lake trout, which prey on smaller fish, are apparently eating large numbers of young cutthroat. Hence, in lakes where lake trout are well established, the outlook for the native is not good.

Ten Thousand Years of Isolation

Pleistocene glaciation has created some unique fish populations in the park. The westslope cutthroat of Avalanche Lake are an example. They are probably a relic population that has been isolated from other indigenous cutthroat for at least 10,000 to 12,000 years. During the Pleistocene, a local montane glacier or a series of temporary ice dams in the drainage may have allowed cutthroat trout to make incremental movements up the gorge, until they eventually reached the lake. When the ice dams broke or the glacier melted, the fish in Avalanche Lake became isolated from other indigenous populations. They have remained that way ever since, the waterfalls of Avalanche Creek posing too much of a barrier for immigrating native trout.

A similar situation exists in Upper Kintla Lake, where the bull trout population shows evidence of its isolation. Probably during the late Pleistocene, ice dams made it possible for bull trout to ascend waterfalls about 2 miles downstream from the lake. Other species native to the drainage apparently didn't make the trip. Without other fish to prey on, the Upper Kintla Lake bulls took to eating plankton, 0.25-inch-long shrimplike amphipods known as scuds. Today scuds are all they eat; they show no evidence of the cannibalism common to other bulls. It is as if mountain lions switched to a diet of grasshoppers.

The small size of Upper Kintla Lake bull trout is probably due to the fact that it takes much more energy to capture a pound of scuds than is required to catch a one-pound fish. Also, Upper Kintla Lake is a very cold lake with a relatively short growing season.

Because of their diet, Upper Kintla bull trout are smaller than the bull trout found in other park waters. A fourteen-year-old might weigh 7 pounds, for example, whereas a similar-aged bull from the North Fork might go 20 to 25 pounds. The reproductive behavior of these plankton eaters differs as well. They spawn at a younger age, for example, and they spawn in lake outlets. Other bull trout use lake inlets. Upper Kintla Lake bulls also spawn later in the season than other bulls, although this probably has more to due with water temperature than anything else. Bull trout

Waterfalls like this one prevent fish from migrating upstream. Ice dams created by glaciers of the last ice age, however, made it possible for fish to pass over some falls. (JOE WEYDT)

spawn in the fall when stream temperatures reach around 48°F. Because of the warming that goes on in the lake, the outlet reaches that temperature well after most inlets of other lakes.

Even with all their differences, Upper Kintla Lake bull trout have not diverged enough genetically from other bull trout to be classified as a distinct subspecies, though they are considered a separate race. The population, at any rate, is an example of evolution at work; of the bull trout that migrated into the lake, those able to eat plankton and spawn in the outlet were more successful at passing on their genes than the fish without those traits.

Fish in Upper and Lower Isabel Lakes in the Middle Fork drainage have also been isolated from other indigenous populations. There, bull trout and westslope cutthroat trout are found together, and the two have developed a peculiar association. The cutthroats are larger than the bulls and tend to be more robust. Elsewhere, where these two species occur together, just the opposite is true, and in a big way: A large cutthroat trout will reach 18 to 20 inches, whereas a big bull trout may exceed 3 feet in length. Further, in the Isabel Lakes, the bull trout have distinctive pumpkin-colored fins that become brilliant crimson during spawning. Some people have speculated that this unusual coloration is the result of the bulls hybridizing with brook trout. Lower Isabel Lake was planted with 2,000 brookies in 1933 in advance of a visit by President Hoover. But bull-brook trout hybrids are usually sterile after the third generation, and genetic and morphologic analyses show no evidence of hybridization. The colors are most likely a consequence of the population's long-term isolation.

The traits exhibited by these stranded populations of cutthroat and bull trout are typical of animals cut off from the main. Populations faced with a restricted diet and a limited gene pool are often small or oddly colored or show variances in their behavior. Sometimes these outlying populations give rise to new species. Who knows, maybe someday one of Glacier's long-isolated populations of native trout will become distinct enough to be considered a separate species. Perhaps one day a population of "pygmy bulls" or "greater cutthroats" will swim out of one of these lakes and find its way into the North Fork or the Middle Fork.

Where to Find Wildlife

Mammals

It is perhaps a quirk of human nature that the animal people most want to see when they visit Glacier National Park is also the one they fear most. "I'd love to see a grizzly," they say, "but only from a safe distance or from my car." Most park visitors, however, never see a **grizzly bear.** Even for hikers the experience is uncommon. As a rule, the species is shy of people. There are, of course, exceptions. When grain spilled along the Burlington Northern Railway began to ferment in 1990, as many as twenty grizzly bears gathered to feed along the 3-mile stretch of U.S. Highway 2 that paralleled the spill. For several summers, people saw grizzly bears on a daily basis. Sometimes, too, grizzlies lose their natural shyness and begin to frequent areas used by people. For instance, in the summer of 1994, a young male grizzly bear hung around the Logan Pass boardwalk for several weeks, forcing periodic closures of the walkway. All bears are potentially dangerous to humans. Grizzlies can attack without warning and are exceptionally fast. A charging adult can cover 60 feet in a second. Please read the section at the end of this book on precautions you should take to avoid encounters with bears and lions. In addition, if you plan a hike, talk with park rangers about bear activity in the area you plan to visit.

Wolves are another animal many visitors would like to glimpse. But like grizzly bears, wolves are secretive animals. The North Fork Valley is the most likely area to see them, winter and spring the best seasons. Wolves, which at a distance are easily mistaken for coyotes, stand about 3 feet high and weigh up to 90 pounds (coyotes are only 2 feet tall and weigh 25 pounds). You're more likely to hear wolves howl, which can be just as thrilling as actually seeing one.

Mountain lions are primarily nocturnal hunters, but they are sometimes seen by visitors. Once again, the North Fork is a good place to look for them. These large animals with long tails can reach 6 to 8 feet in length. In low light, it can be difficult to distinguish one from a wolf or coyote or

During the rut, some bighorns compete for females by butting heads.
(GLACIER NATIONAL PARK)

bear, but if you see a long tail, it's probably a lion. Like bears, lions can be dangerous. Again, consult the section at the end of this book for information on how to behave should you encounter one.

Mountain goats are common in Glacier Park and easy to see. Logan Pass on Going-to-the-Sun Road, Goat Lick on US 2, and Gunsight and Siyeh Passes in the backcountry are all good places to observe and photograph these shaggy, snow-white rock climbers. Keep your distance, however, for goats have been known to gore visitors with their dagger-sharp horns. When you are in goat country, keep an eye out for **Columbian ground squirrels** and **hoary marmots,** mammals that hibernate most of the year. The former is slightly larger than a red squirrel, the latter about the size of a very fat cat.

Bighorn sheep are grayish tan beasts best seen on the east side of the park. The Many Glacier Valley is a good place to go sheep watching. Search the grassy ridges and slopes on the trail to Iceberg Lake. At certain times, bighorns come down to graze right along the road, forcing traffic to back up.

In midsummer, sheep also graze areas along the Continental Divide, such as on the meadows and rocky slopes on Logan Pass and Haystack Butte.

Spring and fall, the North Fork and the east-side aspen parklands provide opportunities to watch **moose, elk,** and **white-tailed deer.** The McDonald Valley, too, is a good place to see moose and deer. Moose sometimes visit the marshy area at the Moose Country Exhibit just above Lake McDonald and similar wet areas in the North Fork and on the east side. Cow moose with calves are as dangerous and unpredictable as a female grizzly with cubs, so be careful. Watch, too, along brushy streams and ponds for **beaver**. Felled aspen, gnawed branches, and lodges are sure signs of this dam-builder at work.

In winter the Belton Hills on the north side of the river along US 2 are important winter range for elk and deer. Two fires earlier this century burned the trees off these low mountains, allowing grasses, shrubs, and deciduous trees to gain a roothold. Wind and sun keep the exposed slopes free of snow much of the winter. Thus the area is favored by wintering wildlife.

Birds

Birders have recorded approximately 260 species in Glacier Park, although 26 of these are considered "accidental" visitors, that is, birds that one would normally not expect to see in Glacier. What you will see depends on the kind of habitat you happen to be in at the moment.

Bottomlands along the North and Middle Forks of the Flathead River and brushy creeksides such as those that meander through the east-side aspen parklands are some of the best places to look for birds. Riparian zones typically shelter more species than any other type of habitat. Often, the birds are concentrated in the relatively narrow strip of creekside willows, cottonwoods, and other water-loving shrubs. In these areas look for **common loons, mergansers, osprey, belted kingfishers, dippers, spotted sandpipers, killdeer, American redstarts,** and **yellow warblers.**

Farther out in the aspen parklands, you might see **ruffed grouse, horned larks**, **McCown's** and **chestnut-collared longspurs, tree swal-**

A female rufous hummingbird feeds one of her nestlings. In the park rufous hummingbirds are found in aspen groves and coniferous forests. (GLACIER NATIONAL PARK)

lows, **flickers, red-naped sapsuckers, western wood-pewees, northern water-thrushes, western tanagers, red-winged blackbirds,** and **dusky** and **least flycatchers.** Really, there are too many species to list here—well over 200 species inhabit the aspen parklands alone. Birding on this mix of prairie and deciduous-coniferous forest can be excellent.

Back on the west side, the area around Lake McDonald harbors the forest dwellers: **sharp-shinned hawks, Cooper's hawks, barred owls, common ravens, Vaux's swifts, calliope hummingbirds, pileated woodpeckers, chestnut-backed chickadees, solitary vireos, warbling vireos, Swainson's thrush, varied thrush, Townsend's warblers, orange-crowned warblers, western tanagers, Hammond's flycatchers, brown creepers,** and **fox sparrows,** to name a few. Also look for **bald eagles** in snags on the lakeshore and **harlequin ducks** on McDonald Creek above the lake.

From Logan Pass, a walk to the Hidden Lake Overlook or a stroll along the Highline Trail can yield glimpses of **white-tailed ptarmigan, blue grouse, Clark's nutcrackers, Steller's jays, water pipits, rosy finches,** and **fox sparrows.**

Reptiles and Amphibians

Because of its cold climate, Glacier National Park has few reptiles and amphibians, and relative to other wildlife, they are seldom seen. Occasionally a **boreal toad** will hop across a trail while you are hiking, or you might hear its birdlike peeps from your tent at dusk. **Garter snakes,** too, are sometimes seen on lower elevation trails and roads, especially when it begins to get cool in the latter part of the summer. The lower McDonald Creek Valley is where you might hear **Pacific tree frogs. Tailed frogs** are hard to find during the day but easy to see at night if you shine a flashlight along a fast-moving stream. However, grizzly bears are also out at night, especially along streams, so this activity is inadvisable in Glacier. In fact, one should never hike in Glacier at night.

Checklist of Selected Animals

Mammals

❑ Masked shrew	*Sorex cinereus*
❑ Vagrant shrew	*Sorex vagrans*
❑ Northern water shrew	*Sorex palustris*
❑ Little brown bat	*Myotis lucifugus*
❑ Long-eared bat	*Myotis evotis*
❑ Long-legged bat	*Myotis volans*
❑ Big brown bat	*Eptesicus fuscus*
❑ Silver-haired bat	*Lasionycteris noctivagans*
❑ Hoary bat	*Lasiurus cinereus*
❑ Bobcat	*Lynx rufus*
❑ Lynx	*Lynx lynx*
❑ Mountain lion	*Felis concolor*
❑ Raccoon	*Procyon lotor*
❑ Black bear	*Ursus americanus*
❑ Grizzly bear	*Ursus arctos*
❑ Red fox	*Vulpes vulpes*
❑ Coyote	*Canis latrans*
❑ Gray wolf	*Canis lupus*
❑ Striped skunk	*Mephitis mephitis*
❑ Badger	*Taxidea taxus*

By damming streams, beavers create habitat for an array of organisms from insects on up to mammals. (JOE WEYDT)

❑ River otter	*Lontra canadensis*
❑ Wolverine	*Gulo gulo*
❑ Least weasel	*Mustela nivalis*
❑ Short-tailed weasel	*Mustela erminea*
❑ Long-tailed weasel	*Mustela frenata*
❑ Mink	*Mustela vison*
❑ Marten	*Martes americana*
❑ Fisher	*Martes pennanti*
❑ Pika	*Ochotona princeps*
❑ Snowshoe hare	*Lepus americanus*
❑ White-tailed jackrabbit	*Lepus townsendii*
❑ Porcupine	*Erethizon dorsatum*
❑ Beaver	*Castor canadensis*

❏ Northern pocket gopher	*Thomomys talpoides*
❏ Hoary marmot	*Marmota caligata*
❏ Least chipmunk	*Eutamias minimus*
❏ Yellow pine chipmunk	*Eutamias amoenus*
❏ Red-tailed chipmunk	*Eutamias ruficaudus*
❏ Golden-mantled ground squirrel	*Spermophilus lateralis*
❏ Columbian ground squirrel	*Spermophilus columbianus*
❏ Thirteen-lined ground squirrel	*Spermophilus tridecemlineatus*
❏ Richardson ground squirrel	*Spermophilus richardsoni*
❏ Northern flying squirrel	*Glaucomys sabrinus*
❏ Red squirrel	*Tamiasciurus hudsonicus*
❏ Western jumping mouse	*Zapus princeps*
❏ Bushy-tailed woodrat	*Neotoma cinerea*
❏ Deer mouse	*Peromyscus maniculatus*
❏ Muskrat	*Ondatra zibethicus*
❏ Northern bog lemming	*Synaptomys borealis*
❏ Red-backed vole	*Clethrionomys gapperi*
❏ Montane heather vole	*Phenacomys intermedius*
❏ Water vole	*Arvicola richardsoni*
❏ Long-tailed vole	*Microtus longicaudus*
❏ Meadow vole	*Microtus pennsylvanicus*
❏ White-tailed deer	*Odocoileus virginianus*
❏ Mule deer	*Odocoileus hemionus*
❏ Elk	*Cervus elaphus*
❏ Moose	*Alces alces*
❏ Bighorn sheep	*Ovis canadensis*
❏ Mountain goat	*Oreamnos americanus*

Reptiles and Amphibians

- Common garter snake — *Thamnophis sirtalis*
- Mountain garter snake — *Thamnophis elegans vagrans*
- Western painted turtle — *Chrysemys picta belli*
- Western toad — *Bufo boreas*
- Spotted frog — *Rana pretiosa*
- Pacific tree frog — *Pseudacris regilla*
- Boreal chorus frog — *Pseudacris triseriata*
- Tailed frog — *Ascaphus truei*
- Long-toed salamander — *Ambystoma macrodactylum*

Fishes

Native Species

- Westslope cutthroat trout — *Oncorhynchus clarki lewisi*
- Bull trout — *Salvelinus confluentus*
- Mountain whitefish — *Prosopium williamsoni*
- Pygmy whitefish — *Prosopium coulteri*
- Lake trout — *Salvelinus namaycush*
- Redside shiner — *Richardsonius balteatus*
- Peamouth — *Mylocheilus caurinus*
- Northern pike minnow — *Ptychocheilus oregonensis*
- Longnose dace — *Rhinichthys cataractae*
- White sucker — *Catostomus commersoni*
- Longnose sucker — *Catostomus catostomus*
- Largescale sucker — *Catostomus macrocheilus*
- Mottled sculpin — *Cottus bairdi*
- Slimy sculpin — *Cottus cognatus*

❑ Shorthead sculpin	*Cottus confusus*
❑ Spoonhead sculpin	*Cottus ricei*
❑ Burbot (Ling cod)	*Lota lota*
❑ Northern pike	*Esox lucius*
❑ Trout-perch	*Percopsis omiscomaycus*

Introduced Species and Subspecies

❑ Rainbow trout	*Oncorhynchus mykiss*
❑ Eastern brook trout	*Salvelinus fontinalis*
❑ Kokanee salmon	*Oncorhynchus nerka*
❑ Yellowstone cutthroat trout	*Oncorhynchus clarki bouvieri*
❑ Lake Superior whitefish	*Coregonus clupeaformis*
❑ Grayling	*Thymallus arcticus*
❑ Fathead minnow	*Pimephales promelas*

Birds

Common loon	Wood duck
Horned grebe	Ring-necked duck
Eared grebe	Common goldeneye
Western grebe	Barrow's goldeneye
Clark's grebe	Bufflehead
Great blue heron	Harlequin duck
Tundra swan	Common merganser
Canada goose	Sharp-shinned hawk
Snow goose	Cooper's hawk
Mallard	Red-tailed hawk
Northern pintail	Rough-legged hawk
Cinnamon teal	Golden eagle
American wigeon	Bald eagle

Mottled ptarmigans blend well with their surroundings. (GLACIER NATIONAL PARK)

Northern harrier
Osprey
American kestrel
Blue grouse
Spruce grouse
Ruffed grouse
White-tailed ptarmigan
American coot
Killdeer
Common snipe
Spotted sandpiper
California gull
Ring-billed gull
Mourning dove
Great horned owl
Northern hawk-owl

Northern pygmy owl
Barred owl
Common nighthawk
Black swift
Vaux's swift
Rufous hummingbird
Calliope hummingbird
Belted kingfisher
Northern flicker
Pileated woodpecker
Lewis' woodpecker
Red-naped sapsucker
Hairy woodpecker
Downy woodpecker
Black-backed woodpecker
Three-toed woodpecker

Eastern kingbird
Western kingbird
Willow flycatcher
Hammond's flycatcher
Dusky flycatcher
Western wood pewee
Olive-sided flycatcher
Horned lark
Violet-green swallow
Tree swallow
Bank swallow
Rough-winged swallow
Barn swallow
Cliff swallow
Gray jay
Steller's jay
Black-billed magpie
Common raven
American crow
Clark's nutcracker
Black-capped chickadee
Mountain chickadee
Boreal chickadee
Chestnut-backed chickadee
Red-breasted nuthatch
Brown creeper
American dipper
House wren
Winter wren
Rock wren
American robin
Varied thrush
Hermit thrush

Swainson's thrush
Veery
Mountain bluebird
Townsend's solitaire
Golden-crowned kinglet
Ruby-crowned kinglet
Water pipit
Bohemian waxwing
Cedar waxwing
Loggerhead shrike
European starling (introduced)
Solitary vireo
Red-eyed vireo
Warbling vireo
Tennessee warbler
Orange-crowned warbler
Nashville warbler
Yellow warbler
Yellow-rumped warbler
Townsend's warbler
Northern waterthrush
MacGillivray's warbler
Common yellowthroat
Wilson's warbler
American redstart
Western meadowlark
Yellow-headed blackbird
Red-winged blackbird
Brewer's blackbird
Brown-headed cowbird
Western tanager
Evening grosbeak
Pine grosbeak

Lazuli bunting

Snow bunting

Cassin's finch

Rosy finch

Common redpoll

Pine siskin

American goldfinch

Red crossbill

White-winged crossbill

Rufous-sided towhee

Savannah sparrow

LeConte's sparrow

Vesper sparrow

Chipping sparrow

White-crowned sparrow

Fox sparrow

Lincoln's sparrow

Song sparrow

Dark-eyed junco

McCown's longspur

Lapland longspur

Chestnut-collared longspur

11

The Human Presence

Ten or twelve thousand years ago, a natural history of the place we now call Glacier National Park would have read quite differently. Descriptions of white-tailed deer, mule deer, elk, and bighorn sheep would have figured alongside, possibly, those of woolly mammoths, giant steppe bison, mountain bison, woodland muskox, stag-moose, Mexican horses, and perhaps camels. Most probably, that narrative would have detailed the relations of these browsers and grass eaters not just with timber wolves and cougars but with dire wolves, giant short-faced bears, saber-toothed cats, scimitar cats, American lions, and cheetahs. And in all likelihood, it would have described the hunting and gathering practices of human beings, those of the Clovis culture, a people believed by many to be the ancestors of modern Native Americans.

A few years ago, an archaeologist found a Clovis spearpoint in the Belly River Valley. Clovis points are easy to recognize; their bases are fluted to fit within the split end of a wooden shaft. The technique typifies a culture that dominated most of North America from about 12,000 to 10,000 years ago. It was during the Clovis period and soon after that most of the large mammals listed above vanished from North America after having thrived here for well over a million years. This raises the possibility that the animals were exterminated by a blitzkrieg of human hunters, an invasion of Clovis people armed with advanced hunting techniques. The mam-

Indian people regularly burned Glacier's grasslands. Fires kept trees from encroaching and improved habitat for game animals. (JOE WEYDT)

moths and giant bison and horses and camels, having evolved with few if any human predators, were unprepared for the onslaught. They vanished in a matter of two or three thousand years. Another good possibility is that a rapidly changing climate is responsible for the extinctions, that human hunters were too few to cause the die-off. Most likely the cause was a combination of both these factors and possibly others. Regardless, it is clear that humans have long been a part of this continent's natural history, and the park is no exception.

Those who have searched have been surprised by the amount of evidence of human presence in the park, especially at high-elevation passes and cirques. Evidence of encampments, of hunting and fishing and gathering dating back to 10,000 years ago have been found at places like Siyeh Pass, Boulder Pass, Hole-in-the-Wall, and Saint Mary Lake. Apparently, mountain bison were the primary game, although bighorn sheep kill sites are common. Lines of cairns were used to funnel migrating herds into narrows and cirques where the animals could be easily dispatched with spears. Blood trace analysis of the spear points found at these sites indicate sheep were the principal prey. The methods used to kill mountain bison were probably similar and involved driving animals into corrals or trapping them in wetlands or forcing them onto frozen lakes where they lost their footing and could be mobbed by spear throwers. Evidence for fishing exists in the form of notched pebbles used as line sinkers. These have been found at several lakes, especially on the east side. In addition, the Clovis people and their descendants probably harvested roots, leaves, berries, mushrooms, barks, pine nuts, and plant medicines here. They most likely held rituals and prayed. The first European-Americans to climb Chief Mountain found a buffalo skull altar at the top, and some of the Blackfeet's most holy sites are still located here. According to tribal elders, these sacred places have been used by the Blackfeet, Pend d'Oreille, and Kootenai for millennia.

Glacier's first inhabitants also systematically burned its forests. Present-day plant communities are, in fact, the legacy of not just lightning fires but of thousands of years of human-caused blazes as well. Interviews with Indian people, journal writings of early explorers and pioneers, and modern research indicate that Indians have been purposefully setting fires on both the east and west sides of Glacier Park for some 7,000 years. Fire served several purposes for them: It kept the brush down in their seasonal campsites, eliminated hiding cover for their enemies, and increased the amount of grass available for their herds of horses. Fire also opened up travel routes through dense timber; enhanced berry production, especially for huckleberries; and, perhaps most importantly, it improved habitat for game animals and thus increased hunting success.

It was probably fire that first formed the prairies of the North Fork, and frequent fires have maintained them through the centuries. Indeed, old fire-scarred trees bordering Big Prairie and Round Prairie show that up until about 1930, low-intensity fires burned through those grasslands as frequently as once every nine to twenty-six years. Lightning-set fires would occur at intervals at least twice that long. A good portion of the North Fork fires were probably set by Indian people camping in the valley. One scenario is that Indian families purposely let their campfires go when they left the valley in the fall. Because of the cool temperatures and low humidities that prevail at that time of year, the resulting fires burned the prairies and savanna and probably large areas of the forest floor but generally stayed out of the forest canopy, yielding the mosaic of forest and grassland we see now.

Indian-lit fires are of more than just a passing interest to today's park managers. If Indian-caused fires altered plant and animal communities for thousands of years prior to the park's establishment, then to restore the park to its "natural" condition, it may be necessary for managers to prescribe regular fires. That argument, in fact, was part of the Park Service's justification for its first prescribed burns on North Fork prairies in the fall of 1992. Since then the Park Service has burned hundreds of acres of prairie and ponderosa pine, western larch, and aspen stands, and more burns will be prescribed in the future for the same reasons, a departure from the policy of the recent past that tried to ensure landscapes would "remain forever unaltered by humans." Our understanding of the natural landscape, then, has come to include the activities of Native Americans because they helped to shape the park into what it was when European-Americans first saw it.

Wild, Perhaps, but Not Pristine

"Natural processes have been virtually undisturbed in most of Glacier National Park. It is one of the most pristine ecosystems on the planet. The park was largely unvisited by nineteenth century European-Americans and was managed as a wilderness park for most of its existence. It was designated a protected reserve by Congress in 1910, and brought into the newly created National Park Service in 1916. The low level of human disturbance that has occurred, such as construction and later removal of backcountry structures, has been well documented . . . Thus, Glacier presents a vignette of pristine nature of unparalleled scientific value as a benchmark for ecosystem studies." These words, from the Park Service's 1993 *Science in Glacier National Park* publication, were written to sell the park as a place to do research. They overstate their case, however, for Glacier, in spite of being one of the wildest places left on the continent, has certainly not been undisturbed by human beings.

Even before 1910, European-Americans had homesteaded in the North Fork and McDonald Valleys and had sunk mine shafts in the Swiftcurrent Valley. They had drilled for oil at Kintla Lake and on Swiftcurrent Creek. They had built villages like Altyn and Saint Mary and Apgar. They had constructed roads and trails and fought forest fires, set traplines, and killed predators. They had introduced plants like common timothy and Kentucky bluegrass. They had cut and milled lumber, ditched and drained wetlands, stocked and netted fish by the tens of thousands. They had run cattle and horses by the thousands, too, and built hotels and chalets fit for royalty. And by the turn of the century, they had eliminated two large mammals from the park: bison and woodland caribou.

After 1910 the focus turned from exploitation of mineral and timber resources to more benign uses, most centered around tourism. The Park Service, the Civilian Conservation Corps, and entrepreneurs put up additional tourist facilities. They built a railroad and more roads and trails, constructed phone lines, picnic tables, and campgrounds. They added fire lookouts and generally beefed up their fire-fighting capabilities. And people poured in. By 1925, 40,000 visitors a year were coming to Glacier Park. In 1936, two years after the Going-to-the-Sun Road was completed and in the depths of the Great Depression, 210,000 people came. By the late 1960s, after more visitor centers, campgrounds, comfort stations, and ranger stations had been added, annual visitation topped a million. Today it is double that. My point is, as natural as Glacier appears, it has not escaped the twentieth century.

Past Human-Caused Disturbances

We start with fire. As discussed in previous chapters, fire suppression has had enormous effects on Glacier's plant and animal communities, especially in the North Fork Valley. Fire frequency can be measured in fire-years, defined as a single year when one or more fires occur. Fire frequency in the North Fork Valley, for example, was twenty fire-years per century from 1650 to 1935 and only two per century after 1935. This tenfold reduction occurred because people fought fires aggressively. Between 1930

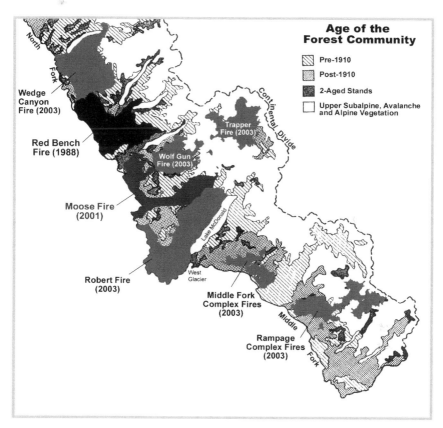

Age of the Forest Community

- Pre-1910
- Post-1910
- 2-Aged Stands
- Upper Subalpine, Avalanche and Alpine Vegetation

Wedge Canyon Fire (2003)

Red Bench Fire (1988)

Trapper Fire (2003)

Wolf Gun Fire (2003)

Moose Fire (2001)

Robert Fire (2003)

West Glacier

Middle Fork Complex Fires (2003)

Rampage Complex Fires (2003)

North Fork

Continental Divide

Lake McDonald

Middle Fork

By suppressing fires, we have altered the age and composition of the park's forests, which in turn has profoundly affected animals. (GLACIER NATIONAL PARK)

and 1987, the Park Service promptly doused ninety-five ignitions. Some would have almost certainly burned large tracts, especially during dry periods. On the east side, fire suppression encouraged conifers to spread onto grassy ridges and parks, and ultimately reduced winter habitat for deer, elk, and sheep. It affected other species, too, everything from insects on up.

Elsewhere in Glacier, fire suppression has changed little. Where fire frequencies are naturally low, communities are still functioning normally. The fact remains, however, that throughout much of Glacier National Park, fire suppression has altered the most basic of natural processes, processes that have been at work for tens of thousands of years. Of course, for those who took Smokey the Bear's message to heart, it's difficult to comprehend that the *absence* of fire can cause problems. Some fifteen years ago, the Park Service started changing its policies to allow fire a more natural place in the park, but the legacy of the past hundred years remains with us, and it will for decades. Ironically many of the major human-caused perturbances go unnoticed by park visitors, while less consequential changes like those caused by fires, the impacts of which are mostly aesthetic and are often beneficial, receive all the attention.

The effects of fish stocking, for example, have been mostly missed by park visitors who either don't fish or would just as soon catch a rainbow trout as a westslope cutthroat. Although the stocking program has ceased, the changes it brought to park waters are probably irreversible. It would be extremely difficult—probably impossible—to selectively rid the park's lakes or streams of alien fish. Some lakes are still being invaded by nonnative migratory species via the North and Middle Forks of the Flathead River. Lake trout and Lake Superior whitefish continue to move into waters currently harboring natives only.

Then there are the park-sanctioned predator control programs of the early part of this century, which rid Glacier of its wolves and decimated grizzly, wolverine, and cougar populations. It took almost half a century for the grizzly bear and wolverine to rebound, and wolves have only recently returned. Early trapping in this region also exterminated the fisher, a large member of the weasel family. Although fishers were reintroduced in 1959 and again in 1988 and 1991, they are still rare. Bobcats, too, are seldom seen anymore. Trapping virtually wiped out the lynx as well, a species now classified by the federal government as threatened, although in the park the species may be on the road to recovery. (A recent survey using DNA sampling techniques identified a minimum of six and as many as eight individuals in the park. For biologists, these numbers offer hope, especially given the periodic abundance in Glacier of snowshoe hare, the animal's chief prey.)

The elimination or reduction of each of these predators caused fluctuations in the size and health of their respective prey populations, which in turn affected plant communities. In most cases, the consequences still res-

For decades park managers fed ungulates and killed predators in the park.
(GLACIER NATIONAL PARK)

onate, although the return of the wolf has demonstrated that recovery is possible as long as corridors connecting Glacier to other wild areas are protected from development. For some time, the nation's attitude toward predators mirrored that held toward fire. Both were seen as destructive and unnecessary. The ideal was to have a park free of killing and catastrophe. But our many well-intentioned interventions only led us astray from our goal of preserving in perpetuity a piece of wild nature. Fortunately, most people now accept the part predators play in Glacier. Most, for example, have applauded the return of the wolf.

The introduction of exotic plants or weeds is another human-caused change many visitors miss. In 1920, 57 alien species grew in Glacier Park; in 1990 the number was 120; by 2002 it was 139. Most are not considered a threat, and only about twenty cause most of the problems in the park. The worst offenders include spotted knapweed, yellow toadflax, Canada thistle, oxeye daisy, St. John's wort, bull thistle, sulfur cinquefoil, leafy spurge, common timothy, and houndstongue. Means of arrival varied: Some were planted in the course of early farming and ranching operations; others came as seeds in bales of hay carried by the park's horse concessions. Still others blew off railroad cars or fell from automobile grills or were carried in gravel used in road construction or hitchhiked in the fur and stomachs of animals migrating in and out of the park. Some escaped from the yards of employee housing. New weeds keep coming, and the ones that are here keep spreading.

Spotted knapweed, leafy spurge, St. John's wort, several of the hawkweeds, sulfur cinquefoil, and oxeye daisy are especially troublesome. All are capable of displacing native grasses, and all have little or no nutritional value for wildlife. Some, like knapweed and leafy spurge, crowd out all other competitors. And because they are growing outside their native environment, they are mostly immune to attack by the park's own insects and diseases. Grasslands, which harbor four times more weeds than the forests do, are most vulnerable. One research team concluded that, if not controlled, spotted knapweed, leafy spurge, common timothy, and Kentucky bluegrass could one day dominate the park's fescue grasslands, areas like Two Dog Flats and Big Prairie. Wildlife populations, everything from elk to butterflies, would suffer.

Exotic plants are difficult to eradicate because they produce huge amounts of seed that stay viable in the soil for years, or because they have extensive underground root systems or rhizomes. With most, complete eradication is impossible; the goal is only containment. The Park Service has tried pulling, cutting, mowing, cultivation, spraying herbicides, and introducing biological controls. Each has limitations. Pulling and cutting are labor-intensive, and pulling disturbs soils, which often causes more weeds to sprout. Mowing can prevent both native plants and exotic plants from flowering and producing seeds. Similarly, chemicals can kill native plants as easily as the exotic plants they are intended to control. Sprays can also contaminate soils and water and cause serious problems for sensitive wildlife. Introducing nonnative diseases and insect pests specific to a given exotic plant is an appealing strategy, but one that can backfire and cause unintended and long-lasting problems for native species. (Thus far, park officials have released two European gall flies to control spotted knapweed and a Eurasian flea beetle to control leafy spurge; no side effects have been documented, and it will take at least a few more years to know how effective these biological strategies are.) Having experimented with all of these methods, the Park Service has settled on the use of chemical sprays along roads (mostly spot spraying) and crews pulling weeds by hand in the backcountry.

The most visible change to come to the park this century is the hundreds of thousands of two-legged beasts called humans that now roam the park each summer. Most of the long-term changes I have mentioned so far have been made for the benefit of park visitors. But the presence of humans has more direct effects, too. Grizzly bears prefer areas void of people. Adult male grizzlies, dominant in grizzly bear society, take the best feeding sites; females with cubs are often relegated to more marginal areas, ones frequented by humans. Thus females often have to cope with a constant flow of hikers and continual disruptions to their feeding. The result is a lower quality of habitat for what is arguably the most important segment of the park's grizzly bear population—reproducing females. Pushed from one marginal site to another, they run the risk of losing their innate fear of humans. They become bold around people and a threat to park visitors as well as themselves.

People have appropriated the habitats of other species as well. Trails and roads typically follow streams or pass through meadows, the most productive zones for many species. Large ungulates and predators tend to avoid people-filled areas to escape harassment. Helicopters filled with sightseers also disturb wildlife, even when the machines stay above their voluntary 2,000-foot limit, which often they don't. I have seen grizzly bears flee mountaintop foraging areas upon hearing a helicopter approach. Thus, sizable chunks of prime habitat, areas that appear pristine, are in effect off limits to many animals. And those species capable of tolerating a human presence may pay a price. Mountain goats at Oberlin Bend near Logan Pass have been seen licking antifreeze from the parking lot, and every year black bears and other animals are shot because they have come to associate people with food. In winter and early spring, emaciated deer and elk are often stressed further, sometimes forced from sheltered areas by curious, picture-taking visitors. Small encroachments such as these add up. Neither do plants escape. In McGee Meadows and Logan Pass, trampling has threatened unique communities that are home to species occurring nowhere else in the continental United States.

Of course, there is another side to this dilemma. If Americans are going to be advocates for protecting wild places, they need to experience them. While there are no simple solutions, preserving additional wilderness offers opportunities to meet the demands of increasing numbers of wildland visitors while at the same time improving the chances for many threatened and endangered species.

And within the park, administrators may one day have to address the problem of an ever-increasing number of visitors with a lottery system, perhaps, or a mandatory shuttle-bus system like the one in Denali National Park in Alaska. In 2007 the park hopes to introduce an optional shuttle-bus system on Going-to-the-Sun Road, a small but important step that can only further Glacier's efforts to meet its mandate.

And it is important to remember exactly what that mandate is. The National Park Service Organic Act spells it out in unambiguous terms: "to *conserve* the scenery and the natural and historic objects and the wildlife therein and to provide for the enjoyment of the same in such manner and by such means as will *leave them unimpaired* for the enjoyment of future generations." According to scholars and the courts, the congressional record is clear about what Congress intended: The duty to conserve comes first. In other words, if the second charge (providing enjoyment) conflicts with the first (conservation), protection of the resource must take precedence. But these two priorities are reversed when it comes to Park Service funding and personnel. For example, in 2005, a typical year, only about 10 percent of the National Park Service (NPS) budget was devoted to natural resource management. Similarly, the proportion of NPS professional staff in natural resource positions was under 10 percent that year. The lion's share of the dollars went to visitor enjoyment—campgrounds, roads, visitor centers, interpretation, and the like. As one biologist put it, "If budgets define priorities, what does that tell us about NPS priorities?"

Why is adequate funding for resource conservation important? There are dozens of reasons, but perhaps the most important is the need to develop proactive management programs based on monitoring and sound science, programs that will help protect the ecological integrity of our parks so we can pass them on unimpaired. Right now in Glacier there is little funding to conduct even the most basic monitoring of wildlife populations. Porcupines, once common in Glacier, are now all but extirpated, according to park biologists. What happened? We simply do not know. Mountain goats are assumed to be doing well. But at Goat Lick, where they have been monitored periodically, their numbers have declined by more than half in twenty-five years. Why? We don't know. Clark's nutcrackers are also in apparent decline, as are pikas at lower elevations and some amphibians. Without monitoring, some species could decline significantly or disappear before we know it. The fact is, in Glacier Park the bald eagle and perhaps the common loon are the only wildlife species for which the park has long-term, parkwide trend data. As we all know, inadequate knowledge can and often does lead to poor decisions. The issue of funding priorities in our parks is an important one and worth talking to your congressional representatives about.

An Island in a Sea of Disturbance?

These internal threats to the park, as significant as they are, will hopefully be overcome. The Park Service occasionally reacts slower than it should, but, all things considered, its record is quite good. That Glacier remains one of the wildest places on the continent is a testament to the Park Service's success and the dedication of its employees. Often, the most serious problems start outside the park, where the agency has little or no control. All park managers can do is watch and worry. Examples abound. A European fungus introduced on the coast of British Columbia more than ninety years ago eventually finds its way to Glacier and kills nearly half of the park's whitebark pine; shock waves radiate through the upper subalpine, where dozens of organisms depend on that tree for food. Nonnative fish migrate up the Flathead River from Flathead Lake and threaten to displace the park's native trout in a dozen lakes. Ongoing habitat destruction in Mexico and Central America threatens warblers and other migratory birds that spend their summers in Glacier Park. Global warming, caused by increasing levels of carbon dioxide and other greenhouse gases in the atmosphere, portends shifts of an altogether different magnitude.

The park's glaciers already show evidence of global warming. Park researchers now estimate that the largest glaciers cover, on average, about one quarter of their previous area. And the current ice thickness of the remaining glaciers are hundreds of meters thinner. According to U.S. Geological Survey scientist Dan Fagre, who since 1991 has studied the park's glaciers and global climate change, the glaciers are shrinking and may be gone within our lifetimes. He reports that several computer models indicate that if current warming trends continue, all the glaciers in the park will be gone between 2030 and 2050.

What are the implications? While it is hard to predict all the consequences, we do know that unglaciated basins contribute much less water to streams than glaciated basins because glaciers buffer the timing and extent of runoff. As glaciers shrink and disappear, scientists expect stream flows parkwide to drop. Many streams will have little or no baseflow in late summer. Stream temperatures will rise, altering the composition of aquatic insect communities. Stoneflies, caddisflies, mayflies, dragonflies, damselflies, water boatmen, gnats, midges, flies, mosquitoes, water beetles—all these critters feed fish, amphibians, and birds, which in turn feed a host of other organisms. As one researcher put it, the changes will cascade throughout the food web. Tinker with the water and you tinker with the life of the park.

So global warming is a concern to park managers. And not just because of the havoc it could wreak on aquatic ecosystems and glaciers. The park's alpine community is at risk and could disappear entirely as could species in other habitats at the southern limits of their range. Fire severity and intensity could and likely will increase. That is to say, forest communities that would normally experience only nonlethal or understory fires will begin to see more and more big, stand-replacing burns. Insects like mountain pine beetles, already on the increase because shorter, milder winters favor them, will reach epidemic levels more often. Millions of trees across large areas of the park and surrounding lands will succumb. That in turn will bump up even further the risk of large, severe fires, events that are outside the normal range of occurence. These are just a few of the most predictable changes that we are likely to see. Undoubtedly there are many others we don't have the tools yet to predict.

Some changes originating outside of the park, changes that are not related to global warming, have already created a cascade of events within. Back in 1916, kokanee, or landlocked sockeye salmon, were planted in Flathead Lake, which sits about 60 miles downstream from Glacier Park. The kokanee, which are not native to the lake, fed primarily on zooplankton, favoring a plump, slow-moving variety of crustacean called *Daphnia*. In the fall of their third or fourth year, they spawned in the lake's tributary streams or in the loose gravel along the shoreline. After spawning, the adults died. The fry made their way back to the lake, and the cycle started again.

Over the years, the kokanee population in Flathead Lake prospered, and the fish began to move into new territories farther upstream to spawn. By 1935 they were migrating into Glacier National Park. They entered via McDonald Creek, where they found the conditions ideal: loose gravel- and cobble-bottomed riffles and water temperatures moderated by the lake. Within a few years, the 2.5-mile reach of stream below Lake McDonald hosted tens of thousands of spawning kokanee each autumn. Bald eagles soon discovered the run. In 1939 thirty-seven birds fished the creek. Each year, the numbers of both fish and eagles migrating into the park grew. By 1981 in excess of 100,000 kokanee spawned there, and the eagle watchers tallied as many as 640 birds in a single count. They estimated at the time that more than 1,000 eagles were stopping at McDonald Creek to feed as they migrated south for the winter from Canada. California gulls, herring gulls, mallards, common mergansers, crows, ravens, jays, and magpies gathered, too, feasting upon spent fish. Common goldeneye, Barrow's

As recently as the 1980s, more than 1,000 eagles stopped off in Glacier National Park each fall to feed on spawning salmon, which had been introduced to Flathead Lake. A short time later, the salmon population crashed, and the eagles stopped coming. (GLACIER NATIONAL PARK)

goldeneye, and dippers fed on the millions of eggs buried in the gravel. Minks, otters, and coyotes patrolled the banks. Even white-tailed deer, which are herbivores, were seen pulling dead fish from the creek and eating them. Grizzly bears, too, worked the stream, chasing and stranding fish in shallow riffles or diving to the bottom of 15-foot-deep pools after dead ones. Some bears lingered beside McDonald Creek long past the time they would have normally entered hibernation to gorge on the thousands of carcasses of decaying fish. And the estimated nine million fry hatching from the eggs fed everything from bull trout to stoneflies. All these organisms flourished and multiplied well beyond what they would have otherwise.

But outside the park, a series of events conspired to make another change. In 1949 British Columbian officials introduced opossum shrimp into Kootenay Lake. They hoped the inch-long shrimp would become food for rainbow trout. But the lake's kokanee benefited the most. Before the introduction, a big Kootenay Lake kokanee salmon went about 12 inches and weighed perhaps a pound. A decade or two after the shrimp had been planted, it was common for kokanee to top 20 inches and weigh 6 pounds or more. News of what had happened spread quickly through fish and game departments in both the United States and Canada, and before long, biologists looking to produce jumbo kokanee for anglers had introduced opossum shrimp into more than one hundred northern lakes. In Montana the Department of Fish, Wildlife & Parks dumped them into fifteen lakes, including three in the upper part of the Flathead drainage: Whitefish and Ashley Lakes in 1968 and Swan Lake in 1975. By 1981 the offspring of the planted shrimp had migrated downstream into Flathead Lake.

At first this was considered good news. Anglers expected Flathead Lake kokanee to reach record lengths, and wildlife viewers in the park expected eagles and bears and other fish eaters to receive yet another boost from the addition of yet another exotic organism. But before long, hopes faded. No other lakes stocked with opossum shrimp in Canada or the United States had benefited the way Kootenay Lake had. In fact, kokanee populations had crashed in all but two or three of those lakes, and where they didn't crash the kokanee showed no signs of increased growth. The odds did not look good for Flathead Lake. Indeed, in a few short years, the bottom fell out of the Flathead system. Kokanee began to starve en masse. The number spawning in McDonald Creek plummeted from 118,000 in 1985 to 50 in 1989. Then there were none. Soon, the entire food chain collapsed—the multitudes that fed on salmon in Glacier Park each fall also diminished. Only a handful of bald eagles now gathered, the rest migrated to more productive feeding grounds farther south. The other fish eaters, all the birds, the bears, the otters, minks, and raccoons, ceased to congregate as well.

What happened? The explanation relates to the differences in feeding behavior between shrimp and kokanee, and to some characteristics unique to Kootenay Lake. Shy of light, shrimp feed at night. During the day, they migrate to deep water, depths of 150 feet or more. But at night, they rise to the surface to prey on *Daphnia*, the kokanee's chief quarry. The kokanee, meanwhile, feed during the day and near the surface. In Flathead Lake they probably never saw the shrimp, their intended prey, which were behaving like bandits cleaning out the cupboard every night. As competitors, the shrimp beat the kokanee at their own game.

In Kootenay Lake upwelling currents pushed the shrimp from their daytime haven in the deep, middle part of the lake into a shallow bay. Without a deep-water refuge, the shrimp became a principal entrée on the kokanee menu. But that, too, turned out to be temporary, lasting only two decades. The government built a major dam upstream from Kootenay Lake, changing flow patterns and nutrient cycles. The salmon population crashed there as well.

Meanwhile, kokanee populations independent of the Flathead Lake population—those in Kintla, Bowman, and Logging Lakes, for example—collapsed in concert with the Flathead Lake kokanee, even in the absence of *Mysis* shrimp. Biologists cannot say precisely why this happened, although they suspect that because kokanee are not native to the park, the populations there are unstable—susceptible to certain environmental factors not found in their native habitats. Kokanee populations in these settings may be cyclic, although now with the presence of lake trout in the park, their recovery is considered unlikely.

The point of this story about kokanee is that Glacier National Park cannot be managed as "an island in a sea of disturbance." Flathead Lake and Lake McDonald are part of the same river system, and so it is predictable that what goes on in one will probably affect the other. Other connections are not as obvious. For example, a good portion of the park's grizzlies put on winter fat stores by eating moths that migrate from the Great Plains some 600 miles away. Thus, what affects the moths when they are on the plains can conceivably impact the park's grizzlies. It is something biologists and managers have had to think about. Some feared pesticides sprayed on crops in North Dakota might be tainting moths eaten by bears. But recent studies in Yellowstone Park indicate that army cutworm moths migrating onto peaks in that park contain only trace or undetectable levels of those toxins.

Activities at even greater distances can and do have substantial impacts. Researchers have learned that air pollution coming from as far away as Southeast Asia is having a measurable impact on lakes in Waterton and probably Glacier. Specifically, the concern is volatile organochlorine compounds (VOCs), which are light enough to be transported across the Pacific. They then fall in minute quantities on glaciers, snowfields, and cold lakes in the Rockies where they accumulate, ultimately showing up in fish tissue samples at levels that exceed standards for safe human consumption. Another air-pollution concern: Low-level ozone produced in urban settings west of the park is now reaching levels high enough in Glacier to cause damage to ponderosa pine and aspen trees and certain species of lichen. It's clear that stresses originating far beyond the Rocky Mountains are affecting and will continue to affect Glacier Park.

The Importance of Adjacent Habitats

Elk, moose, grizzly bears, and wolves survive today on the east side of Glacier because they are able to forage in aspen parklands in Canada and on the Blackfeet Indian Reservation. Wolves and elk exist in the North Fork in the numbers they do because they, too, can drift back and forth across the international border or onto private and National Forest lands in the United States. Logging, livestock grazing, residential and commercial development, and other activities on lands adjacent to Glacier can ruin seasonal habitats; wildlife populations in the park will decline as a result.

In the late 1980s a number of grizzly bears in the Middle Fork died because of a series of train derailments on the Burlington Northern line just outside the park. In the past, no one paid much attention when a train derailed and spilled corn or wheat or barley. The company simply buried the grain or left it for bears and other animals to clean up. Then in the winter of 1988–89, three major derailments occurred. Altogether, 110 freight cars, each filled with 250,000 pounds of corn, jumped the tracks along Bear Creek. Some cars spilled their contents in the derailment; BN purposely dumped the rest in its rush to reopen the line. The result was thousands of tons of corn covering the ground in 10- to 15-foot-deep piles along a 3-mile stretch of track. As salvagers winched bent and broken freight cars from the creek, they tore deep furrows in the loose soils along the banks. After vacuuming up the accessible piles of corn, they buried the rest in the furrows, as they had always done in the past. With the cars removed, the corn out of sight, and the land roughly restored to its original contours, BN considered the job finished.

The following summer, a few bears were seen licking up spilled corn from the scattered piles left along the tracks, but no one suspected a problem. By the next summer, however, the buried grain had fermented and begun to smell, attracting bears, mostly grizzlies. On a good day, you could count fifteen to twenty silvertips digging along the tracks. People gathered to watch. Automobiles backed up along U.S. Highway 2. Concerned for human safety, the highway department made it illegal for cars to stop. Meanwhile, the bears, working the veins of buried corn, excavated 4- and 5-foot-deep caverns. In places they undermined the ballast supporting the tracks. BN refilled those. They began to fear the digging might cause more derailments.

And then bears were beginning to be hit by trains and automobiles. In a span of a few months, nine grizzlies had been hit and killed at the Bear Creek spill. After a female and three cubs died, public and agency outrage forced BN to contract with a Texas firm to have the site cleaned well. Over an eight-month period, a crew hauled away 1,400 truckloads of rotten corn, which they dumped in a landfill near Shelby.

Since then, spills have continued. In December of 1993, six cars filled with wheat went off the tracks 1.5 miles east of West Glacier. Twelve more cars derailed 3 miles farther east in March of 1994. Together, more than a million pounds of wheat were dumped. This time BN responded quickly, thoroughly vacuuming the grain and firing propane-cannon guns continuously during the cleanup to frighten away bears.

To its credit, BN avoided a repeat of the Bear Creek disaster. And to prevent future derailments, the company, now called Burlington Northern and Santa Fe Railway, has replaced wooden ties with concrete ones and installed seamless rail from East Glacier to West Glacier. They have also developed emergency spill procedures and an emergency communications network in case a future derailment spills more than just grain. They have worked hard to eliminate bear attractants along railroad tracks, including significantly reducing the trickle of grain that leaks from hopper cars.

Another draw for bears on the train line is carrion. In winter the BNSF line forms an uninterrupted snow-free corridor, a travel route used by deer, elk, and moose as they move from one wintering area to another. Cattle, too, use the tracks. From time to time these animals get hit by trains. Their rotting carcasses then attract grizzlies as they emerge from their dens in the spring. Occasionally, the bears get hit. Lately, the Burlington Northern and Santa Fe Company has begun using experimental technology to make collisions with wildlife less likely, and they have lowered the speed limit through the corridor to 35 mph.

But other concerns remain. In January of 2004 an avalanche crossed the tracks and stopped an empty 119-car freight train on the west side of Marias Pass. While stopped, another avalanche hit the train, derailing fifteen cars. A third nearly missed cleanup crews and a fourth hit a truck traveling on US 2. Following this incident, BNSF notified the park that it wanted to set up an avalanche hazard reduction program. As I write, an Environmental Impact Statement is being written to analyze potential impacts on park resources and values of blasting to reduce avalanche hazard. The EIS will also examine various alternative approaches to reduce avalanche hazards on park and Flathead National Forest lands.

Burlington Northern Santa Fe transports an average of 125 million tons of material a year through the Middle Fork corridor. (The company averages twenty-eight to thirty-four trains a day—most more than a mile long.) Add to that the cargo carried by all the trucks that travel US 2, which parallels the railroad. A significant portion of the material hauled by both train and truck is toxic. What if a derailment or accident spilled hazardous chemicals instead of grain into the Middle Fork of the Flathead River? It could destroy a fishery that is one of a kind. Perhaps even more threatening, it could poison the subterranean river community so critical to the functioning not only of the Middle Fork but also to the wildlife of Glacier Park and the Bob Marshall Wilderness Complex and the water quality of Flathead Lake.

The portion of the BNSF line bordering Glacier National Park is steep and winding, more so than any other segment on the line from Chicago to Seattle. As frequent as they have been, derailments seem inevitable in the future, even with ribbon rail and cement ties. The same is true of the potential for accidents involving trucks hauling dangerous loads on US 2. Like the railroad, the highway is full of curves, and in winter it's icy. A toxic spill could easily occur. No one advocates closing the BNSF line or the highway, but perhaps dangerous chemicals could be transported through Montana's other east-west corridors, which run through less critical habitat. Or maybe speed limits could be reduced further and other steps taken to reduce the chance of spills.

Protecting Connections with Other Wild Places

As homesite and commercial development and logging on private lands eat up habitat for park grizzly bears, wolves, wolverines, elk, moose, mountain goats, and dozens of other, less charismatic species, the Department of Interior has granted permits to oil companies to drill for oil and gas just 4 miles south of Glacier Park, in country along the Continental Divide as wild as any in the lower forty-eight states. There is a moratorium on drilling now, but that could change at any time. And north of the border on tributaries to the Flathead River, Canadian companies have proposed enormous coal strip mines, mine-mouth coal-fired electrical generating plants, and coalbed methane development. This industrialization of the Canadian portion of the North Fork of the Flathead poses enormous threats to the long-term welfare of the park.

Also in Canada, the area around Waterton has seen terrific amounts of development in recent years—logging, grazing, second homes, and oil and gas—so much so that scientists fear bears from Glacier and other wildlands that travel into the area may not make it back out. A major residential development recently constructed near the entrance of Waterton will result in the deaths of more bears and wolves and even greater habitat fragmentation.

Wolves returned to the park in the 1980s after half a century of absence because corridors of undeveloped land still linked Glacier with

If Glacier Park is to stay the wild place that it is, we cannot manage it as an island. Plants and animals need adjacent habitats and corridors that connect the park to other large wild areas. (JOE WEYDT)

wild areas in central Canada. Wolverines managed a similar feat a few years earlier. Now, one by one, those corridors are being blocked, clear-cut, roaded, subdivided, mined, industrialized, or converted into commercialized zones for casinos, go-kart tracks, and zoos. If the trend continues, Glacier will be cut off, isolated from other wildlands by development.

Major transportation corridors, like US 2, are becoming more of a concern for biologists because they can fragment habitats and populations. Recent research on Glacier's southern end has shown that grizzly bears strongly avoid areas within 500 meters of US 2. When grizzlies do cross the road, they cross at night, when traffic volumes are lowest (about ten vehicles per hour). These researchers concluded that as traffic increases over the next thirty years or so, which it will do, the highway could become a significant barrier to grizzly bears traveling between Glacier Park and the Great Bear and Bob Marshall wilderness areas. That has large implications for the long-term welfare of the population.

In the east, where development has reduced and fragmented large tracts of deciduous forest, many species have disappeared. A similar decline has been found on islands formerly connected to a mainland by land bridges. Fragmentation reduces the size and types of available habitats. A fragment may lack a winter range for an ungulate, for example, or spring range for grizzly bears, or snags for cavity-nesting birds. At the same time, fragmentation influences immigration rates because it creates gaps or barriers difficult for many organisms to cross. Thus, if a species is wiped out within a fragment, there is little chance the fragment will be recolonized. Also, surviving organisms are an isolated gene pool, their populations less adaptable to change. Undesirable traits accumulate through inbreeding. In the end, the organisms are rendered less fit. For some, extinction is inevitable. And the decline of each individual species destabilizes others, as the ebbing of whitebark pine has done in Glacier's subalpine.

In the words of author and biologist Doug Chadwick, "We cannot tuck species away in little preserves as if we were storing pieces in a museum, then come back a century later and expect to find them all still there." For Glacier National Park to succeed as we have intended, we need to maintain the corridors connecting it to other large wild areas. For instance, we need to ensure, through careful land-use planning, that the thousands of acres of private land along US 2 do not become full of second homes and businesses that cut Glacier off from the Great Bear, the Bob Marshall, and the Scapegoat Wildernesses to the south. I mentioned that there are fears US 2 could also become a barrier to grizzly bears. Preventing that from happening could be as simple as constructing well-designed wildlife crossings at key locations, crossings that allow bears and other animals to feel secure as they move unseen beneath the road. We need to ensure that that kind of improvement occurs when the opportunity presents itself. We need to protect de facto wilderness adjacent to the park from oil and gas development, and our government needs to work hard to ensure that the Canadian headwater reaches of the North Fork remain free of coal strip mines, giant generating plants, and coalbed methane development. We need to ensure that logging and road building in Canada and on the neighboring Flathead National Forest does not harm threatened grizzly bear populations and that logging, oil and gas development, and cattle grazing on the Blackfeet Indian Reservation do not destroy winter, spring, and fall habitats for elk, moose, grizzlies, and wolves. These are not radical proposals. Only 5 percent of the continental United States now lies within protected preserves. We must strive to save these remaining wild areas, to do the best job we can managing the human activities threatening them.

There is a major initiative under way that, if successful, would accomplish many of these goals and help to ensure Glacier's future as a wild park. The Yellowstone-to-Yukon Conservation Initiative, or Y2Y, would build and maintain a system of protected reserves stretching from Yellowstone National Park in the south to Yukon Territory in the north. These areas would be stitched together by wildlife movement corridors, which in turn would be protected by transition zones. It is envisioned that existing parks and wilderness areas would provide the foundation for this system, while the creation of new protected areas and the conservation and restoration of existing areas would fill the gaps and provide the needed corridors. The goal: to protect key habitats across 1,800 contiguous miles of the Rocky, Columbia, and Mackenzie Mountains and thereby ensure that the plant and animal communities in places like Glacier Park are maintained for future generations. The Y2Y vision—to maintain the natural integrity and connectivity of what remains a fully functional mountain system—is shared by 200 organizations, institutions, and foundations.

Already it is becoming more than a vision. For example, Canada is now contemplating the expansion of Waterton Lakes National Park. The addition would bring Waterton's west boundary all the way to the Flathead River. Glacier would benefit through the protection of important adjacent habitats. While the idea of expanding Waterton has been around since 1911, it looks as though it might actually happen this time.

A second development, this time in the United States, also shows we are making progress. More than a decade ago a group of agencies and other cooperators, including Glacier National Park, the Blackfeet Indian Nation,

Burlington Northern and Santa Fe Railway Company, Flathead National Forest, and the state of Montana, joined together in an effort to protect the Middle Fork of the Flathead River corridor. Recognizing the importance of the area as a connecting bridge between Glacier National Park and the Bob Marshall Wilderness Complex, the group is striving to protect and conserve its fish and wildlife populations and habitats and to reduce the barrier effects of the railroad and highway for wildlife movement and migration. The corridor is now designated the Great Northern Environmental Stewardship Area. Through conservation easements, special management, and a number of other steps, the area is on the way to receiving the attention and protection it deserves.

All these efforts bode well for the future. Glacier's value as a wilderness will only increase as time goes on. Our task is to pass on a place at least as wild as the one we have enjoyed. Our children expect nothing less.

Hiking in Bear Country

Most hikers never see a bear, but all of the park is bear country, and people have been seriously injured, maimed, and killed. Whether you plan to hike for days or just a few hours, take the time to learn about the special trail conditions presented by bears.

Don't Approach or Surprise Bears!

Bears are exceptionally fast and can run 180 feet in three seconds. A minimum safe distance from bears is 500 to 1,000 feet, although there is no guarantee of your safety.

Bears will usually move out of the way if they hear people approaching, so make noise to let them know you are coming. Bells are not as effective as many people believe; talking loudly, clapping hands, and calling out are all better ways to make your presence known. Sometimes trail conditions make it hard for bears to see, hear, or smell approaching hikers. Be careful when hiking by a stream, against the wind, or in dense vegetation. A blind corner or a rise in the trail also requires special attention by hikers.

Inform Yourself about Bears

Park staff can tell you of recent bear activity in the area where you plan to hike. They can also help identify signs of bear activity like paw prints, torn-up logs, trampled vegetation, droppings, and overturned rocks. Bears spend a lot of time eating, so try to avoid hiking in obvious feeding areas such as berry patches, cow-parsnip thickets, or fields of glacier lilies.

- All bears are dangerous and should be respected equally. A female with cubs, a bear with a fresh kill, and a bear conditioned to human food are the most dangerous.

- When hiking in bear country, leave an itinerary with friends or leave one in your car that includes beginning and ending times.

- Never hike alone or at night.

- Never feed animals or leave food or garbage unattended.

What Should You Do If You See a Bear?

Bears, like people, react differently to different situations depending on their mood, the weather, the time of year, and many other factors. Bears may appear tolerant of people and then attack without warning. A bear's body language can help you determine its mood. In general, bears show agitation by swaying their heads, huffing, and clacking their teeth. Lowered head and laid-back ears also indicate aggression. Bears stand on their hind legs to get a better view.

If you encounter a bear:

- Talk quietly or not at all.

- Never run from a bear; it may instinctively chase you. Back away slowly, but stop if it seems to agitate the bear.

- Assume a nonthreatening posture. Turn sideways, or bend at the knees to appear smaller.

- Use peripheral vision. Bears appear to interpret direct eye contact as threatening.

- A bear may "bluff charge." If the bear does not stop, fall to the ground in a fetal position to reduce the severity of an attack. Do not move until you are sure the bear has left.

Camping, Picnicking, and Bears

Odors attract bears. Park regulations require that all edibles (including pet food), food containers (empty or not), and cookware be stored in a hard-sided vehicle or food locker, or hung from a food pole or cable when not in use, day or night. Improperly stored and unattended food will be confiscated and the owner ticketed.

- Inspect campsites for bear sign and for careless campers nearby.

- Place all trash in bear-proof trash containers.

- Pets, especially dogs, must be kept under physical restraint.

- Use a flashlight when walking at night.

- If a bear enters your campsite, inform park staff immediately.

- Don't feed the bears! When animals are fed, they can become aggressive toward humans, cause injuries, and often must be destroyed. A fed bear is a dead bear.

Pepper Spray

This aerosol pepper derivative triggers temporary incapacitating discomfort in bears. It is a nontoxic and nonlethal means of deterring bears. There have been cases where bear spray apparently repelled aggressive or attacking bears, and accounts where it has not worked as well as expected. Factors influencing effectiveness include distance, wind, rainy weather, temperature extremes, and product shelf life.

If you decide to carry bear spray, use it only in situations where aggressive bear behavior justifies its use. **Under no circumstances should bear spray create a false sense of security or serve as a substitute for standard safety precautions in bear country.**

Bear spray should not be confused with anti-personnel defense sprays. Antipersonnel defense sprays are not suited for bears. Likewise, bear spray is intended as a deterring mechanism for bears, not humans. Some brands of bear spray may be transported across the U.S./Canada border while others may not; check before attempting.

Mountain Lions

Mountain lions are big, beautiful, wild cats, known by many names including cougar, puma, and panther. Adult mountain lions weigh between 90 and 150 pounds and are about 6 to 8 feet in length. The long tail, one third the body length, is a distinguishing characteristic. Sightings of these large predators have increased in recent years. A glimpse of one of these magnificent cats would be a vacation highlight, but you need to take precautions to protect yourself and your children from an accidental encounter. Don't hike alone; make noise to avoid surprising a lion.

- Keep children close to you at all times.
- If you do encounter a lion, do not run. Talk calmly, avert your gaze, stand tall, and back away.
- If attack by a lion seems imminent, act aggressively. Do not crouch, and do not turn away. If you have small children with you, pick them up.
- Lions may be scared away by being struck with rocks or sticks, or by being kicked or hit.

Lions are primarily nocturnal, but they have attacked in broad daylight. Mountain lions rarely prey on humans, but such behavior occasionally does occur; children and small adults are particularly vulnerable.

Notes to Chapters

Chapter 1: The Rock of the Park

Nature of the Belt Sea: in Winston and Link, "Middle Proterozoic Rocks of Montana, Idaho and Eastern Washington: The Belt Supergroup." Also D. Winston, "Evidence for Intracratonic, Fluvial and Lacustrine Settings of Middle to Late Proterozoic Basins of Western U.S.A.," in C. F. Gower, T. Rivers, and B. Ryan, (eds.), *Mid-Proterozoic Laurentia-Baltica,* Spec. Pap. 38:535–564.

Origin of Belt Sediments: G. M. Ross, R. R. Parrish and D. Winston, "Provenance and U-Pb geochronology of the Mesoproterozoic Belt Supergroup (northwestern United States): implications for age of deposition and pre-Panthalassa plate reconstructions," *Earth and Planetary Science Letters,* 113:57–76, 1992.

Belt Formation Descriptions: *Belt Supergroup: A Guide to Proterozoic Rocks of Western Montana and Adjacent Areas,* edited by Sheila M. Roberts, Montana Bureau of Mines and Geology, Special Publication 94. Also Wipple's "Geologic map of Glacier National Park, Montana," published by the U.S. Geological Survey; and the Glacier Natural History Association's *Geology along Going-to-the-Sun Road Glacier National Park, Montana* by O. Raup and others. On the Appekunny "string-of-beads" fossils, see Ychelson and Fedonkin (2000). On the Purcell Lava see R. G. McGimsey, "The Purcell Lava, Glacier National Park, Montana," U.S. Geological Survey Open File Report 85-543.

Stromatolites and other Fossils, Molar Tooth Structures, and Oolites: M. R. Walter, "Interpreting stromatolites," *American Scientist* Vol. 65 no. 5, 1977:563–571. Also R. J. Horodyski, "Stromatolites from the Middle Proterozoic Altyn Limestone, Belt Supergroup, Glacier National Park, Montana," in Walter, M. R. (ed.), *Developments in Sedimentology 20: Stromatolites,* 1976, Amsterdam: Elsevier Sci. Publ. Co. Also the opening chapters of D. Winston, R. J. Horodyski and J. W. Whipple, "Middle Proterozoic Belt Supergroup, Western Montana," *Field Trip Guidebook T334, Great Falls, Montana to Spokane, Washington,* 28th International Geol. Cong., Amer. Geophys. Union, Washington D.C., 1989.

Chapter 2: Shoving the Park into Place

Laramide Orogeny and events preceding it: *Modern Physical Geology* by G. Thompson and J. Turk (Philadelphia: Sanders College Publishing, 1991).

Lewis Thrust Fault: "Development of Normal Faults During Emplacement of a Thrust Sheet: An Example from the Lewis Allochthon, Glacier National Park, Montana (U.S.A.)," by An Yin and Thomas Kelty, *J. of Struct. Geol.* Vol. 13 no. 1, 1991:37–47. Also "Duplex Development and Abandonment During Evolution of the Lewis Thrust System, Southern Glacier National Park, Montana" by An Yin, Thomas K. Kelty and Gregory Davis, *Geology,* Vol. 17, 1989:806–810.

Formation of the North Fork Valley: K. N. Constenius, "Stratigraphy, Sedimentation, and Tectonic History of the Kishenehn Basin, Northwestern Montana" (Master's thesis University of Wyoming, Laramie, 1981).

Chapter 3: An Ice-Age Park

Pleistocene Glaciation: C. A. Matsch, *North America and the Great Ice Age* (New York: McGraw Hill Book Co., 1976). Also P. E. Carrara, "Surficial Geologic Map of Glacier National Park, Montana," U.S. Geological Survey Miscellaneous Investigation Series Map I-1508-D, 1990; and P. E. Carrara and R. G. McGimsey, "Map Showing Distribution of Moraines and Extent of Glaciers from the Mid-19th Century to 1979 in the Mount

Jackson Area, Glacier National Park, Montana," U.S. Geological Survey Miscellaneous Investigation Series Map I-1508-C, 1988.

Human Remains: R. E. Taylor and others, "Major Revision in the Pleistocene Age Assignments for North American Human Skeletons by C-14 Accelerator Mass Spectrometry: None Older Than 11,000 C-14 Years B.P.," *American Antiquity 50*, 1985:136–40.

Volcanic Ash: P. E. Carrara and R. G. McGimsey, "Map Showing Distribution of Moraines and Extent of Glaciers from the Mid-19th Century to 1979 in the Mount Jackson Area, Glacier National Park, Montana," U.S. Geological Survey Miscellaneous Investigation Series Map I-1508-C, 1988.

Glacial Features: R. P. Sharp, *Living Ice: Understanding Glaciers and Glaciation* (New York: Cambridge University Press, 1988).

Modern Glacial Recession: A. Johnson, "Grinnell and Sperry glaciers, Glacier National Park, Montana—a record of vanishing ice," U.S. Geological Survey Professional Paper 1180, 1980. Also P. E. Carrara, "Glaciers and Glaciation in Glacier National Park," U.S. Geological Survey Open File Rpt. 93-510, 1993.

Chapter 4: A Place to Live

Soil Influences on Plants: D. Lynch, "Ecology of the Aspen Groveland in Glacier County, Montana," *Ecological Monographs,* Vol. 25 no. 4, 1955: 321–344. J. DeSanto discusses lime-loving alpine plants in his *Alpine Wildflowers of Glacier National Park and Waterton Lakes National Park, Alberta,* which is unpublished but available in the Glacier National Park Library. Also S. Arno and Ramona P. Hammerly's *Timberline: Mountain and Arctic Forest Frontiers.*

Fire Influences: H. B. Ayres, *The Flathead Forest Reserve.* U.S. Geological Survey 20th Annual Report, Part V (1898–1899):245–316. Also J. R. Habeck, *Fire ecology investigations in Glacier National Park, historical considerations and current observations,* Missoula: Dept. of Botany, University of Montana, 1970.

Glaciation Influences: J. DeSanto's *Alpine Wildflowers of Glacier National Park and Waterton Lakes National Park, Alberta.*

Weather: A. I. Finklin's *A climate handbook for Glacier National Park—with data for Waterton Lakes National Park.*

Chapter 5: The Aspen Parklands

Aspen Parklands: D. Lynch, "Ecology of the Aspen Groveland in Glacier County, Montana," *Ecological Monographs,* Vol. 25 no. 4, 1955:321–344.

Red Belt: S. Arno and Ramona P. Hammerly, *Timberline: Mountain and Arctic Forest Frontiers.*

Aspen Groves: *Aspen: Ecology and Management in the Western United States,* N. V. DeByle and R. P. Winokur, eds., USDA Forest Service, Gen. Tech. Rpt. RM-119, 1985. Also E. B. Peterson, E. B. and N. M. Peterson, *Ecology, Management, and Use of Aspen and Balsam poplar in the Prairie Provinces, Canada,* Forestry Canada, Northwest Region, Special Rpt. 1, Edmonton, Alberta, 1992. See also David S. Shea, Susan Olin, and Jennifer Asebrook, 2004, *Glacier National Park Eastside Grasslands Ecology Project, Final Report,* West Glacier: Glacier National Park.

Birds of the Parklands: T. McEneaney's *Birding Montana.* Also Peterson and Peterson, *Ecology, Management, and Use of Aspen and Balsam poplar in the Prairie Provinces, Canada,* Forestry Canada. Background on ruffed grouse and sapsuckers in A. C. Bent, *Life Histories of North American Birds*, Gallinaceous Birds (1932) and Woodpeckers (1939), United States National Museum: Washington, D.C.

Beavers and Hares: Peterson and Peterson, *Ecology, Management, and Use of Aspen and Balsam poplar in the Prairie Provinces, Canada,* Forestry Canada.

Buffalo: J. DeSanto, "Historical status of the bison in Glacier National Park," *Glacier Natural History Report,* 1971, photocopy available in the Glacier National Park Library.

Bears in the Parklands: Unpublished data collected by Dan Carney, biologist for the Blackfeet Tribe, Browning, Montana.

Ups and Downs of Elk: C. J. Martinka's paper, "Wildlife Management in Glacier National Park," in R. C. Scace, and C. J. Martinka (eds.), 1983, *Proceedings—Towards the biosphere reserve: exploring relationships between parks and adjacent lands,* Washington D.C.: National Park Service. Also C. J. Martinka, "An Incidence of Mass Elk Drowning," *Journal of Mammology,* Vol. 50 no. 3, 1969:640–641.

East-Side Wolves: Unpublished notes of Carter Neimeyer, a wolf management specialist with the Animal Damage Control Division of the USDA.

Chapter 6: The North Fork Valley Bottom

Floodplain Plants: H. L. Allen, *Floodplain plant communities of the North Fork, Flathead River, Montana,* West Glacier, Mont.: Glacier National Park, Resource Management Report Series, No. 1, 1980.

Spruce Hybrids: J. R. Habeck and T. W. Weaver, "A chemosystematic analysis of some hybrid spruce (*Picea*) populations in Montana," *Canadian Journal of Botany,* Vol. 47, 1969:1565–1570.

North Fork Prairies: W. D. Koterba and J. R. Habeck, "Grasslands of the North Fork Valley, Glacier National Park, Montana," *Canadian Journal of Botany,* Vol. 49, 1971:1627–1636.

Ponderosa Pine: J. S. Lunan and J. R. Habeck, "The effects of fire exclusion on ponderosa pine communities in Glacier National Park, Montana," *Canadian Journal of Forest Research,* Vol. 3, 1973:574–579.

Fens and Fen Plants: Unpublished notes of Peter Lesica, botanist in Missoula, Montana. Also *Peatlands* by P. D. Moore and D. J. Bellamy (New York: Springer-Verlag, 1974) and *The Audubon Society Field Guide to North American Wildflowers, Western Region,* by Richard Spellenberg (New York: Alfred A. Knopf, 1979).

Birds of the North Fork: T. McEneaney's *Birding Montana.* Also D. Richie, "Underwater Flyer—The Water Ouzel," *Montana Outdoors,* Vol. 23 no. 4, 1992:4–7.

Small Mammals: C. A. Long, "Notes on habitat preference and reproduction in pigmy shrews, Microsorex," *Canadian Field-Naturalist,* Vol. 86, 1972:155–160; Sara Churchfield, *Natural History of Shrews* (Ithaca: Comstock Pub. Assoc. 1990); and E. B. Kritzman, *Little mammals of the Pacific Northwest* (Seattle: Pacific Search Press, 1977). Also C. H. Key, "Mammalian utilization of floodplain habitats along the North Fork of the Flathead River in Glacier National Park" (Master's thesis, University of Montana, Missoula, 1979), and J. D. Reichel and S. G. Beckstrom, *Northern Bog Lemming Survey,* USDA Forest Service, Kootenai National Forest, 1992.

Moose: M. Langley, "Habitat selection, mortality and population monitoring of Shiras moose in North Fork of the Flathead River Valley, Montana" (Master's thesis, University of Montana, Missoula 1993). Also R. L. Peterson, *The North American Moose* (Toronto: University of Toronto Press, 1955).

Competition between Similar Species: R. H. MacArthur, "Population ecology of some warblers of northeastern coniferous forests," *Ecology* 39, 1958:599–619. Also K. J. Jenkins, "Winter habitat and niche relationships of sympatric cervids along the North Fork of the Flathead River, Montana" (Ph.D. dissertation, University of Idaho, Moscow, 1985), and F. J. Singer, "Habitat partitioning and wildfire relationships of cervids in Glacier National Park, Montana," *Journal of Wildlife Management,* Vol. 43, 1979:437–444.

North Fork Ungulates and Predators: D. Pletscher, R. Ream, W. Brewster, E. Bangs, and R. DeMarchii, "Managing wolf and ungulate populations in an international ecosystem," Transactions 56th North American Wildlife and Natural Resource Conference, 1991:540–549. J. Rachael, 1992, "Mortality and seasonal distribution of white-tailed deer in an area recently recolonized by wolves" (Master's thesis, University of Montana, Missoula). Also R. R. Ream, M. W. Fairchild, A. J. Blakesley, and D. K. Boyd, "First Wolf Den in Eastern U.S. in Recent History," *Northwestern Naturalist,* Vol. 70, 1989:39–40; R. R. Ream, M. W. Fairchild, D. K. Boyd, and D. H. Pletscher, *Wolf Monitoring and Research in and Adjacent to Glacier National Park,* Sec. 6 Final Report (1984–87), submitted to Montana Department of Fish, Wildlife & Parks, Helena, 1987; M. J. Bureau, "Mortality and Seasonal Distribution of Elk in an Area Recently Colonized by Wolves" (Master's thesis, University of Montana, Missoula, 1992); R. W. Krahmer, "Seasonal habitat relationships of white-tailed deer in northwestern Montana" (Master's thesis, University of Montana, Missoula 1989); D. A. Boyd, R. R. Ream, D. H.

Pletscher, and M.W. Fairchild, "Prey Taken by Colonizing Wolves and Hunters in the Glacier National Park Area," *Journal of Wildlife Management,* Vol. 58 no. 2, 1994:286–295; K. E. Kunkel and D. H. Pletscher, "Cervid-wolf relationships in the North Fork of the Flathead River," Progress Report for 1993, School of Forestry, University of Montana. Missoula; and P. A. White and D. K. Boyd, "A cougar (*Fells concolor*) kitten killed and eaten by gray wolves (*Canis lupus*) in Glacier National Park, Montana," *Canadian Field-Naturalist,* Vol. 103 no. 3, 1989:408–409.

Bears in the North Fork: F. J. Singer, "Seasonal Concentrations of Grizzly Bears, North Fork of the Flathead River, Montana," *Canadian Field-Naturalist,* Vol. 92, 1978:283–286. Also Harry Carriles, "Black Bears in the North Fork of the Flathead River Valley, Montana" (Master's thesis, University of Montana, Missoula, 1990), and the National Wildlife Federation's *Grizzly Bear Compendium.*

On Cow-parsnip and Bears: R. D. Applegate, L. Rogers, D. Castell, and J. Novack, "Germination of Cow-Parsnip seeds from Grizzly Bear feces," *Journal of Mammology,* Vol. 60, 1979:655; and S. Schaffer, "Some ecological aspects of grizzly bears and black bears in Glacier National Park" (Master's thesis, University of Montana, Missoula, 1971).

Chapter 7: The McDonald Creek Valley

Old Growth Redcedar-Hemlock Forest: J. R. Habeck, "The composition of several climax forest communities in the Lake McDonald area of Glacier National Park," *Proceedings of the Montana Academy of Science,* Vol. 23:37–44, 1963. Also Arno and Hammerly's *Northwest Trees* and Norse's *Ancient Forests of the Pacific Northwest.* On succession in the community, see J. R. Habeck, "Forest succession in the Glacier National Park cedar-hemlock forests," *Ecology 49,* 1968:872–880, and on fire, see Agee, *Fire ecology of Pacific Northwest forests.*

Checkerspot Butterflies and Biodiversity: D. M. Debinski, "Inventory and monitoring of biodiversity: an assessment of methods and a case study of Glacier National Park, Montana" (Ph.D. dissertation, Montana State University, Bozeman 1991), and Kellert and Wilson, *The Biophilia Hypothesis.*

Mycorrhizal Fungi and Mycotrophs: Norse's *Ancient Forests of the Pacific Northwest* and Miller's *Mushrooms of North America.*

Birds: T. McEneaney's *Birding Montana*; P. R. Erlich, D. S. Dobkin, and D. Wheye, *The Birder's Handbook: A Field Guide to the Natural History of North American Birds;* and E. L. Bull and C. T. Collins, "Vaux's Swifts (*Chaetura vauxi*)," *The Birds of North America,* No. 77 (A. Poole and F. Gill, eds.), Philadelphia: the Academy of Natural Sciences; Washington, D.C.: The American Ornithologists' Union, 1993.

Mammals: E. B. Kritzman, *Little mammals of the Pacific Northwest.* (Seattle: Pacific Search Press, 1977); and R. A. Powell, *The Fisher; Life History, Ecology, and Behavior* (Minneapolis: University of Minnesota Press, 1982). Also R. P. Weckwerth and P. L. Wright, "Results of Transplanting Fishers in Montana," *Journal of Wildlife Management* Vol. 32, 1968: 977–980.

Chapter 8: Glacier's Subalpine

Lower and Upper Subalpine Forests: Habeck's *The vegetation of Glacier National Park, Montana,* an unpublished manuscript in the Glacier Park Library. Also S. Barrett, S. Arno, and C. Key, "Fire regimes of western larch—Lodgepole pine forests in Glacier National Park, Montana," *Canadian Journal of Forest Research,* Vol. 21, 1991:1711–1720; J. K. Agee, *Fire ecology of Pacific Northwest forests;* Arno and Hammerly's *Northwest Trees;* and J. DeSanto, "Subalpine larch of Glacier National Park," Glacier Natural History Report, photocopy, no date.

Factors affecting Treeline: S. Arno and Ramona P. Hammerly, *Timberline: Mountain and Arctic Forest Frontiers.* Also J. R. Habeck, "An analysis of a timberline zone at Logan Pass, Glacier National Park," *Northwest Science,* Vol. 43, 1969:65–73.

Whitebark Pine and Nutcrackers: Various papers in W. C. Schmidt and F. K. Holtmeier (eds.), *Proceedings—International Workshop on Subalpine Stone Pines and their Environment: Status of our Knowledge,* USDA Forest Service General Technical Report GTR-309, 1992, and W. C. Schmidt and K. McDonald (eds.), *Proceedings—Symposium on Whitebark*

Pine Ecosystems: Ecology and Management of a High Mountain Resource, USDA Forest Service, Intermountain Research Station General Technical Report INT-270, 1990. Also S. F. Arno and Ray Hoff, *Silvics of Whitebark Pine (Pinus albicaulis),* Ogden: USDA Forest Service, Intermountain Research Station General Technical Report INT-253, 1989.

On Indian use of whitebark pine, see Bud Cheff's book, *Indian trails and grizzly tales.* In "The black bear in the spruce-fir forest," Jonkel and Cowan write about black bear use of whitebark.

Huckleberries: P. A. E. Martin, "Productivity and taxonomy of the *Vaccinium globulare-Faccinium membranaceum* complex in western Montana" (Master's thesis, University of Montana, Missoula, 1979).

Bear Trees: S. Schaffer, "Some ecological aspects of grizzly bears and black bears in Glacier National Park" (Master's thesis, University of Montana, Missoula, 1971).

Chapter 9: The Alpine

Alpine Plant Communities: J. DeSanto's *Alpine Wildflowers of Glacier National Park and Waterton Lakes National Park, Alberta* and Habeck's *The vegetation of Glacier National Park, Montana*; both are in the Glacier National Park Library. Also Bamberg and Major, "Ecology of the vegetation and soils associated with calcareous parent materials in three alpine regions of Montana"; Lesica and McCune, *Monitoring effects of global warming using peripheral rare plants in wet alpine tundra in Glacier National Park, Montana*; and Zwinger and Willard, *Land above the trees: a guide to American alpine tundra.*

Birds of the Alpine: T. McEneaney's *Birding Montana* and P. Erlich's *The Birder's Handbook.* Also T. S. Choate, "Ecology and population dynamics of white-tailed ptarmigan (*Lagopus leucocurus*) in Glacier National Park" (Ph.D. dissertation, University of Montana, Missoula, 1960).

Mammals: J. O. Whitaker, *The Audubon Society Field Guide to North American Mammals* (New York: Alfred A. Knopf, 1980). Also D. R. Butler, "The grizzly bear as an erosional agent in mountainous terrain," *Z. Geomorph. N. F,* Vol. 36 no. 2, 1992:179–189.

Bears and Bugs: D. White, *The ecology and bear use of high elevation insect aggregation sites in Glacier National Park, Montana,* Progress Report, Dept. of Biology, Montana State University, Bozeman, 1992. Also J. DeSanto, "Alpine Bears," Glacier Natural History Report, photocopy, no date.

Goats and Sheep: D. Chadwick's *A Beast the Color of Winter.* Also R. A. Riggs, "Winter Habitat Use Patterns and Populations of Bighorn Sheep in Glacier National Park" (Master's thesis, University of Idaho, Moscow, 1977); and R. A. Riggs and J. M. Peek, "Mountain sheep habitat-use patterns related to post-fire succession," *Journal of Wildlife Management,* Vol. 44 no. 4, 1980:933–938.

Chapter 10: Lakes and Streams

Aquatic Insect Communities: J. A. Stanford and J. V. Ward, "The Hyporheic Habitat of River Ecosystems," *Nature,* Vol. 335, 1988:64–66. Also R. K. Pennak, *Freshwater Invertebrates of the United States* (New York: Ronald Press, Co. 1953).

Amphibians: Unpublished data, Glacier National Park; J. L. Behler, *The Audubon Society Field Guide to North American Reptiles and Amphibians* (New York: Alfred A. Knopf, 1979); and R. Nussbaum, *Amphibians and Reptiles of the Pacific Northwest* (Moscow, University Press of Idaho, 1983).

Fish: L. F. Marnell, "Status of the westslope cutthroat trout in Glacier National Park, Montana"; Marnell, Behnke, and Allendorf, "Genetic identification of cutthroat trout, *Salmo clarki,* in Glacier National Park, Montana"; and Trotter, *Cutthroat: Native Trout of the West.*

Chapter 11: The Human Presence

Archaeology: Telephone interview with Dr. Brian Reeves of the University of Calgary who is conducting a four-year ethnographic and archaeology study of the park.

Indian Fires: S. W. Barrett and S. F. Arno, "Indian Fires as an Ecological Influence in the Northern Rockies," *Journal of Forestry*, Vol. 80 no. 10, 1982:647–651.

Early Twentieth-Century Human Impacts: C. W. Buchholtz, *Man in Glacier*. Also S. Barrett, S. Arno, and C. Key, "Fire regimes of western larch—Lodgepole pine forests in Glacier National Park, Montana"; L. F. Marnell, "Impacts of hatchery stocks on wild fish populations," in R. H. Stroud (ed.), *Fish Culture in Fisheries Management* (Bethesda: American Fisheries Society, 1986).

Weeds: R. W. Tyser and C. Key, "Spotted Knapweed in Natural Area Fescue Grasslands: An Ecological Assessment," *Northwest Science*, Vol. 62, 1988:151–160. Also R. W. Tyser and C. A. Worley, "Alien flora in grasslands adjacent to road and trail corridors in Glacier National Park, Montana (U.S.A.)," *Conservation Biology*, Vol. 6 no. 2, 1992:253–262; P. Lesica, K. Ahlenslager, and J. DeSanto, "New vascular plant records and the increase of exotic plants in Glacier National Park, Montana," *Madrono*, Vol. 40, 1993:126–131; and David Lange, *Exotic Vegetation Management Plan*, 1991, West Glacier: Glacier National Park.

Kokanee and Eagles: C. N. Spencer, B. R. McClelland, and J. A. Stanford, "Shrimp stocking, salmon collapse and eagle displacement: Cascading interactions in the food web of a large aquatic ecosystem," *BioScience* 41 (1991):14–21

Train Derailments: Telephone interviews with Tim Manley of Montana Department of Fish, Wildlife & Parks in Kalispell and Kate Kendall, U.S. Biological Survey, West Glacier.

Information on the effects of fire on bird distribution: N. B. Kotliar, S. J. Hejl, R. L. Hutto, V. A. Saab, C. P. Melcher, and M. E. McFadzen, "Effects of Fire and Post-Fire Salvage Logging on Avian Communities in Conifer-Dominated Forests of the Western United States," *Studies in Avian Biology*, No. 25:49–64, 2002.

Bibliography

Agee, J. K. 1993. *Fire Ecology of Pacific Northwest Forests.* Washington, D.C.: Island Press.

Alpha, T. R. and Willis H. Nelson. 1990. "Geologic Sketches of Many Glacier, Hidden Lake Pass, Comeau Pass, and Bears Hump Viewpoint, Waterton-Glacier International Peace Park, Alberta, Canada, and Montana, United States." U.S. Geological Survey Miscellaneous Investigation Series Map I-1508-E.

Arno, Stephen and Ramona P. Hammerly. 1984. *Timberline: Mountain and Arctic Forest Frontiers.* Seattle: The Mountaineers.

Arno, Stephen F. and Ray Hoff. 1989. *Silvics of Whitebark Pine (Pinus albicaulis).* Ogden: USDA Forest Service. Intermountain Research Station. Gen. Tech. Rpt. INT-253.

Bamberg, S. A. and J. Major. 1968. "Ecology of the vegetation and soils associated with calcareous parent materials in three alpine regions of Montana." *Ecological Monographs* 38(2):127–167.

Bangs, Edward E., S. H. Fritts, J. A. Fontaine, D. W. Smith, K. M. Murphy, C. M. Mack, and C. C. Niemeyer. "Status of Gray Wolf Restoration in Montana, Idaho, and Wyoming." *Wildlife Society Bulletin 26* (4):785–798.

Barrett, S., S. Arno, and C. Key. 1991. "Fire regimes of western larch—Lodgepole pine forests in Glacier National Park, Montana." *Canadian Journal of Forest Research* 21:1711–1720.

Borror, D. J. and R. E. White. 1970. *Insects: A Field Guide to Insects America north of Mexico.* Boston: Houghton Mifflin Company.

Brown, C. J. D. 1971. *Fishes of Montana.* Bozeman: Big Sky Books.

Buchholtz, C. W. 1976. *Man in Glacier.* West Glacier: Glacier Natural History Association.

Carrara, P. E. 1993. "Glaciers and Glaciation in Glacier National Park." U.S. Geological Survey. Open File Rpt. 93-510.

Chadwick, Douglas H. 1991. *Introduction to Landscape Linkages and Biodiversity.* (Wendy E. Hudson, ed.) Washington, D.C.: Island Press.

––––––. 1983. *A Beast the Color of Winter.* San Francisco: Sierra Club Books.

Cheff, Bud. 1994. *Indian Trails and Grizzly Tales.* Stevensville, Mont.: Stoneydale Press.

Contreras, G. P. and K. E. Evans (comps.). 1986. *Proceedings—Grizzly Bear Habitat Symposium.* USDA Forest Service Intermountain Research Station Gen. Tech. Rep. INT-207.

Davis, G. A., M. R. Hudec, E. A. Jardine, T. Kelty, M. R. Hudec, and A. Yin. 1989. "The Lewis Thrust Fault in Glacier National Park, Montana: Geologic Surprises From a Classic Fault and its Allochthon." *Geol. Soc. of Amer. Abstr. with Prog.* 21(5):72.

DeSanto, J. 1971. "Historical status of the bison in Glacier National Park." Glacier Natural History Report.

––––––. 1988. "Orchids of Glacier Park." *Montana Magazine.*

––––––. 1989. *Alpine Wildflowers of Glacier National Park and Waterton Lakes National Park, Alberta.* Unpublished Manuscript.

Erhart L. R., O. B. Raup, J. W. Whipple, A. L. Isom, and G. A. Davis. 1989. "Geologic Maps, Cross Section, and Photographs of the Central Part of Glacier National Park, Montana." U.S. Geological Survey Miscellaneous Investigation Series Map I-1508-B.

Erlich, P. R., D. S. Dobkin, and D. Wheye. 1988. *The Birder's Handbook: A Field Guide to the Natural History of North American Birds.* New York: Simon and Schuster, Inc.

Fagre, Daniel B. "Changing Mountain Landscapes in a Changing Climate: Looking into the Future." *Changing Landscape.* Summer 2000.

Fagre, Daniel B., P. L. Comanor, J. D. White, F. R. Hauer, and S. W. Running. "Watershed Responses to Climate Change at Glacier National Park." *Journal of the American Water Resources Association.* 33(4):755–765.

Fagre, Daniel B. "Understanding Climate Change on Glacier National Park's Natural Resources." *Status and Trends of the Nation's Biological Resources—Volumes 1 and 2.* U.S. Department of the Interior, U.S. Geological Survey, Reston, Va.

Fagre, Daniel B. and David L. Peterson. M. 2000. "Ecosystem Dynamics and Disturbance in Mountain Wildernesses: Assessing Vulnerability of Natural Resources to Change." *Wilderness Science in a Time of Change, Volume 3: Wilderness as a Place for Scientific Inquiry.* USDA Forest Service Proceedings RMRS-P-15-Vol-3.

Fagre, D. B. and D. L. Peterson. (2002) "Modeling and monitoring ecosystem responses to climate change in three North American mountain ranges." Pages 249–59 in Korner, C. and E. Spehn (eds.), *Global Mountain Biodiversity: changes and threats.* Springer-Verlag, Berlin.

Finklin, A. I. 1986. *A climate handbook for Glacier National Park—with data for Waterton Lakes National Park.* USDA Forest Service Gen. Tech. Rpt. INT-204.

Habeck, J. R. 1969. "An analysis of a timberline zone at Logan Pass, Glacier National Park." *Northwest Science* 43:65–73.

_____. 1970. *The Vegetation of Glacier National Park, Montana.* Missoula: Dept. of Botany, University of Montana, 132 pp.

Hitchcock, C. L. and A. Cronquist. 1973. *Flora of the Pacific Northwest.* Seattle: University of Washington Press.

Holterman, J. 1985. *Place Names of Glacier/Waterton National Parks. 1985.* West Glacier: Glacier National History Association.

Howard, Janet L. 1996. "Populus tremuloides." In Fire Effects Information System [Online]. U.S. Department of Agriculture, Forest Service, Rocky Mountain Research Station, Fire Sciences Laboratory (Producer).

Jonkel, C. J. and I. M. Cowan. 1971. "The black bear in the spruce-fir forest." *Wildlife Monographs*, No. 27.

Key, Carl H., D. B. Fagre, and R. K. Menicke. 2001. "Glacier Retreat in Glacier National Park, Montana. Satellite Image Atlas of Glaciers of the World: Glaciers of the United States." U.S. Geological Survey.

Kellert, S. R. and Wilson, E. O. 1993. *The Biophilia Hypothesis*. Washington, D.C: Island Press.

Kendall, K. C. and R. E. Keane. 2001. "Whitebark pine decline: Infection, mortality, and population trends." Pages 221–242 in D. F. Tomback, S. F. Arno, and R. E. Keane (eds.). *Whitebark pine communities: Ecology and restoration*. Washington, D.C.: Island Press.

Kendall, K. C., L. Waits, D. Roon, M. Murphy, and J. Stetz. "Non-invasive genetic sampling of grizzly bear and black bear population status at an ecosystem scale." Defenders of Wildlife, Carnivores 2000 Conference. Boulder, Colo. November 12, 2000.

Kendall, K. C., S. Gniadek, and A. Edmonds. "Detecting lynx in Glacier National Park, Montana." Defenders of Wildlife, Carnivores 2000 Conference. Boulder, Colo. November 12, 2000.

Kotliar, N. B., S. J. Hejl, R. L. Hutto, V. A. Saab, C. P. Melcher, and M. E. McFadzen. "Effects of Fire and Post-Fire Salvage Logging on Avian Communities in Conifer-Dominated Forests of the Western United States." *Studies in Avian Biology* 25:49–64, 2002.

Kuijt, Job. 1982. *A Flora of Waterton Lakes National Park*. Edmonton: University of Alberta Press.

LeFranc, M. N. Jr., M. B. Moss, K. A. Patnode, W. C. Sugg. 1987. *Grizzly Bear Compendium*. Washington, D.C.: National Wildlife Federation.

Lesica, P. 1996. *Checklist of the Vascular Plants of Glacier National Park Montana, U.S.A.* (second edition). West Glacier, Mont.: Glacier Natural History Association.

_____. 2002. *Flora of Glacier National Park.* Corvallis: Oregon State University Press.

Lesica, P. and B. McCune. 1992. *Monitoring effects of global warming using peripheral rare plants in wet alpine tundra in Glacier National Park, Montana.* Final report. West Glacier: Glacier National Park.

Lopez, B. H. 1978. *Of Wolves and Men.* New York: Charles Scribner's Sons.

McClelland, B. Riley, L. S. Young, David S. Shea, Patricia T. McClelland, Harriet L. Allen, and Elizabeth B. Spettigue. "The Bald Eagle Concentration in Glacier National Park, Montana: Origin, Growth, and Variation in Numbers." *The Living Bird,* Nineteenth Annual, 1980–81. Cornell Laboratory of Ornithology.

Marnell, L. F. 1988. "Status of the westslope cutthroat trout in Glacier National Park, Montana." In R. Jenkins (ed.). *Biology and Management of the Interior Cutthroat Trouts.* Bethesda: American Fisheries Society.

Marnell, L. F., R. J. Behnke, and F. W. Allendorf. 1987. "Genetic identification of cutthroat trout, *Salmo clarki,* in Glacier National Park, Montana." *Canadian Journal of Fisheries and Aquatic Sciences* 44(11): 1830–1839.

McEneaney, Terry. 1998. *Birding Montana.* Guilford, Conn.: The Globe Pequot Press.

Mech, D. L. 1970. *The Wolf, the ecology and behavior of an endangered species.* New York: Natural History Press.

Miller, Orson K., Jr. 1978. *Mushrooms of North America.* New York: E. P. Dutton.

Norse, E. A. 1990. *Ancient Forests of the Pacific Northwest.* Washington, D.C.: Island Press.

Pfister, R. D., B. Kovalchik, S. Arno, and R. Presby. 1977. *Forest Habitat Types of Montana.* USDA Forest Service Intermountain Research Station Gen. Tech. Rpt. INT-34

Pletscher, D., R. Ream, W. Brewster, E. Bangs, and R. DeMarchii. 1991. "Managing wolf and ungulate populations in an international ecosystem." Transactions 56th N. A. Wildlf. & Nat. Res. Conf.:540–549.

Raup, O. B., R. L. Earhart, J. W. Wipple, and P. E. Carrara. 1983. *Geology along Going-to-the-Sun Road Glacier National Park, Montana.* West Glacier: Glacier Natural History Association.

Schmidt, W. C. and Holtmeier, F. K. (eds.). 1992. *Proceedings—International Workshop on Subalpine Stone Pines and Their Environment: Status of Our Knowledge.* USDA Forest Service Gen. Tech. Rep. GTR-309.

Schmidt, W. and K. McDonald (eds.). 1990. *Proceedings—Symposium on Whitebark Pine Ecosystems: Ecology and Management of a High Mountain Resource.* USDA Forest Service Intermountain Research Station Gen. Tech. Rpt. INT-270.

Shaw, Richard J. and Danny On. 1979. *Plants of Waterton-Glacier National Parks and the Northern Rockies.* Missoula: Mountain Press Publishing Co.

Shea, David S. 1973. "White-tailed Deer Eating Salmon." *The Murrelet.* May–August, 1973: 52–54.

_____. 1976. *A Wintertime Ecological Evaluation of the North Fork Flathead River Drainage, Glacier National Park.* West Glacier: Glacier National Park.

_____. 1995. *Birds of Glacier National Park: Field Check List.* West Glacier: Glacier National Park.

_____. 1995. *Mammals of Glacier National Park: Field Check List.* West Glacier: Glacier National Park.

_____. 2000. *Animal Tracks of Glacier National Park.* West Glacier: Glacier Natural History Association.

Shea, David S., Susan Olin, and Jennifer Asebrook. 2004. "Glacier National Park Eastside Grasslands Ecology Project, Final Report." West Glacier: Glacier National Park.

Simonin, Kevin A. 2000. "*Vaccinium membranaceum.*" In Fire Effects Information System [Online]. U.S. Department of Agriculture, Forest Service, Rocky Mountain Research Station, Fire Sciences Laboratory (Producer). Available: www.fs.fed.us/database/feis/ [2006, March 14].

Spencer, C. N., B. R. McClelland, and J. A. Stanford. 1991. "Shrimp stocking, salmon collapse and eagle displacement: Cascading interactions in the food web of a large aquatic ecosystem." *BioScience* 41:14–21.

Stanford, J. A. and J. V. Ward. 1988. "The hyporheic habitat of river ecosystems." *Nature* 335:64–66.

Trotter, P. 1987. *Cutthroat: Native Trout of the West.* Boulder: Colorado Association University Press.

Whipple, James W. 1992. Geologic map of Glacier National Park, Montana. U.S. Geological Survey Miscellaneous Investigation Series Map I-1508-F.

Willis, B. 1902. "Stratigraphy and Structure, Lewis and Livingston Ranges, Montana." *Bulletin of the Geological Society of America.* 13: 305–352.

Winston, Don. 1986. "Sedimentation and Tectonics of the Middle Proterozoic Belt Basin and Their Influence on Phanerozoic Compression and Extension in Western Montana and Northern Idaho." In *Paleotectonics and Sedimentation.* James A. Peterson, ed. *American Association of Petroleum Geologists Memoir* 41:87–118.

_____. 1990. "Evidence for Intracratonic, Fluvial and Lacustrine Settings of Middle to Late Proterozoic Basins of Western U.S.A." In C. F. Gower, T. Rivers, and B. Ryan, eds. *Mid-Proterozoic Laurentia-Baltica: Geol. Assoc. of Can., Spec. Pap.* 38:535–564.

Winston, D. and M. Woods. 1986. "Road Log No. 3: A traverse across the northern Belt basin from East Glacier Park, Montana to Bonners Ferry Idaho." In *Belt Supergroup: A Guide to Proterozoic Rocks of Western Montana and Adjacent Areas.* Sheila M. Roberts, ed. Montana Bureau of Mines and Geology, Special Publication 94:47–68.

Winston, D. and P. K. Link. 1992. "Middle Proterozoic Rocks of Montana, Idaho and Eastern Washington: The Belt Supergroup." In *The Geology of North America.* Geological Society of America 487–517.

Zwinger, Ann and B. E. Willard. 1972. *Land above the Trees: A Guide to American Alpine Tundra.* New York: Harper and Row.

Index

taxol, 157
temperatures, 61, 68, 71
three-flowered rushes, 217
topography, 61–62
tourism, 268
Trail of the Cedars, 141, 149, 171
train derailments, 281–84
Trapper Fire, 140
Triple Divide Peak, 66
tundra, 66, 211, 212–13, 217–18
Two Dog Flats, 138
Two Medicine Glacier, 39–40

U
Upper Kintla Lake, 249–51
U.S. Highway 2, 57–58

V
vegetation, 65–66
voles, 170, 224

W
warblers, 107–9
water pipits, 220
Waterton Lakes National Park, 287
weather, 68–72
Wedge Canyon Fire, 143
western hemlocks, 149, 159–60
western jumping mice, 224–25
western larch, 103, 142, 177–78, 179
western red cedars, 149
westslope cutthroat trout, 235,
    241–43, 246, 248, 249, 251
whitebark pines, 138, 184,
    186–200, 275

white pine blister rust, 76, 166,
    186–88
white spruce, 100, 143
white-tailed ptarmigans, 218–20
*Wildflowers of Glacier National Park
    and Surrounding Area* (Kimball
    and Lesica), 145
wildlife
    birds-viewing, 254–55
    checklist of birds, 260–63
    checklist of fishes, 259–60
    checklist of reptiles and
        amphibians, 259
    checklist of selected mammals,
        256–58
    mammals-viewing, 252–54
    reptiles and amphibians-viewing,
        255–56
Wolf Ecology Project, 120
wolves
    Aspen Parklands, 93–96
    Blackfeet Indian Reservation, 95
    North Fork Valley, 120–21,
        126–32
    viewing, 252
woodland caribou, 268
woodpeckers, 107

Y
Yellowstone checkerspots, 156
Yellowstone cutthroat trout, 245,
    246–48
Yellowstone-to-Yukon Conservation
    Initiative (Y2Y), 287
yellow sweetvetches, 212

About the Author

David Rockwell has worked in the field of natural resource management and education for thirty years. Much of his work has been with the Salish and Kootenai Tribes of the Flathead Indian Reservation, which is located just south of Glacier National Park. He is the author of two other books: *The Nature of North America: A Handbook to the Natural History of the Continent* and *Giving Voice to Bear: North American Indian Myths, Rituals, and Images of the Bear.* He lives with his wife and two children in Dixon, Montana, near the lower Flathead River and the Mission Mountains.

Outfit Your Mind

falcon.com

log in

learn more

falcon.com/davidrockwell